Trade, Poverty,

MW01118170

This work looks beyond the seemingly endless deadlock in the WTO's Doha round of trade negotiations that began in November 2001 and which were first scheduled to conclude by 1 January 2005. As well as offering an incisive analysis of the ills of the round, with particular attention directed at the poorest and least developed countries, the book expands on how the round could be moved forward.

The work as a whole provides the reader with a critical analysis of the implications of the negotiations for development and poverty reduction as well as proposals for moving beyond the current impasse. The volume brings together contributions from serving and former ambassadors to the WTO, key practitioners, and civil society representatives and leading scholars. Each chapter explores an area of critical importance to the round; and together they stand as an important contribution to debates not only about the Doha round but also about the role of trade in the amelioration of poverty in the poorest countries.

Rorden Wilkinson is Professor of International Political Economy in the School of Social Sciences and Research Director of the Brooks World Poverty Institute, both at the University of Manchester.

James Scott is Hallsworth Research Fellow with the Brooks World Poverty Institute at the University of Manchester.

Routledge Global Institutions Series

Edited by Thomas G. Weiss
The CUNY Graduate Center, New York, USA
Rorden Wilkinson and James Scott
University of Manchester, UK

About the series

The Routledge *Global Institutions Series* has two "streams." Those with blue covers offer comprehensive, accessible, and informative guides to the history, structure, and activities of key international organizations, and introductions to topics of key importance in contemporary global governance. Recognized experts use a similar structure to address the general purpose and rationale for specific organizations along with historical developments, membership, structure, decision-making procedures, key functions, and an annotated bibliography and guide to electronic sources. Those with red covers consist of research monographs and edited collections that advance knowledge about one aspect of global governance; they reflect a wide variety of intellectual orientations, theoretical persuasions, and methodological approaches. Together the two streams provide a coherent and complementary portrait of the problems, prospects, and possibilities confronting global institutions today.

Related titles in the series include:

The Millennium Development Goals and Beyond (2012)
edited by Rorden Wilkinson and David Hulme

The United Nations Development Programme and System (2011)
by Stephen Browne

African Economic Institutions (2011)
by Kwame Akonor

Global Poverty (2010)
by David Hulme

Trade, Poverty, Development

Getting beyond the WTO's Doha deadlock

Edited by
Rorden Wilkinson and James Scott

Routledge
Taylor & Francis Group

LONDON AND NEW YORK

First published 2013
by Routledge
2 Park Square, Milton Park, Abingdon, Oxon OX14 4RN

Simultaneously published in the USA and Canada
by Routledge
711 Third Avenue, New York, NY 10017

Routledge is an imprint of the Taylor & Francis Group, an informa business

British Library Cataloguing in Publication Data
A catalogue record for this book is available from the British Library

Library of Congress Cataloging in Publication Data
Trade, Poverty, Development: getting beyond the WTO's Doha deadlock / edited by Rorden Wilkinson & James Scott.
  p. cm. – (Routledge global institutions series; 67)
  Includes bibliographical references and index.
  1. World Trade Organization. 2. Doha Development Agenda (2001–)
3. Commercial treaties–Developing countries. 4. Economic development–Developing countries. 5. Poverty–Developing countries. 6. International trade. I. Wilkinson, Rorden, 1970- II. Scott, James.
  HF1385.T725 2013
  382'.92–dc23
                  2012006608

ISBN: 978-0-415-62449-7 (hbk)
ISBN: 978-0-415-62450-3 (pbk)
ISBN: 978-0-203-10214-5 (ebk)

Typeset in Times New Roman
by Taylor & Francis Books

MIX
Paper from
responsible sources
FSC
www.fsc.org FSC® C004839

Printed and bound in Great Britain by
TJ International Ltd, Padstow, Cornwall

Contents

Illustrations

Figures

Tables

Contributors

Yonov Frederick Agah is Nigeria's Ambassador and Permanent Representative to the World Trade Organization and is the current Chair of the Special Session of the Council for TRIPs. Until his appointment as Permanent Representative, he had served as Deputy Director (Multilateral) from 1991 to 2001 and Director (External Trade) from 2002 to May 2005, during which period he was responsible for coordinating Nigeria's participation in major bilateral and multilateral trade negotiations under the auspices of the WTO, United Nations Conference on Trade and Development (UNCTAD), Global System of Trade Preferences, ACP-EU Cotonou Partnership Agreement, and the African Growth and Opportunity Act. Agah has also served as the Chair of the following WTO Bodies: Council for Trade in Goods 2006; Council for TRIPs 2007; Trade Policy Review Body 2008; Council for Trade in Services 2009; Dispute Settlement Body 2010; and General Council in 2011. He holds the following degrees: BSc (Economics); MSc (Economics); MBA; PhD in International Trade; and the Bachelor of Laws (LLB). His PhD thesis is on trade policy reform and economic growth in Nigeria since 1986.

Ujal Singh Bhatia was India's Ambassador and Permanent Representative to the World Trade Organization between 2004 and 2010. He joined the Indian Administrative Service in 1974 and served in a number of senior positions in the Central government in Delhi as well as in the State government of Orissa in eastern India between 1976 and 2004. Between 1995 and 2000 he was posted as Joint Secretary in the Ministry of Commerce and Industry in the Central government in Delhi. In this capacity, he was involved in a number of bilateral and regional trade negotiations including the India-Sri Lanka Free Trade Agreement and the South Asian Free Trade Agreement. He also served briefly in the Ministry of Information and Broadcasting in 2004. Educated in Jamshedpur and Delhi, he was awarded a Master's degree in Economics from Delhi University in 1973. He also spent a year in Manchester in 1990–91 and acquired a Master's degree in Economics from the University of Manchester.

Bipul Chatterjee is Deputy Executive Director of the Consumer Unity and Trust Society (CUTS International), a leading economic policy research, advocacy and networking, non-governmental group in India with offices in Nairobi, Lusaka, Hanoi, and Geneva. He has an MA (Economics) from the Delhi School of Economics, and a BSc (Economics) from the University of Calcutta. Bipul represents CUTS at various fora, including presenting papers and conducting training workshops, particularly of civil society organizations on economic reforms (policy as well as practice aspects). His other responsibilities include fundraising and financial management of the organization and management of trade-related projects (in an advisory capacity) of overseas centers of the organization. He has published/edited several books and papers on the political economy of trade and development.

Jennifer Clapp is a Professor in the Environment and Resource Studies Department at the University of Waterloo, Canada. Her research covers the themes of global food and agriculture governance, food aid, agricultural trade, and the global food crisis. Her most recent books include *Food* (Polity, 2012); *Hunger in the Balance: the New Politics of International Food Aid* (Cornell, 2012); (with Peter Dauvergne) *Paths to a Green World: The Political Economy of the Global Environment* (MIT Press, 2011), second edition; (co-edited with Rorden Wilkinson), *Global Governance, Poverty and Inequality* (Routledge, 2010); (co-edited with Marc J. Cohen), *The Global Food Crisis: Governance Challenges and Opportunities* (WLU Press, 2009); and (co-edited with Doris Fuchs), *Corporate Power in Global Agrifood Governance* (MIT Press, 2009). She is co-editor of the journal *Global Environmental Politics* (MIT Press).

Peter Draper joined the South African Institute of International Affairs as Trade Research Fellow and Project Head of the "Development through trade" program in 2003. He previously headed the Department of Economics and Economic History at the University of Durban-Westville; the Asia and Mercosur desks at the Department of Trade and Industry (DTI); and Economic Analysis and Research in the DTI's International Trade and Economic Development Division. He is a member of Business Unity South Africa's trade committee and lectures in international business at the Wits Business School.

He is a board member and non-resident senior fellow of the Brussels-based European Centre for International Political Economy; a member of the IMD-Lausanne's Evian group including its "Brains trust"; and a board member of the Botswana Institute for Development Policy Analysis. He holds a Master's degree in Economics from the University of Kwazulu-Natal and is based in Pretoria.

Memory Dube is a researcher and project manager in the Economic Diplomacy Programme at the South African Institute of International Affairs (SAIIA). She holds an LLM (*cum laude*) in International Trade and Investment Law from the University of Pretoria. Memory's areas of research interest include trade policy reform; WTO policy; global economic governance; regional economic integration; as well as trade and sustainable development.

Joseph George has an MPhil degree in Applied Economics from Jawaharlal Nehru University, India, with a specialization in the participation of developing countries in the WTO, specifically in the area of trade in services. He has undertaken extensive studies and has published on the implications of the General Agreement on Trade in Services (GATS) for regulatory authorities governing financial services in India, with a research fellowship at the Indian Institute of Foreign Trade, New Delhi. His expertise lies in the economic interpretations of the provisions of GATS and their intersections with the priorities of developing and least developed countries in services trade. Currently occupying the position of research associate at CUTS Centre for International Trade, Economics and Environment, he is in charge of projects on trade issues concerning the South Asian subregion. His latest research work at CUTS encompasses comparative analyses of the negotiating positions of South Asian countries in the Doha Development Round as well as various economic and political aspects of functioning of the South Asian Free Trade Agreement.

Bernard Hoekman is the Sector Director of the Trade Department in the Poverty Reduction and Economic Management Vice-Presidency at the World Bank. Before taking up his present position he managed the team on trade and international integration in the Development Research Group in the Development Economics Vice Presidency, and the international trade and global integration activities of the World Bank Institute's Economic Policy division. He has worked extensively in countries in the Middle East and North Africa. Between 1988 and 1993 he was on the staff of the General Agreement on Tariffs and Trade Secretariat in Geneva. He is a graduate of the

Erasmus University Rotterdam, holds a PhD in Economics from the University of Michigan and is a Research Fellow of the London-based Centre for Economic Policy Research. His current research focuses on the functioning of the multilateral trading system, international transactions in services, the relationship between competition and trade policy, the economics of regional economic integration, and channels of international technology diffusion.

Faizel Ismail is currently Ambassador and Permanent Representative of South Africa to the World Trade Organization. He is author of, among other things, two books on the multilateral trading system: *Mainstreaming Development in the WTO: Developing countries in the Doha Round* (CUTS International, 2007), and *Reforming the World Trade Organization: Developing Countries in the Doha Round* (CUTS International, 2009). He is an Associate Editor of the *Journal of World Trade.*

Donna Lee is Professor in the Department of Politics and International Studies, University of Birmingham. She has published widely on economic negotiations, economic diplomacy, and the WTO. She has a particular interest in the activities and influence of the Africa Group and small states in the WTO. Donna is currently Director of the research project "African activism in the WTO," based at the University of Birmingham.

Pradeep S. Mehta is the founder Secretary-General of the Jaipur-based Consumer Unity and Trust Society (CUTS International), a leading economic policy research, advocacy and networking, non-governmental group in India with offices in Nairobi, Lusaka, Hanoi, and Geneva. CUTS was established in 1983. He has studied commerce at Calcutta University and law at Rajasthan University, Jaipur. Mehta serves on several policy-making bodies of the Government of India, related to trade, investment, competition, environment, and consumer affairs, and has been Honorary Adviser to the Commerce and Industry Minister of India and NGO Adviser to the WTO Director-General, Dr Supachai Panitchpakdi. He chairs the advisory committee of the South Asia Watch on Trade, Economics, and Environment, Kathmandu. In the past, he has served on the governing boards of the International Centre for Trade and Sustainable Development (ICTSD), Geneva; Consumer Coordination Council, New Delhi; and on the Global Policy and Campaigns Committee on Economic Issues of Consumer International, London.

Richard E. Mshomba is Professor of Economics at La Salle University in Philadelphia, USA. Born and raised in Arusha, Tanzania, he received a PhD in Economics from the University of Illinois at Urbana-Champaign. Mshomba is the author of *Africa in the Global Economy* (Lynne Rienner Publishers, 2000), a *Choice* Outstanding Academic Book, and *Africa and the World Trade Organization* (Cambridge University Press, 2009).

Morisho Nene is a doctoral candidate in Economic Geography at Bayreuth University, Germany, and a junior lecturer at the Catholic University of Bukavu, Democratic Republic of Congo, and at the Independent University of Kigali. His areas of expertise are development economics with a particular interest in poverty analysis, international trade, and regional integration. His main geographical focus is Central and Eastern Africa. He holds two Master's degrees: one in Macroeconomics and another in Development Studies from the Catholic University of Louvain-La-Neuve, Belgium.

James Scott is Hallsworth Research Fellow with the Brooks World Poverty Institute at the University of Manchester. He works on issues of trade, aid, and emerging powers. He holds a BA in Physics and Philosophy from the University of Oxford, an MA in Development Studies from the University of Manchester and a PhD in International Political Economy also from the University of Manchester. His principal research area is international trade, in particular developing countries' participation in the General Agreement on Tariffs and Trade and the World Trade Organization.

Jomo Kwame Sundaram has been Assistant Secretary-General for Economic Development in the United Nations' Department of Economic and Social Affairs since January 2005, and (Honorary) Research Coordinator for the G24 Intergovernmental Group on International Monetary Affairs and Development since December 2006. In 2007 he was awarded the Wassily Leontief Prize for Advancing the Frontiers of Economic Thought. Jomo has authored over 35 monographs, edited over 50 books and translated 12 volumes besides writing many academic papers and articles for the media.

Brendan Vickers is Director of Research and Policy, International Trade and Economic Development at the Department for Trade and Industry, South Africa, and an Associate of the Institute for Global Dialogue.

Rorden Wilkinson is Professor of International Political Economy in the School of Social Sciences and Research Director in the Brooks World Poverty Institute, both at the University of Manchester. He is author of, among other things, *The WTO: Crisis and the Governance of*

Global Trade (2006) and *Multilateralism and the World Trade Organisation* (2000); co-editor (with Jennifer Clapp) of *Global Governance, Poverty and Inequality* (Routledge, 2010); (with Donna Lee) of *The WTO after Hong Kong* (Routledge, 2007) and (with Steve Hughes) of *Global Governance: Critical Perspectives* (Routledge, 2002); and editor of *The Global Governance Reader* (Routledge, 2005). He co-edits (with Thomas G. Weiss) the *Global Institutions Series* in which this book appears.

Sun Zhenyu was born in Hebei Province of China in March 1946 and graduated from Beijing Foreign Languages Institute in July 1969. From 1973 to 1985 he served successively as staff member, Deputy Director and Director in the Third Department for Regional Affairs of the Ministry of Foreign Trade. During this period, he worked on bilateral trade relations between China and the UK and later between China and the European Community. From 1985 to 1990, he worked as Vice President of China National Cereals, Oil and Foodstuff Import and Export Corporation, focusing on the company's business with Japan and South-east Asian Countries. In 1989, he attended a one-year program of a management training course for senior executives sponsored by the United Nations Development Programme in cooperation with the University of British Colombia, Canada, and the University of Manchester, UK. From 1990 to 1994, he served as Deputy Director-General and Director-General of the Department of American and Oceanic Affairs of the Ministry of Foreign Trade and Economic Co-operation (MOFTEC), working on bilateral trade relations with the United States, Canada, Australia, New Zealand, and Latin American countries. During this period, he participated on separate occasions in Sino-US bilateral negotiations on market access, textiles and intellectual property rights. Since 1994, he served as Vice Minister of MOFTEC, responsible for regional policy, foreign investment, and reform of state trading enterprises. From 2002 to 2010 he was Ambassador and Permanent Representative of China to the World Trade Organization, the period immediately after China became a member of the WTO.

Foreword

Rorden Wilkinson and James Scott's edited book is the seventh in what we anticipate will be a growing number of research volumes in our Global Institutions Series that examines crucial global problems and possible global policies and solutions. As with the previous volume in this research stream, *The Millennium Development Goals and Beyond* (2012) that was edited by Rorden Wilkinson and David Hulme, the current volume, *Trade, Poverty, Development: Getting beyond the WTO's Doha deadlock*, grew out of the inaugural Global Poverty Summit organized in Johannesburg, South Africa, in January 2011.

In addition to these longer research volumes, the series strives to provide readers with user-friendly and short (usually 50,000 words) but definitive guides to the most visible aspects of what we know as "global governance" as well as authoritative accounts of the issues and debates in which they are embroiled. We now have over 60 books that act as key reference points to the most significant global institutions and the evolution of the issues that they face. Our intention has always been to provide one-stop guides for all readers—students (both undergraduate and postgraduate), interested negotiators, diplomats, practitioners from non-governmental and intergovernmental organizations, and interested parties alike—seeking information about most prominent institutional aspects of global governance.

The new research stream incorporates lengthier and more specialized works by key authors as well as edited compilations, the collective wisdom from which helps push out the envelope on important topics linked to global institutions. In this case, Wilkinson and Scott have assembled essays by a group of expert participants at the Johannesburg conference, one of whose purposes was to look beyond the seemingly endless deadlock in the WTO's Doha round of trade negotiations that began in November 2001 and were first scheduled to conclude by 1 January 2005. As well as offering an incisive analysis of the ills of the round, with particular attention directed at the poorest and least developed countries, the book expands on how the round could be moved forward, elaborating on the Statement on the Doha Development Agenda that was negotiated in Johannesburg (see the appendix to this book).

We are delighted to put forward the essays in this volume, expertly assembled by the editors. Rorden Wilkinson is Professor of International Political Economy in the School of Social Sciences at the University of Manchester and Research Director of the Brooks World Poverty Institute. James Scott is Hallsworth Research Fellow at the Brooks World Poverty Institute at the University of Manchester. The essays as a whole provide the reader with a critical analysis of the implications of the negotiations for development and poverty reduction as well as proposals for moving beyond the current impasse. The volume brings together contributions from serving and former ambassadors to the WTO, key practitioners, and civil society representatives along with those of leading scholars. Each essay explores an area of critical importance to the round; and together they stand as an important contribution to debates not only about the Doha round but also about the role of trade in the amelioration of poverty in the poorest countries.

Ideally, this and other volumes in the research stream will be used as complementary readings in courses in which other specific titles in this series are pertinent—in this case, we naturally point readers to a host of books on trade, poverty, and development already published in the series, a selection of which can be found in the "About the series" section at the front of this book. Our aim is to enable topics of importance to be dealt with exhaustively by specialists as well as enabling collected works to address issues in ways that bring more than the sum of the individual parts, while at the same time maintaining the quality of the series.

As always, we look forward to comments from our readers.

Thomas G. Weiss
The CUNY Graduate Center, New York, USA
February 2012

Acknowledgments

This book—and its sister volume[1]—emerges from our collective motivation, and scholarly and professional endeavors, to make a small difference to improving the world we know. As concerned academics and practitioners our efforts are designed to offer a credible way forward in the current round of World Trade Organization (WTO) negotiations— the Doha Development Agenda (DDA)—that puts the development of realizable trade gains for the least developed countries at the heart of the negotiations, with particular reference to the economic and developmental circumstances of Africa.

This book emerges from the inaugural Global Poverty Summit that was held in Johannesburg, South Africa, between 17 and 19 January 2011. A thoroughly stimulating event, the Summit brought together more than 50 of the world's foremost authorities on poverty, trade, and development to press for substantive action in, and find innovative ways to move forward on, the DDA and the Millennium Development Goals (MDGs); and to share knowledge with, and learn from, those interested and engaged in poverty issues but who do not normally have access to global policymaking.

The Johannesburg Global Poverty Summit, the website that accompanies it (www.povertydialogue.org), and our ongoing efforts to effect change in global public policy would not have been possible without the kind and generous support of Rory and Elizabeth Brooks and their Foundation. Rory and Elizabeth are rare among those people who can make a difference. They act on word, lead in deed, engage with passion. They also provided invaluable advice and assistance throughout the process. We are also grateful to the University of Manchester for its part in funding this initiative, as well as for the resources and support of the Ralph Bunche Institute at The City University of New York's Graduate Center and CUTS International and to their respective executive heads—Thomas G. Weiss and Pradeep Mehta.

We are also grateful to Bridget Fury for her tireless work in overseeing the logistics of the Summit, for helping shape the event, and for sharing the burden in crafting the process by which we were able to bring together such a stellar array of right thinking individuals to push for global change. Without the ceaseless energy and hard work of Emma Leach in managing the Summit we would also not have been able to produce such a successful event and two books of such high quality—our sincerest thanks. We would also like to extend our gratitude to Ereshnee Naidu, Fredrick Njehu, Nomvuyo Nolutshungu, Di Sutherland, and Abednigo Twala who provided valuable help and assistance in the run-up to, and during, the Summit.

The Summit, the Statements on the DDA and the MDGs that we worked so hard to produce, the books that have come out of our collective endeavors, and the events to come, would not have been possible without the industry, enthusiasm, intellect, and energy of the gathered participants. We are indebted to, among others, Yonov Frederick Agah, Charles Abugre Akelyira, Miriam Altman, Samuel Amehou, Margaret Joan Anstee, Yusuf Bangura, Walden Bello, Ujal Singh Bhatia, Debapriya Bhattacharya, Tendai Biti, H. Russel Botman, Rashad Cassim, Bipul Chatterjee, Admos Chimhowu, Jennifer Clapp, Peter Draper, Sakiko Fukudo-Parr, Aida Girma, Sophie Harman, Bernard Hoekman, Faizel Ismail, Rosebud Violet Kurwijila, Donna Lee, Liepollo Lebohang Pheko, Katherine Marshall, Ricardo Melendez-Ortiz, Pradeep Mehta, Richard E. Mshomba, Craig N. Murphy, Supachai Panitchpakdi, Ilaria Regondi, Nigel Richards, Jomo Kwame Sundaram, Frances Stewart, Joseph E. Stiglitz, Melanie Stravens, Ramesh Thakur, Brendan Vickers, Thomas G. Weiss, Alan Whiteside, Agostinho Zacarias, Fikre Zewdie, and Sun Zhenyu. Thanks are also due to Rudi Dicks, Alan Hirsch, Uma Kothari, Neva Makgetla and Herbert Mkhize who offered their kind assistance in helping shape aspects of the Global Poverty Summit. And we owe a debt of thanks to Denise Redston and all those at the Brooks World Poverty Institute who supported our efforts, as well as to our families for their help and support throughout this and other endeavors.

One final note of thanks is due to the publishers for allowing us to include a revised and updated version of James Scott and Rorden Wilkinson, "The Poverty of the Doha Round and the Least Developed Countries," *Third World Quarterly* 32, no. 4 (2011): 611–27.

James Scott and Rorden Wilkinson
Manchester, UK
January 2012

Note

1 Rorden Wilkinson and David Hulme, *The Millennium Development Goals and Beyond: Global Development after 2015* (London: Routledge, 2012).

Abbreviations

A4T	aid for trade
ACP	Africa, Caribbean, and Pacific
AMS	aggregate measure of support
ANC	African National Congress
APEC	Asia-Pacific Economic Cooperation
ATC	Agreement on Textiles and Clothing
BITs	bilateral investment treaties
BRICS	Brazil, Russia, India, China, South Africa
CGE	computable general equilibrium
CSC	Cotton Sub-Committee
CTD	Committee on Trade and Development
CTDSS	Committee on Trade and Development Special Session
DDA	Doha Development Agenda
DFQF	duty free quota free
DSB	Dispute Settlement Body
DSM	Dispute Settlement Mechanism
DSU	Dispute Settlement Understanding
EC	European Community
EITI	Extractive Industries Transparency Initiative
EU	European Union
FAO	Food and Agriculture Organization
FDI	foreign direct investment
FTA	Free Trade Agreement
GATS	General Agreement on Trade in Services
GATT	General Agreement on Tariffs and Trade
GDP	gross domestic product
GSP	Generalized System of Preferences
GTAP	Global Trade Analysis Project
IATP	Institute for Agriculture and Trade Policy
IBRD	International Bank for Reconstruction and Development

ICTSD	International Centre for Trade and Sustainable Development
IFPRI	International Food Policy Research Institute
IGDC	Informal Group of Developing Countries
IMF	International Monetary Fund
ITO	International Trade Organization
LDCs	least developed countries
LIFDCs	low income food deficit countries
MC	Ministerial Conference
MDGs	Millennium Development Goals
MFN	most favored nation
NAMA	Non-Agricultural Market Access
NEDLAC	National Economic Development and Labour Council (South Africa)
NGO	non-governmental organization
NFIDCs	net food importing developing countries
NTBs	non-tariff barriers
ODA	official development assistance
ODI	Overseas Development Institute
OECD	Organization for Economic Cooperation and Development
OTDS	overall trade-distorting domestic support
PTA	Preferential Trade Agreement
RTA	Regional Trade Agreement
SACU	Southern African Customs Union
SCM	Subsidies and Countervailing Measures
SDT	special and differential treatment
SSM	special safeguard mechanism
SVEs	small and vulnerable economies
TACB	technical assistance and capacity building
TPP	Trans-Pacific Partnership
TRIMs	Trade-Related Investment Measures
TRIPs	Trade-Related Aspects of Intellectual Property Rights
UN	United Nations
UNCTAD	United Nations Conference on Trade and Development
UNDP	United Nations Development Programme
UNECA	United Nations Economic Commission on Africa
WTO	World Trade Organization
WWII	World War Two

Introduction

The promise of "development" and the Doha Development Agenda

James Scott and Rorden Wilkinson

As 2011 drew to a close the World Trade Organization's (WTO) Doha Development Agenda (the DDA—but what is universally known as the Doha round) entered a second decade of negotiations much like it had left the last: in deadlock. While a stasis continues to afflict the DDA, dramatic changes have occurred in the external environment. When the DDA was launched, robust growth, low inflation and low interest rates were evident in most of the developed economies. The US budget surplus built up by the Clinton administration looked like it might create a situation in which the United States paid off its national debt.[1] And China's emergence as an economic powerhouse had begun, but had not yet generated the alarm among the established powers— particularly the United States—that would subsequently emerge.

Ten years later MC8, the WTO's eighth Ministerial Conference, was held amid unprecedented turbulence in the Euro zone, worries over a downgrading of France's credit rating (following a similar downgrading of a number of major economies, including the United States), rising unemployment and snowballing public debt in most Organization for Economic Cooperation and Development (OECD) countries, sharply falling investment rates in China, growing tensions between the West and Iran, persistent and seemingly intractable US trade and budget deficits, growing global food insecurity among already precariously placed populations, and threats of yet another housing bubble collapse, this time in China with potentially severe consequences for growth in both China and its international suppliers.[2] Indeed, the only positive news appeared to be the modest success of the December 2011 COP17 Durban Climate Change Conference in agreeing to a limited amendment and extension of the Kyoto Protocol (despite Canada's decision to withdraw from the Protocol shortly thereafter),[3] a commitment to the adoption of a universal climate change treaty by 2015, and the establishment of an ad hoc Working Group on the Durban Platform for Enhanced Action.[4]

Matters were little better inside "the onion."[5] While MC8 delivered a number of side agreements—notably the accessions of the Russian Federation, Samoa, Vanuatu, and Montenegro, the conclusion of the revision to the plurilateral Government Procurement Agreement,[6] and seven official decisions on minor issues primarily covering small changes with respect to the treatment of least developed countries (LDCs) and pledges to continue work on specific issue areas[7]—they did little to hide the Conference's inability to find a way forward in the DDA. In a break from the normal "spin" given to these affairs at times of crisis and intransigence,[8] WTO Director-General Pascal Lamy told the gathered delegates: "You have failed in your endeavors to amend the WTO rulebook to make global trade fairer and more open. The Doha Development Round is at an impasse."[9]

Lamy's firm admonishment of WTO members for their failure to move the round forward since the negotiations broke down in July 2008 was not the only evidence of malaise that underpinned a meeting that on the surface appeared convivial. On the morning the Conference opened, a statement was released by ministers and heads of delegation from the Informal Group of Developing Countries (IGDC)[10]—a group of 120 developing countries that is the successor grouping to the G-110 formed at the 2003 Cancún Ministerial Conference.[11] In a sad reflection of how little progress had been made in the two years since the IGDC released a similar statement at the 2009 Ministerial Conference, and echoing a declaration made by Brazil, Russia, India, China, and South Africa (the BRICS) a day before MC8,[12] the statement reiterated the need to pursue a conclusion to the DDA on the basis of the original mandate, underscored the importance of the single undertaking (that is, all aspects of the negotiations should be treated as an indivisible whole and "nothing is agreed until everything is agreed"),[13] highlighted the need to agree an "early harvest" for LDCs, and bemoaned the lack of political commitment by key industrial members (principally the United States). Importantly, and in a strong reminder of the longevity of key disagreements in the round, the IGDC statement also recalled the necessity of adopting the proposals in Annex C of the Draft (but never adopted) 2003 Cancún Ministerial Declaration on Special and Differential Treatment,[14] and refraining from overburdening acceding countries with commitments that are inappropriate to their levels of development and go beyond those commonly applied to existing members.

Sharper criticism came in the form of a statement issued by Bolivia, Cuba, Ecuador, Nicaragua, and Venezuela, which bemoaned the continuing lack of transparency, effective participation, and sufficient preparation in the day-to-day work of the WTO; the "increasingly sophisticated methods ... used to prevent the participation of all Members and to give the appearance of an inclusive and consensual process"; the persistent presentation of the views of a small group as those of the majority; and the intentional omission of a formal statement on the causes of the impasse in the DDA.[15]

The opening day of MC8 also saw trade ministers from 22 member states plus the 27 members of the European Union hold a press conference at which they made the case for including in the Chair of the Ministerial Conference's statement a pledge to "refrain from raising new barriers to trade in goods and services, imposing new export restrictions, or implementing WTO-inconsistent measures in all areas, including those that stimulate exports."[16] And the United States reiterated its position that the DDA could not be completed unless China and India, among others, were more ambitious in their market access offers in agricultural and non-agricultural goods. As US Trade Representative Ron Kirk put it in his plenary address: "[t]he world has changed profoundly since this negotiation began a decade ago, most obviously in the rise of the emerging economies. The results of our negotiations thus far do not reflect this change, and yet they must if we are to be successful."[17]

In many ways, the tensions in evidence during MC8 and the deadlock that currently afflicts the negotiations are all-too-familiar.[18] Yet, this familiarity masks the threat that the current impasse poses to any likelihood that the DDA's conclusion will bring much needed trade gains for developing countries generally, and the least developed in particular. Recognizing the need to move beyond this stasis, the contributors to this volume were among a group that came together in Johannesburg in January 2011 during the inaugural Global Poverty Summit with the specific intention of mapping out a path that would better enable the round to progress and, crucially, to deliver trade gains to some of the poorest and most vulnerable populations. We gathered as a broad group of practitioners, scholars, and civil society representatives united by a conviction that enduring poverty and widening inequalities were unacceptable features of an affluent world and that the DDA had to play its part in addressing these ills. Our discussions focused both on the Doha round generally as well as on the relationship between the DDA and Africa— the most marginalized, poorest and least developed continent on earth.

In the course of our deliberations we were able to set aside intellectual and substantive differences and craft a way forward that we believe offers real gains for the poorest. The result is appended to this volume in the form of *The Johannesburg Statement on the DDA*. We also wanted to find a way of discussing some of the issues that we each believe to be important in a longer, more involved way—hence we revised our original submissions to the Global Poverty Summit DDA working group and produce them here for the first time.

The essays that follow make compelling reading. Together they offer a forensic analysis of the current state of play and a set of prescriptions on what is to be done to move beyond the WTO's Doha deadlock. In the remainder of this chapter we set out how the book unfolds. In so doing we detail how the chapters hang together and highlight moments of convergence and disagreement thereby setting out the context in which the rest of the book unfolds.

How the book unfolds

The contributions that follow are organized into four broad parts: "The round," "Key issues," "The view from inside," and "Focus on Africa." The first part comprises two chapters that offer broad analyses of the negotiations to date and their potential value were they to be concluded on the basis of what is currently on offer. The second part explores two issues that came to prominence during the round and which are of key importance to the poorest LDCs: food security and cotton. Part III brings together the views of four key past and serving developing country Ambassadors, and one nationally based Director of Policy and Research, involved in the Doha negotiations, thereby providing an insiders' view frequently missing from scholarly works on the DDA. Part IV focuses our attention on the experiences of African countries in the DDA and the problems and opportunities they face.

The round

We begin the analysis in Chapter 1 with an examination of the capacity of the DDA to deliver development gains for the poorest countries. Fusing insights from the economic (specifically that based on computable general equilibrium [CGE] simulations) and political economy literatures the chapter reveals just how limited the benefits of the DDA would be if the negotiations were to be concluded on the basis of what is currently "on the table." More worryingly, however, we point to an outcome that is not only poor in terms of the overall gains (or indeed for some regions, the losses) projected by CGE simulations, but one that is potentially disastrous for the future development of these countries. As we put it, the "outcome for developing countries ... is not only poor in the aggregate ... [it also] locks them into a particular kind of [production] ... which crowds out the possibilities for diversification." Our argument, in extension, is that to deliver realizable gains for the poorest, the negotiations need to encompass ways of tackling the invisible barriers to industrial diversification that are created by particular patterns of negotiating.

In Chapter 2, Bernard Hoekman considers where the Doha negotiations go from their current impasse. He argues that three acknowledgements are necessary before the round can be successfully concluded: (i) that reductions in applied levels of protection do not constitute the sum of the benefits that would flow from a concluded DDA; (ii) that the source of the deadlock in the negotiations is understood to be a disagreement among a small number of large players on market access; and (iii) that a forward looking process and accompanying work program need to be identified and agreed upon. He argues that the hiatus that will inevitably prevail in the negotiations over the course of 2012 and 2013 (the result of electoral cycles in key member states) should provide a window of opportunity to discuss these issues under the auspices of WTO committees with a view to being able to forge an agreement once the turbulence of the election cycles has settled; and in the interim we should resist tinkering with core aspects of the institution—such as the principles of non-discrimination and consensus decision-making—in a misguided attempt to get the major players back to the negotiating table.[19]

Hoekman's argument is compelling. His cautioning against viewing reduced trade barriers as the sole measure by which to gauge a DDA outcome is important, and his call for the construction of a forward looking agenda that brings key players back to the table a welcome one. Yet his most significant contribution is to cut through the hyperbole and high-stakes drama that has come to surround the negotiations and to call for a period of contemplation and reassessment that takes *advantage* of the round's hiatus and results in a more appropriate outcome for all of the round's participants.

Key issues

The first two chapters provide the general analytical context in which the rest of the book unfolds. The second part of the book narrows the focus to two issues that are of critical importance to the poorest and most vulnerable WTO members and that have emerged over the course of the round: food security and cotton. In Chapter 3, Jennifer Clapp leads us through the complexities of the linkages between food security and the DDA. Clapp begins her analysis by exploring the way the dramatic food price rises of 2007–2011, and the direct and indirect insecurities generated by these rises, have been used as a lever for increasing pressure on member states for a conclusion of the Doha round.[20] She then shows that behind the linkage between food prices and the DDA—which is indicative of many other issues that have been used to add gravity to the call for the round's conclusion—lie more complex relationships between food security and international trade. As Clapp argues, food crises and episodes of price volatility are not simply the consequences of supply and demand imbalances. As such, they require corrective measures that go beyond merely removing barriers that restrict the flow of food across state boundaries. Her conclusion is that if the round were to be concluded on the basis of what is on the table it is unlikely to attenuate food insecurity. Indeed, as she puts it, a DDA concluded on this basis might actually "exacerbate some of the key factors that have *contributed* to both volatility in prices and the vulnerability of developing countries to food price shifts."[21] In calling into question the simple linkage between supply and demand factors and food price volatility, Clapp deftly challenges us to think harder about how we deal with the insecurities that vulnerable populations face and address these in multilateral frameworks. In so doing, she also shines a light on some of the more obscure and deleterious factors affecting food security—of which financialization of food commodities is perhaps the most worrisome—and makes a compelling argument for the inclusion of a robust special safeguard mechanism in any Doha deal to help protect vulnerable communities against food insecurity (see paragraph 17 of *The Johannesburg Statement on the DDA*).

In Chapter 4 Donna Lee moves the discussion on to look at a second issue that has come to prominence: cotton. Cotton has received more headline attention than issues of food security in the Doha round. The discussion to date, however, has been equally unsatisfactory. Lee begins her exploration of the cotton issue with a sobering claim: that "[t]he singular most important recommendation to the Doha Development Agenda ... that will help alleviate poverty among some of the poorest farming communities in a sustainable way is that developed country cotton subsidization, which in recent years has topped $6 billion annually, must be removed expeditiously." She also suggests that adjustments need to be made to the WTO's dispute settlement process so that members are compelled to provide financial compensation to injured parties in disputes to offset the damage done by large scale subsidy programs. Lee paints a bleak picture of the plight of cotton farmers in West and Central Africa and makes a compelling case for tackling income poverty in the region through the reduction of US and European subsidy regimes.

Taken together, Clapp and Lee's chapters make a powerful case for directing some of the attention in the DDA to promoting food security (or at least putting in place mechanisms to enable member states to mitigate food insecurity) and securing vital income flows for some of the world's most precariously placed people. Inevitably, these two issues featured prominently in our discussion in Johannesburg and this is reflected in the collective *Statement* we produced.

The view from inside

The third part of the book offers an unique insight into the problems, possibilities, and challenges of the Doha round from two serving and two former Ambassadors to the WTO as well as one nationally based Director of Policy and Research. The contributions to this part come from permanent representatives of three of the most significant "emerging powers" in the multilateral trading system—China, India, and South Africa—and the 2011 Chair of the WTO's General Council (the Organization's highest level decision-making body in Geneva), Nigeria's permanent representative to the WTO. In Chapter 5, former Indian Permanent Representative and Ambassador to the WTO, Ujal Bhatia, looks beyond the macro aspects of the Doha stalemate—which he attributes to a deadlock between the United States and developing countries; shifting global power relations; and a crisis of multilateralism—to highlight the consequences of the impasse in the negotiations for the poorest and smallest economies, particularly those in Africa. Bhatia begins his insightful examination of the plight of the poorest and most vulnerable in the DDA by mapping out the principal challenges facing these countries: the rise of preferential trading arrangements; the erosion of tariff preferences; food security; and the rise of natural resource prices. It is in the context of these challenges that Bhatia then examines the likely gains for the least developed from the Doha negotiations. Here, echoing others in this book, he highlights a number of areas of possibility and of concern: agriculture, cotton, the identification of special products and the special safeguard mechanism, proposals for further expanding duty-free quota-free access for LDCs, the challenge of standard setting and the harmonization of standards, the services waiver, trade facilitation, fisheries, flexibilities in the Trade-Related Intellectual Property Rights (TRIPs) Agreement and its relationship with the Convention on Biological Diversity, the role of supply side factors, and aid for trade. But it is the stalemate, he reminds us, that poses the biggest threat to the poorest and most vulnerable countries. As he puts it:

> [t]he stalemate in the Doha round is bad news for Africa. The issue is not so much the trade gains for Africa, which by all accounts

will be fairly modest, but the implications this has for the multilateral process in general, and the capacity of the WTO to intervene on the behalf of the poorest and smallest countries in the world.

Chapter 6 sees South Africa's Permanent Representative and Ambassador to the WTO, Faizel Ismail, and Director of Research and Policy at South Africa's Department for Trade and Industry, Brendan Vickers, shift the focus to the role that norms and values can play in the multilateral trading system. Ismail and Vickers show how South Africa's unique values, as a country moving away from the inequities of apartheid, have been key to its advancement of the DDA's trade and development objectives as well as to its commitment to processes of inclusive consultation, fairness, and sustainable development. They argue that these values have enabled South Africa to play a key role as a middle power "facilitator" and "mediator" in the negotiations, and cite five areas in support of their case: TRIPs and Public Health; the formation of the Group of 20 (G-20) developing country alliance; the special and differential treatment negotiations; and the Non-Agricultural Market Access coalition (NAMA-11). Ismail and Vickers provide a powerful argument for the need to look beyond the habitual focus on, and narrow confines of, material self-interest when examining trade politics. Though South Africa has naturally sought to pursue its own interests, it has also actively sought to accommodate the interests of smaller, less powerful countries and represent them within small group meetings. This chapter forms a timely reminder that if the DDA is to reflect and deliver on the interests of poor countries a more normatively driven and inclusive politics is necessary. Crucially, the case of South Africa explored by Ismail and Vickers demonstrates that this is possible.

In Chapter 7, Yonov Frederick Agah, Nigeria's Ambassador and Permanent Representative to the WTO and former Chair of the WTO's General Council, makes a vital contribution to understanding the position of Africa in the negotiations. To appreciate the extent to which the DDA is responding to Africa's demands, it is essential to examine what African countries themselves have been demanding in the negotiations. Agah provides a comprehensive analysis of the positions adopted by African countries, articulated through their submissions to the WTO—an analysis that he is uniquely placed to provide. The chapter makes clear that Africa has been active in all areas of the negotiations, with African delegates providing comprehensive proposals across the range of negotiating areas. Agah then goes on to examine the pathway that has led the DDA to its current impasse. In his final section he makes a strong case for the importance of concluding the round in a manner that respects the mandates contained in the Declarations of the Doha and Hong Kong Ministerial Conferences, and sets out how such an outcome can be achieved. Agah argues that, for the DDA to be concluded, the process of negotiation must be inclusive, fully multilateral, and supported by greater political will at the level of trade ministers. If this is achieved, along with the correct sequencing of issue areas to allow cross-linkages and trade-offs, the progress to date can be built on and a successful conclusion can be reached that addresses the needs of developing countries.

Chapter 8 comprises insights from the former Ambassador and Permanent Representative of China to the WTO, Sun Zhenyu. On each of the core elements of the DDA—agriculture, NAMA, and services—he demonstrates compellingly that the current draft texts require considerable concessions from developing countries, in some regards exceeding those required of developed members. Pressure from the rich countries, particularly the United States, for the emerging powers to contribute greater market opening is, he argues, misplaced, particularly given that the principles of special and differential treatment and less than full reciprocity are the explicit basis of the Doha mandate. As meaningful concessions are already on the table, Sun argues, it would be a great mistake to abandon the DDA, particularly since there is no feasible alternative should it be abandoned that would not damage the WTO irrevocably. With this in mind, Sun concludes his chapter with an exposition of how China's participation in the DDA is likely to evolve over subsequent years and how China will contribute to future WTO negotiations. He argues that China will continue to support the multilateral negotiation process, arguing that the proliferation of bilateral trade deals is only a symptom of the impasse in the WTO. China will also continue to work closely with India, Brazil, and the other emerging powers and make contributions with them that are consistent with their current levels of development. Lastly, China will continue to support other developing countries and try to further their interests. Overall, Sun argues that China has made a full commitment to the DDA and given significant concessions in the negotiation process, and will continue to support both the WTO and the DDA in the future.

Focus on Africa

The final part of the book brings together four contributions from close followers of the DDA, with a particular focus on the impact on Africa. Taken together, they provide both cause for concern and hope that Africa can benefit from the multilateral trade system. In Chapter 9, Jomo Kwame

Sundaram offers a powerful challenge to prevailing development ortho-doxy that trade liberalization, particularly with regard to agriculture, will benefit Africa. He uses three approaches to substantiate his claim. First, he examines the lessons from past periods of trade reform in Africa as a basis for considering how the DDA will impact on the continent. Here he shows that the DDA as currently constituted is likely to repeat the mistakes of trade opening in the 1980s and 1990s in which tariff liberalization undertaken in the absence of competitive agricultural and industrial sectors led to deindustrialization and declining food produc-tion, turning Africa from a net food exporter into a net food importer. Second, he draws from the wealth of studies using CGE modeling to examine the likely impacts of the DDA. Throughout Sundaram shows that Africa is likely to make at best insignificant gains, and is more likely to be left billions of dollars worse-off by the current DDA package. This analysis, through focusing on Africa, complements that of Scott and Wilkinson in Chapter 1. Third, Sundaram examines recent advances in trade theory to underscore the point that Africa's development is unlikely to be furthered by the current trade liberalization agenda. The chapter offers a telling critique of the current WTO agenda and illus-trates the need for a wholesale rethink of our current approach to trade-led development and poverty alleviation.

In Chapter 10 Richard Mshomba focuses on the capacity of African states to negotiate beneficial deals both historically within the General Agreement on Tariffs and Trade and presently within the WTO. In a nuanced and insightful analysis, he elucidates the severe disadvantage that African states operate under in the negotiation process and the implications this has both for those countries and for the DDA. In particular, Mshomba highlights the lack of technical and negotiating capacities that most African states suffer, precluding their full partici-pation in the multilateral trade system. The result has been agreements that African states did not fully understand and have struggled to implement, reducing their willingness to sign new deals. In the DDA negotiations Mshomba demonstrates that African states have been helped by greater use of coalitions and by technical assistance provided by the United Nations Conference on Trade and Development (UNCTAD) and civil society organizations, placing them in a better negotiating position than in previous rounds. However, several problems remain. Mshomba highlights Africa's lack of economic strength, its dependency on aid, and the difficulties of operating a successful coalition strategy among countries with divergent interests, all of which undermine the capacity of African states to participate in the DDA negotiations and secure deals that reflect their own interests. Though mindful of these disadvantages, Mshomba forcefully argues that African states must engage fully with the process of trade reform because trade, when combined with the correct domestic policies, can be an important driver of economic growth. Africa, he argues, must resist adopting overly mercantilist positions, demanding only greater market access for their products while refusing to engage in a process of trade policy reform. Such a path, he warns, would lead Africa further down the road of dependency.

In Chapter 11 Pradeep Mehta, Bipul Chatterjee, and Joseph George provide a rich analysis of the unfolding of the DDA, the challenges that stand in the way of its completion, and how these challenges may be overcome. The chapter demonstrates the problematic way in which the agenda of the Doha round has shifted away from its original mandate of tackling development issues towards a more traditional bargaining over market access between the major powers. The result has been a marginalization of core development issues and an exclusion of measures that benefit African countries. They argue that if the DDA is to deliver benefits to poorer WTO members there must be improvements in the current draft package across the range of negotiation areas. Mehta, Chatterjee, and George examine several of the most important—namely agriculture, NAMA and services—and highlight what is needed to bring the DDA back into line with its original aims. They then go on to examine the interests of Africa more specifically and set out how these interests can be integrated into the DDA package, in line with *The Johannesburg Statement*. Mehta, Chatterjee, and George also discuss the importance of increased aid for trade being integrated into the DDA package to assist African states in overcoming domestic supply-side constraints. The chapter then makes the case for focusing on the needs of the LDCs and African states.

In the final chapter, Peter Draper, Memory Dube, and Morisho Nene provide a thought-provoking analysis of the relationship between the DDA and Africa's needs. They begin their analysis by highlighting the development challenges faced by sub-Saharan Africa and the key areas of interest within the DDA to the region. Draper, Dube, and Nene highlight a number of new issues that threaten Africa's ability to gain from trade, such as "climate protectionism" and "murky protectionism" being introduced by the rich countries in response to the global economic crisis. Despite these problems, however, like Richard Mshomba in Chapter 10, they demonstrate that Africa could use the multilateral trade system to its advantage if it engages in negotiations in a positive and well-informed manner. Many areas of the DDA negotiations are of critical importance to sub-Saharan Africa, such as the agreement on trade facilitation, which remains "one of the biggest hurdles to trade in Africa." Furthermore, Draper, Dube, and Nene argue that Africa could gain significantly from participating in a plurilateral agreement on investment. This would help to avoid the current proliferation of bilateral investment treaties in which African countries have their domestic interests subordinated to the interests of foreign investors. The WTO thus is seen both to offer constraints on Africa's achievement of its development goals as well as opportunities if African negotiators can build an offensive trade agenda.

Together these chapters highlight problems in the substance of the negotiations, the manner in which they are conducted, the relations of power upon which they sit (and the tensions thrown up by shifts therein) and the congruity of the pattern the negotiations have taken with the development needs of the poorest, particularly in Africa. Moreover, they highlight the seriousness and urgency with which the development needs of the poorest must be treated and the role that the DDA must play in addressing these.

Where to now?

Appended to this book is the *Statement* we crafted in Johannesburg in response to the stasis in, and the problematic direction of, the DDA negotiations. Our *Statement* stands as a collation of our heartfelt contributions, a declaration of what we should do now, and an advocacy tool for pressing, with the greatest urgency, for a reorientation in the round. In it we identify a number of issues that pose significant threats to livelihoods within the poorest countries that need to be treated with the greatest seriousness, of which the pursuit of food security and sustainable forms of development, and putting in place safeguards that enable vulnerabilities to external shocks to be mitigated, are perhaps the most pressing. We argue that the length of time that the negotiations have taken threatens to render aspects of the agenda obsolete; that a concerted effort is required to bring the DDA to an early and satisfactory conclusion; and that a successful conclusion to the round requires commitment, willingness, and flexibility from all WTO members. But we also warn against the pursuit of a conclusion for the sake of urgency alone. To this end, we encourage WTO members to remain faithful to the DDA's original mandate, redouble their efforts to place development at the heart of the negotiations, and bear in mind that the business of enhancing the contribution of trade to the development of the poorest and most vulnerable will not halt with the conclusion of a development-centred outcome to the round.

Notes

1 This possibility, and the associated problems that it would create for investment funds, was actively worked on by the US government in 2000. See www.npr.org/blogs/money/2011/10/21/141510617/what-if-we-paid-off-the-deb t-the-secret-government-report.

2 Jamil Anderlini, "Chinese Property: A Lofty Ceiling," *Financial Times*, 13 December 2011, www.ft.com/intl/cms/s/0/6b521d4e-2196-11e1-a1d8–00144f eabdc0.html#axzz1gcE1c74h.

3 Ian Austen, "Canada Announces Exit from Kyoto Climate Treaty," *New York Times*, 12 December 2011, www.nytimes.com/2011/12/13/science/earth/cana da-leaving-kyoto-protocol-on-climate-change.html?_r=1.

4 www.cop17-cmp7durban.com/en/news-centre/media-releases/cop17-president-closing-statement.html.

5 This is the South African Permanent Representative to the WTO Ambassador Faizel Ismail's phrase likening the WTO to an onion in that the core of its decision-making, and knowledge about what is *actually* going on, is obscured and distorted by multiple layers. Personal conversations with the authors.

6 Tom Miles, "WTO Agrees Procurement Deal, US Urges China to Join," *Reuters*, 15 December 2011, www.reuters.com/article/2011/12/15/wto-procur ement-idUSL6E7NF2QS20111215.

7 These seven were (with WTO document number in brackets) "TRIPs and Non-violation and Situation Complaints" (WT/L/842), "Work Programme on Electronic Commerce" (WT/L/843), "Work Programme on Small Economies" (WT/L/844), "Transition Period for LDCs under Article 66.1 of the TRIPs Agreement" (WT/L/ 845), "Accession of Least-Developed Countries" (WT/L/846), "Preferential Treatment to Services and Service Suppliers of Least-Developed Countries" (WT/L/847), and on the "Trade Policy Review Mechanism" (WT/L/848).

8 See James Scott and Rorden Wilkinson, "What Happened to Doha in Geneva? Re-engineering the WTO's Image while Missing Key Opportunities," *European Journal of Development Research* 22, no. 2 (2010): 141–153; and Rorden Wilkinson, "The WTO in Hong Kong: What it Really Means for the Doha Development Agenda," *New Political Economy* 11, no. 2 (2006): 291–303.

9 Pascal Lamy, "Stand Up for the Values of Multilateralism," opening address to the Eighth Ministerial Conference of the World Trade Organization, 15 December 2011, www.wto.org/english/news_e/sppl_e/sppl212_e.htm.

10 See WTO, "Dominican Republic: Statement by Sr César Dargam Espaillat Vice Minister of Foreign Relations for Economic Affairs and Trade Negotiations," 15 December 2011, document WT/MIN(11)/ST/16. For the 2009 statement, see http://ictsd.org/downloads/2009/12/igdc-communique.pdf.

11 "Developing Countries Reassure Support for Doha Round," ShanghaiDail y.com, 16 December 2011, www.shanghaidaily.org/article/article_xinhua. asp?id=39254. For commentary on the Cancún ministerial conference, see Rorden Wilkinson, "Crisis in Cancun," *Global Governance* 10, no. 2 (2004): 149–155.

12 The Declaration is available at www.brics.utoronto.ca/docs/111214-trade.html.

13 www.wto.org/english/tratop_e/dda_e/work_organi_e.htm.

14 The draft Cancún Declaration is available at www.wto.org/english/thewto_ e/minist_e/min03_e/draft_decl_annex_e.htm.

15 "Communication from the Plurinational State of Bolivia, The Republic of Cuba, The Republic of Ecuador, The Republic of Nicaragua and the Bolivarian Republic of Venezuela," 14 December 2011, document WT/MIN(11)/W/4.
16 ICTSD, "Bridges Daily Update," issue no. 2, 16 December 2011.
17 WTO, "Remarks by U.S. Trade Representative Ron Kirk at the Opening Plenary Session at the World Trade Organization Ministerial Conference," 15 December 2011, document WT/MIN(11)/ST/53.
18 See Rorden Wilkinson, *The WTO: Crisis and the Governance of Global Trade* (London and New York: Routledge, 2006) for an extended discussion of the politics of crisis in the GATT/WTO.
19 For a complementary view of the need to resist reform impulses as responses to the DDA impasse, see Rorden Wilkinson, "Four Principles for Reforming the WTO," plenary address to the International Centre for Trade and Sustainable Development (ICTSD) Trade and Development Symposium, Geneva, 16 December 2011, www.ictsdsymposium.org/sites/default/files/Book_4_Wilkinson.pdf.
20 See, for instance, "Lamy rebuts UN rapporteur's claim that WTO talks hold food rights 'hostage'," WTO News, 14 December 2011, www.wto.org/english/news_e/news11_e/agcom_14dec11_e.htm.
21 Our emphasis.

Part I
The round

1 The poverty of the Doha round and the least developed countries

James Scott and Rorden Wilkinson[1]

The November 2010 meeting of the G-20 in Seoul concluded with a familiar "must do harder" refrain on the World Trade Organization's (WTO) Doha round (DDA—the Doha Development Agenda). Couched in terms of a belief that "trade can be an effective tool for reducing poverty and enhancing growth in developing countries [and] LICs [low income countries] in particular"[2] and of "recognizing the concerns of the most vulnerable," the leaders of the G-20 countries publicly stated their commitment to a "successful, ambitious, comprehensive, and balanced conclusion" consistent with the original Doha mandate, encouraging WTO members to build on "the progress already achieved" with a view to reaching a conclusion to the round in 2011.[3] Few commentators took this aspect of the Seoul Declaration seriously, taking it to be a well meaning, but nonetheless overly optimistic, attempt to paper over the deep divisions that had emerged among member states over key aspects of the negotiations.

Just 12 months later, at the G-20's November 2011 meeting in Cannes, attempts to paper over the cracks were conspicuous by their absence. The *Final Declaration* put it bluntly: "It is clear that we will not complete the DDA if we continue to conduct negotiations as we have in the past ... we need to pursue in 2012 fresh, credible approaches to furthering negotiations, including the issues of concern for Least Developed Countries and, where they can bear fruit, the remaining elements of the DDA mandate."[4]

The G-20's Cannes Declaration is a sobering acknowledgement of the stasis currently afflicting the round. The negotiations have coughed and spluttered since the round was launched in 2001, passing through the not-as-yet-repeated high point of July 2008 when they came closest to an agreement before abruptly coming to a halt shortly thereafter. A number of the leading players, particularly the United States, have shown little in the way of the kind of engagement required to conclude the negotiations. Moreover, what we previously identified as an "emerging consensus"[5] on the likely results of the round for the poorest countries has since been consolidated and few now believe the round would offer the least developed countries (LDCs) much, if anything, of value.

Yet, while this consensus has crystallized, just how little the poorest countries would gain from the round is not wholly apparent. The results of most computable general equilibrium (CGE) simulations (more-often-than-not the preferred method of estimating how much is to be gained from concluding a trade round) offer little comfort for LDCs.[6] Since the round was launched these simulations have steadily predicted that the outcome of the DDA for developing countries will be small, with the poorest and most vulnerable faring worst. Moreover, as the round has progressed the predicted gains for both of these groups have fallen significantly.

That said, the extent of just how poor the gains are for developing and least developed countries as a group is not fully captured by economic models. While they offer useful insights into the aggregate picture of the projected Doha gains (or losses as is increasingly the case), CGE models often lack the kind of specificity that enables a detailed insight into not only the projected gains but also the consequences and congruity of particular kinds of liberalization for particular developing and least developed countries.

A second body of literature has taken a different approach to exploring the likely outcome of the DDA.[7] Rather than focusing on the projected gains from liberalization based on scenarios drawn from different points in the negotiations, these studies use detailed examinations of the pattern and progress of the negotiations as a basis for exploring the likely opportunities accruing to different countries from a concluded trade deal. This literature too, however, is not entirely satisfactory; though like the CGE models it nonetheless conveys a sense of the poverty of the Doha round. The strength of these studies is that they have been able to offer more precise and tailored analyses of the impact of particular kinds of liberalization for specific countries. Their weakness, however, is that they have only been able to talk in vague terms about the relative imbalance of opportunities resulting from a potentially concluded DDA without offering a detailed and precise global portrait.

There has, however, been little engagement between these two bodies of literature—their methodological and disciplinary differences more often than not proving too great a divide. One result is that few modeling the likely outcome of the round connect their studies to the political machinations of the negotiations in pursuit of a cogent answer as to why the structure of the round is likely to yield such poor results.

Likewise, few political economy approaches engage with the econometric literature beyond a fleeting reference to poor aggregate projections as a means of reinforcing the point that Doha is unlikely to result in significant gains. This lack of engagement presents something of a problem. While both literatures agree that the likely results of the round will be poor, what neither offers alone is a pointed appreciation of just how poor, and indeed problematic, the results are likely to be and how such a situation has come about.

Our aim in this chapter is to get a more complete sense of just what the poorest countries are likely to gain from the DDA by bringing together the insights of the econometric and political economy literatures. We do this by fusing a review of the CGE projections of the likely gains from the DDA with an examination of the passage of the Doha negotiations. We find that, when viewed in combination, the econometric and political economy literatures point to an outcome for developing countries that is not only poor in the aggregate but also locks them into a particular kind of (largely raw material-based) production and crowds out the possibilities for diversification. Thus, we argue that the focus of negotiations in the round should not only be on finding ways of increasing the liberalization "cut" to enhance the projected aggregate gains for the least developed. It should also be on addressing the invisible barriers to industrial diversification that are thrown up by particular patterns of negotiating. In extension, we argue that for the Doha round to be more successful, and to better approximate the sentiments of the G-20 statement quoted earlier, a qualitative shift in the negotiations is required. In pursuit of our aim, the next section reviews the econometric literature on the projected gains from Doha. Thereafter, the paper turns to the passage of the negotiations before offering our concluding comments.

Simulating the DDA

Since their introduction around the time of the Tokyo round (1973–1979)[8] estimates of the prospective economic gains from trade liberalization based on CGE and partial equilibrium modeling have ballooned. Hess and von Cramon-Taubadel compiled a set of 1200 such studies published between 1994 and 2006.[9] Most of these studies utilize the freely available model developed by the Global Trade Analysis Project (GTAP), or else they are based on the World Bank's LINKAGE model (which also uses GTAP datasets).

Inevitably (both because of the proliferation of these models but also their claim to offer more precise assessments of the outcome of any prospective trade deal), CGE modeling has come to play an increasing role in WTO negotiations, informing the negotiating positions of the member states.[10] It is unsurprising, then, that peaks in the production of these studies have arisen at key moments in the negotiations, such as in the immediate run-up to WTO Ministerial Conferences. What is interesting about these studies is that there has been a marked diminution in the predicted gains arising from the DDA across the course of the negotiations[11]—a factor that has contributed to the relatively agnostic approach that many negotiators have developed to the round's conclusion. The average predicted global welfare gains made by the studies sampled by Hess and von Cramon-Taubadel preceding the launch of the DDA, for instance, peaked in 1998 at $250 billion, before falling to a trough in 2003 of around $35 billion, and subsequently climbing again to around $90 billion in 2006 (see Figure 1.1). These figures, of course, mask wide variations. For example, for full liberalization of goods and services Brown, Deardorff, and Stern (2003) claim global welfare gains of some $2,080 billion, while Francois, van Meijl, and van Tongeren (2003) predict only $367 billion.[12] Similarly, when examining a likely DDA outcome on trade in goods (that is, through agricultural and Non-Agricultural Market Access [NAMA] liberalization), Harrison et al. (2003) predict global welfare gains of $186 billion, with non-Organization for Economic Cooperation and Development (OECD)

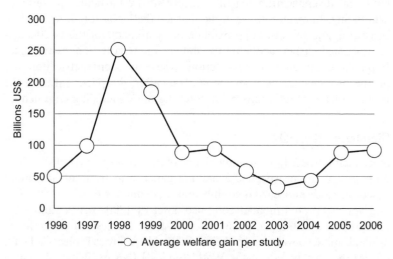

Figure 1.1 Average welfare gains predicted by CGE studies, 1996–2006
Source: Adapted from Sebastian Hess and Stephan von Cramon-Taubadel, "A Meta-Analysis of General and Partial Equilibrium Simulations of Trade Liberalisation under the Doha Development Agenda," *The World Economy* 31, no. 6 (2008): 812.

countries receiving $97 billion; while Anderson and Martin (2005) predict only $38.4 billion globally with a meager $6.7 billion going to developing countries.[13]

There are several reasons for the wide spread in predicted gains, though this is not the place for a detailed analysis.[14] The principal differences lie with the assumptions made, particularly the choice of Armington elasticity (which sets the elasticity of substitution between products of different countries), and whether or not tariff cuts are assumed to be made on bound or applied rates. As with all CGE modeling, the outcome is highly dependent on the assumptions made. The gains for developing countries in particular are highly dependent on the Armington elasticity chosen.[15] Doubling the Armington elasticity, for instance, increases predicted global welfare gains by 96 percent, gains of developing countries as a group by 119 percent, and gains for sub-Saharan Africa by 423 percent. The Armington values in the standard GTAP model are taken from estimates made for seven countries (Argentina, Brazil, Chile, New Zealand, Paraguay, United States, and Uruguay).[16] It is an open question how valid they are for the rest of the world and across sectors,[17] and the Armington elasticities used in key World Bank studies have been argued to be greater than justified by econometric evidence.[18] As noted earlier, their choice has profound implications for the expected distribution and size of benefits from the DDA. Notably for Africa, the choice of Armington values can have dramatic consequences for the continent's predicted gains, or indeed convert predicted gains into losses.[19]

Compounding the issue of falling returns, some of the assumptions in the standard GTAP model are inappropriate for developing countries and correcting these anomalies can further reduce the expected gains. First, in many developing countries tariff revenues constitute a significant portion of total tax revenue. Tariff liberalization will lead to falling tariff revenue, which must be made up elsewhere if government spending levels are to be maintained.[20] Valenzuela, Anderson, and Hertel have examined the effect of modifying the GTAP standard model such that tariff revenue losses are balanced by increased indirect consumption taxes (since most developing countries lack the capacity to raise direct taxes). They find that the expected welfare gains in developing countries as a group fall by 17 percent, and for sub-Saharan Africa by 25 percent.[21]

Second, CGE models usually assume either full or less than full but fixed employment. That is, the model assumes that any person who loses his or her job will find new employment in a different sector. This removes by assumptive fiat the central political issue with regard to trade liberalization—how trade liberalization affects the level of employment. Particularly in developing countries, which tend to have high levels of un- or under-employed labor, a more realistic situation might be for displaced workers ending up joining the ranks of the unemployed.[22] Some attempts have been made to integrate employment into CGE models,[23] but the caveat applies that the effects of trade reforms on employment are too complex and context specific to be readily modeled. A broad outline can be drawn that in countries in which production is falling, employment will likewise fall.[24] For some countries, notably China and Vietnam, a reduction in agricultural employment as a result of the DDA is likely to be counterbalanced by an increase in employment in manufacturing, because these two countries are frequently found to be the biggest potential beneficiaries of liberalization in non-agricultural goods (so-called NAMA). Other countries that are not competitive in manufactures, particularly in Africa, are likely to see unemployment rise. So countries that are already expected to be net losers from the DDA, particularly if they are seeing both shrinking agricultural and manufacturing sectors, may be expected to suffer greater losses if employment effects were included. Even for those countries that are expected to benefit from liberalization, there are impacts on the quality and distribution of jobs that are of political significance but are lost in the CGE framework.

Third, there is a mismatch between the model of development (and particularly within that, of industrialization) that developing countries generally subscribe to and which underlies CGE models. A key element of development, or at the very least a key aim of developing countries, is to change the range of products that they produce, either to industrialize or to move into higher value added sectors. Though it finds little support within neo-classical economics, one of the most important policies used to this end among all industrialized (both old and new) countries has been the use of trade restrictions to support the growth of new and infant industries.[25] CGE simulations calculate the welfare gains from moving factors of production into those in which the country has, at present, a comparative advantage, and from allowing consumers access to goods at the cheapest price. This sits uneasily, however, with the aims developing countries have of creating new areas of comparative advantage, often through the use of targeted trade restrictions, and of sacrificing present consumption for higher future returns through repositioning their economy within the global trade system. Of course, this tension merely reflects the ongoing debate concerning the role of liberalization within development, but it highlights the disparity between the politics surrounding trade negotiations, the economic analysis typically found in CGE simulations and, as we show in the following section, the constraints placed on developmental trajectories by particular patterns of negotiating.

As noted earlier, the gains predicted for developing countries by CGE simulations have fallen substantially over the course of the DDA, with the large gains being predicted in the years before the Doha Ministerial Conference giving way to much more modest expectations, especially for developing countries. One reason for this development has been the introduction of updated data. Before 2005, the data being put into the models described the world as it was in 1997. The updated data has included several important changes in levels of protectionism, including: (i) the substantial reduction in tariffs undertaken by some countries, particularly China as it acceded to the WTO; (ii) the phasing out of quotas on textiles and clothing; (iii) the completion of Uruguay round tariff liberalization; and (iv) the expansion of the European Union. The result is that, because there is now less protectionism to remove, there are fewer gains to be made through liberalization.[26]

A second reason for the decline in predicted gains is that as the Doha round got underway studies began to model the likely outcome of the negotiations based on draft texts and negotiation positions, rather than examining complete liberalization as was the previous norm. The outcome has been that the gains to be had from further trade liberalization have been reduced to what are, in some simulations, insignificant quantities. Ackerman and Gallagher, for instance, predict the DDA to be worth "less than $1 per person per year, or less than a quarter of a penny per person per day" in the developing world.[27]

The point here is that, despite some noted limitations, CGE modeling predictions point to diminishing returns for developing countries as a group from a concluded DDA. And while it is the case that some of these diminished gains result from models that utilize assumptions related to progress made in the negotiations, without a detailed account of how the round has progressed, an appreciation of how little the predicted gains are, as well as what those gains constitute (and the impact they may have on the future development trajectories of the poorest), is incomplete. The next section turns to developments in the negotiations and marries this to the aggregate picture explored earlier in pursuit of a more fulsome account.

Negotiating Doha

It is not just the fall in the aggregate levels of gain predicted by CGE models that is alarming when considering the potential outcome of Doha for LDCs. What is also clear is that the passage of the negotiations has seen the development content of the round whittled away from a concern with issues of implementation, less than full reciprocity and enhanced special and differential treatment, among other things, to one that concentrates primarily on agriculture.[28] What makes this particularly problematic is that any liberalization of agriculture under Doha is likely to be limited; and a focus on agriculture as the primary vehicle for development will lock LDCs into an agriculture-based development strategy that simultaneously yields little but which also reduces the incentives (and, indeed, puts in places barriers) to diversify into higher value, leading-edge sectors. Thus, when viewed in tandem, the poor aggregate gains predicted by the CGE studies, and the lack of opportunity for gains from agriculture and for industrial diversification, illustrate just how problematic the conclusion of the DDA is likely to be for the least developed. But to appreciate how the opportunities available to the least developed have been constrained, and to highlight just how poor the results of Doha are likely to be, we need to explore how the negotiations have unfolded and how the development content of the DDA has been steadily whittled away. To do this, we first need to revisit the run-up to the round's launch before looking at the pattern of the negotiations themselves.

The launch of the Doha round was by no means a certainty. Indeed, European Union Trade Commissioner Leon Brittan's hopes that the 1999 Seattle Ministerial Conference would result in the launch of what was then known as a millennium round were dashed by a walkout of developing country delegates and mass demonstrations. Indeed, in the run-up to the Seattle conference most developing countries declared themselves to be at best ambivalent and at worst hostile to the launch of another round.[29] Much of the reticence towards the launch of a new round coalesced around the problematic nature of the previous Uruguay round and a widespread desire not to repeat an outcome that clearly favored the advanced industrial countries. As the then Indian Minister of Commerce and Industry, Murasoli Maran, put it in the opening session of the Seattle conference, developing countries felt that there were "asymmetries and inequities in several of the agreements" and the special and differential treatment clauses had "remained virtually inoperative."[30] African member states, in particular, were fearful of a comprehensive new round in which they would be required to take on further obligations, particularly if this included new areas such as the environment and labor standards as well as the "Singapore issues" of investment, government procurement, trade facilitation, and competition policy. Stung by an outcome to the Uruguay round that had been costly to implement and had failed to bring them the benefits they had expected, developing countries on the whole felt that they lacked the resources and technical capacity to undertake negotiations in these new areas.

Implementation issues

When the DDA was launched in 2001, two months after the 11 September attacks, these concerns remained. Most developing countries remained convinced that the round should redress the imbalance of the Uruguay round and previous General Agreement on Tariffs and Trade (GATT) agreements, enable developing countries to negotiate on the basis of less than full reciprocity, and give special consideration to the interests of developing countries.[31] Their concerns have focused primarily on the way the industrial countries had implemented key agreements, particularly the Agreement on Agriculture and the Agreement on Textiles and Clothing (ATC). Both had been executed in such as way as to minimize the liberalization of the heavily protected markets. This included, within the Agreement on Agriculture, increasing the effective level of protection by an estimated 61 percent in the European Union and 44 percent in the United States when converting non-tariff barriers into tariffs (known as "dirty tariffication"),[32] and making use of the tariff cutting modalities to ensure that the minimum liberalization was achieved. In the ATC, liberalization was heavily back-loaded towards the latter stages in such a way that almost no meaningful greater market access was given before the third stage on 1 January 2002.[33] In Seattle, the Like Minded Group (eight developing countries that had come together to oppose the Singapore issues) put forward a list of nearly 100 "implementation issues" covering almost every Uruguay round agreement. Their concerns fell into three broad categories:

- Those stemming from an inadequate or faulty implementation of agreements in letter or spirit;
- Those arising from incorrect implementation of the provisions of these agreements; and
- Those which reflected inherent asymmetries and imbalances within the WTO agreements themselves.[34]

In the run-up to the Doha conference, the implementation issues had been split into two categories: those to be dealt with in the run-up to launch of a new round; and those that "could" be negotiated during the round.[35] Hopes that the implementation issues might be dealt with in this fashion were, however, dashed when the decision on "Implementation Related Issues and Concerns," reaffirming the pre-Doha General Council Agreement of December 2000, was agreed at the Ministerial Conference. This gave no meaningful concessions and comprised instead of "best endeavor" (but non-binding and almost always empty) clauses.[36]

Even the relatively innocuous demands of developing countries—such as a proposal that no country should be able to start a new anti-dumping suit against another country within one year of an unsuccessful anti-dumping case in that product—were watered down into best endeavor clauses.[37]

However, matters quickly worsened for the developing countries. Once the round was launched, the industrial countries pursued a tactic of "filibustering" within the Committee on Special and Differential Treatment by consistently postponing the discussions on implementation issues and on making the special and differential treatment clauses in the WTO agreements more operable. Such was the success of this tactic, that by the time of the September 2003 Cancún Ministerial Conference almost nothing had been agreed.[38] This was to the great frustration of the African countries in particular, who, at the end of the marathon special sessions in the previous December seeking an agreement ahead of Cancún, felt that the whole process had been a net loss to them because of the disproportionate amount of human resources consumed, preventing their small delegations from attending other negotiations, but with no end product.[39]

This lack of progress continued in the subsequent years. By the Hong Kong ministerial of 2005 little of substance had been achieved, and the Ministerial Declaration only agreed to "redouble … efforts to find appropriate solutions as a priority to outstanding implementation-related issues."[40] Finally, by the 2009 Geneva Ministerial Conference implementation had been quietly dropped, with only the LDC group mentioning the issue.[41] What had once been seen as a requirement before the developing countries would enter into a new round of multilateral trade negotiations had first been relegated to being part of a new set of negotiations and then quietly forgotten.

While the implementation issues went nowhere, developing countries had greater success with resisting the Singapore issues, though the successes for developing countries in this area ensured that they have had to give ground in other areas, thereby contributing further to the emptying out of the development content of the round. Many developing countries had been deeply opposed to the negotiations of the Singapore issues, but they had been included in the DDA primarily at the insistence of the European Union, with support from Japan and South Korea, among others. Indeed, it was largely because of the lack of support from the United States (except on the issue of government procurement), and therefore the lack of a united front by the two most powerful WTO members, that developing countries were able successfully (and eventually) to oppose their negotiation. However, this was only after the developing countries had played a key role in forcing the collapse of the Cancún ministerial resulting in the ejection of three of the Singapore issues from the negotiations, with only trade facilitation continuing.

Agriculture

Following the removal of the contentious Singapore issues after Cancún, the focus within the DDA negotiations switched towards agriculture. Although discussions have continued on NAMA, it has been tacitly accepted that the eventual numbers used (determining the extent of market opening) will be determined only after agreement is reached on agriculture, and will depend on the extent of "ambition" achieved therein. We return to this below.

Agriculture has taken a special position in the DDA because of its history in the GATT. For the duration of the GATT, agriculture was largely excluded from multilateral oversight. Agricultural liberalization within the GATT's first seven rounds was minimal and huge subsidy regimes in the European countries and United States were constructed without contravening GATT rules and without regard to their effects on other countries. The Uruguay round Agreement on Agriculture was supposed to liberalize agriculture and bring it under multilateral oversight. However, as Sylvia Ostry has noted, this was one half of the developing countries' side of the Uruguay round "grand bargain" which saw them agree to a set of negotiations that was, by everyone's reckoning, not in their interests.[42]

The DDA was meant to rectify these flaws and deliver the liberalization that the Uruguay round had failed to generate. Members committed themselves in the DDA to "comprehensive negotiations aimed at: substantial improvements in market access; reductions of, with a view to phasing out, all forms of export subsidies; and substantial reductions in trade-distorting domestic support."[43] However, over the course of the ensuing negotiations, the likely outcome will deliver at best only the letter, rather than the spirit, of these aims. At the time of the first major breakdown in negotiations in July 2006 (when the DDA was temporarily put on ice), the European Union had offered cuts in aggregate measure of support (AMS)[44] of 75 percent if the United States would cut theirs by 65 percent, while the United States offered a 60 percent reduction if the European Union and Japan would agree to 83 percent.

These figures sound dramatic, but when examined in more detail they become less impressive. This is because of the flawed nature of the Agreement on Agriculture. The Agreement created three categories of subsidies: (i) the "amber box" of trade distorting measures, in which the level of subsidy is directly related to the quantity of the good produced; (ii) the "green box" of subsidies that are "decoupled" from production and are considered minimally trade distorting; and (iii) the "blue box" measures, which are "partially decoupled" from production and are exempt from limits in most circumstances. Only amber box and some blue box payments contribute to the AMS. The critical issue is the level at which the AMS was bound (see Figure 1.2). Because of an agreement between the United States and European Union, the base-year from which bound rates of AMS were calculated was chosen to be the peak years of support (1986–1988). As a result, coupled with subsidy reforms to shift subsidies out of the limited amber box into the unconstrained blue and green boxes, there is a huge gap between the level of AMS bound by the subsidizing countries in the WTO and the level that they actually pay each year (see Figure 1.2). Consequently, cuts in AMS of up to 75 percent would be required before making any impact on current spending programs.[45] Moreover, high world food prices and hence low subsidies in recent years have increased the required cut even further.

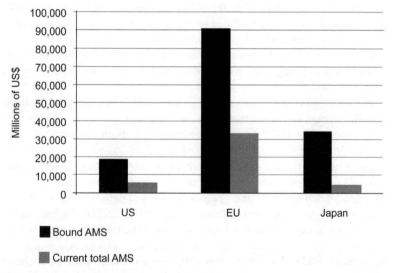

Figure 1.2 Bound and current AMS
Sources: WTO, "Committee of Agriculture – Notification – United States – Domestic Subsidies," G/AG/N/USA/77, 2010; WTO, "Committee of Agriculture – Notification – European Union – Domestic Subsidies," G/AG/N/EEC/64, 2010; WTO, "Committee of Agriculture – Notification – Japan – Domestic Subsidies," G/AG/N/JPN/137, 2008.

In addition, if a final agreement reflects the current status of the negotiations as reflected in the July 2008 drafts prepared by the chairs of the various negotiating committees, as is likely, the United States has been successful in its demands to expand the blue box to include its counter-cyclical payments introduced in the 2002 Farm Bill.[46] This allows the United States to shift around $7 billion of its amber box (and therefore limited) subsidies into the blue box (largely unrestricted).[47]

The green box is also to remain unlimited in the July 2008 draft. This is justified by the claim that green box measures are not (or at most are minimally) trade distorting. However, a series of studies have cast doubt on this assertion.[48] Subsidies, even when decoupled from production, affect the level of production. They reduce risk and provide insurance through assuring an income floor, with the result that farmers are able to take on greater risk than would otherwise be the case and are encouraged to place more marginal land under production. Subsidies for such things as research and extension services, conservation and funding structural changes to farm size and infrastructure, have an effect on productivity. Agricultural output is therefore greater than would be the case if there were no subsidies. That even green box subsidies increase output is shown by the experience of the EU and US subsidy regimes. Since the completion of the Uruguay round both the European Union and United States have shifted subsidies towards the green box, but this has had no detrimental effect on their market share of world exports, despite the fact that the market share for both would be significantly smaller if subsidies were reduced.[49] The effect of high subsidies paid by the rich countries is thus to reduce the economic opportunities for developing countries and lower world prices, such that farmers in the developing world receive less for their produce. The DDA negotiations, as they currently stand, have failed to tackle this issue.

Cotton

Cotton has achieved particular prominence in the DDA negotiations because of the detrimental effects of high subsidies in the United States on world cotton prices and the livelihoods of millions of cotton farmers in West and Central Africa. Four African countries—Benin, Burkina Faso, Mali and Chad, known as the Cotton Four—have consistently pushed the issue in the DDA and are demanding that cotton receive special and more urgent treatment that goes beyond the agricultural deal.[50] This has, rhetorically at least, been agreed in the decision of 1 August 2004 that cotton would be treated "ambitiously, expeditiously and specifically" within the agriculture negotiations.[51] Director-General

Lamy has noted that "cotton has become a litmus test of the commitment to make the WTO Doha round of global trade negotiations a truly development round."[52] So far, however, the commitment to this aim has been lacking, with the United States in particular seeking to delay addressing the issue. In the July 2008 push for a conclusion to the DDA, which came unexpectedly close to a deal, of the 20 critical issues identified by Director-General Lamy that needed agreement, 18 were resolved, the negotiations broke down over the 19th—a special safeguard mechanism to protect food security and rural livelihoods in developing countries—while cotton, the 20th, was not even discussed.

Leaving cotton until last poses dangers for the Cotton Four (and others with an interest in the sector). Once all other pieces of a deal are put in place, there will be huge pressure to finalize the negotiations. Though the Cotton Four have thus far received a considerable amount of support from other members in their demands, this is likely to diminish rapidly when cotton is the last roadblock preventing the conclusion of the round. If they are to have any chance of getting the issue addressed, the Cotton Four will need to maintain the support of the big emerging economies. This will be hampered by China's cotton subsidies having overtaken those of the United States to become the largest in the world.[53] If a few poor African countries find themselves isolated against massive US (and other) opposition, they will find it almost impossible to withstand the pressure to accept a compromise, however weak.

NAMA

NAMA is a critical area for developing countries because it affects their ability to industrialize and shift their economies away from a reliance on agricultural and raw material production. However, it is also a sector in which the industrialized countries continue to have a comparative advantage, particularly in high technology and high value goods. The United States, and to a lesser extent the European Union, have been pushing for a strong deal in NAMA to open up the economies of the emerging nations, particularly India, China, and Brazil. With the exception of China, which bound its tariffs at an average of 10 percent when it acceded to the WTO, these countries have relatively high levels of bound tariffs. The European Union and United States, in marked contrast to their offers on agricultural subsidies, are demanding that the NAMA agreement should go beyond cutting out the water in developing countries' tariff schedules and bite into applied tariffs. They have repeatedly argued that this is essential for the "development" content of the DDA to be realized—that is, that the deal should create new market access into those countries that are achieving the highest rates of growth.[54] This conflicts with the DDA stipulation that the developing countries would be required to give "less than full reciprocity in reduction commitments,"[55] and would severely hamper their ability to pursue a flexible trade regime to promote industrialization.[56] This is also a problem for LDCs. Though they are not being required to make cuts into applied tariffs, the proposed NAMA deal will require them to bind a high percentage of their tariff lines and to cut some of the water from their current tariff schedule. Again, the effect is to restrict their capacity to apply tariffs as part of an industrialization strategy.

LDCs

Focusing on achieving results for LDCs plays a prominent role in the DDA Work Programme.[57] However, offers in this area have been less than hoped, particularly in the area of granting developing countries duty-free and quota-free market access. The United States offered at the Hong Kong ministerial meeting to grant LDCs duty-free quota-free access on 97 percent of tariff lines, and has steadfastly refused to go beyond this. As a result, many of the exports of LDCs are excluded. Around 300 US tariff lines will be excluded, with two-thirds of Bangladesh's exports, for instance, concentrated in just 25 lines.[58] As such, the agreement effectively grants LDCs duty-free quota-free market access on products that they do not export, while excluding most of those on which they are able to compete.

What we see across the range of issues examined here, then, is that the "development" content of the round has been whittled away over the course of the negotiations, and pressure has been applied by the industrial countries to subvert the original meaning of the DDA Work Programme. The DDA, as the likely agreement currently stands, will not deliver development, nor increased trading opportunities for the developing world, particularly the least developed. Agriculture remains the most important area for many people across the developing world and is a critical area to get right if the DDA is to deliver on its promises; but equally, a focus on agriculture alone will serve to lock developing countries into a particular kind of production, precluding diversification into other areas.

Conclusion

In fusing together the insights of economic models on the predicted outcome of the DDA with an analysis of the patter and pattern of the progress of the negotiations we see that the likely gains for the LDCs from the Doha round are both small and deeply problematic. The introduction of new data on declined levels of protection and the running of projections on the basis of draft texts clearly shows that the overall size of the Doha pie is smaller than initially envisaged and considerably less for LDCs. This situation is made worse when the pattern of the negotiations unfolding is taken into account. Implementation issues, a key requirement for the developing countries in the run-up to the launch of the DDA, have been squeezed out of the negotiations. The move towards a focus on agriculture as the core development content of the round has been problematic because of a lack of ambition and commitment on the part of the United States and European Union, the capacity for subsidy box shifting to undermine any agreement that might be reached, and the inadequacy of the attention paid to issues like cotton. In addition, the focus on liberalization does little to address the crucial agricultural issues for LDCs, such as how to ensure greater food security and self-sufficiency. Likewise, the pressure many developing countries have come under in the NAMA negotiations highlights the conflict between the liberalization agenda and the need of developing countries to maintain flexibility in trade policies. Moreover, little comfort can be found elsewhere in the DDA as the questionable value of commitments on duty-free and quota-free access illustrate.

Without a dramatic refocusing of the content of the DDA, there is little substance to maintain continued LDC participation in the round. And given that LDC participation is necessary for a deal to be agreed on the basis of a single undertaking, the need to ensure their continued participation in this and any future round is crucial. At a bare minimum, the negotiations must provide the least developed with a means to protect, in the short term, their agricultural sectors in times of import shortages, space to pursue an industrialization strategy, offer real market openings in areas of immediate and future value, and address outstanding implementation issues (see *The Johannesburg Statement on the DDA*, in the appendix to this volume, for a more comprehensive list of how the content of the DDA needs to be refocused if it is to deliver for LDCs). The chances of even this bare minimum resulting, however, look slight. Moreover, given the head of steam that is emerging for some kind of "variable geometry" or "plurilateralism" to feature in the final deal (in which some members agree to some, but not necessarily all, aspects of a deal thereby abandoning the single undertaking commitment that every member must agree to every aspect of an agreement), any influence that LDCs have in the outcome will be eroded further. Should this prove to be the case, Doha is likely to be remembered as just another asymmetrical multilateral trade deal.

Notes

1 This is a revised and updated version of James Scott and Rorden Wilkinson, "The Poverty of the Doha Round and the Least Developed Countries," *Third World Quarterly* 32, no. 4 (2011): 611–627.

2 G-20 2010, *The Seoul Summit Document*, paragraph 44, www.g8.utoronto.ca/g20/2010/g20seoul-doc.pdf.

3 G-20 2010, *Seoul Summit Leaders' Declaration*, paragraphs 5 and 9, www.g8.utoronto.ca/g20/2010/g20seoul.pdf.

4 G-20 2011, *Cannes Summit Leaders' Declaration*, paragraph 66, www.G-20.org/Documents2011/11/Cannes%20Declaration%204%20November%202011.pdf.

5 See Scott and Wilkinson, "The Poverty of the Doha Round," 611–612.

6 See, for example, Drusilla K. Brown, Alan V. Deardorff, and Robert V. Stern, "Multilateral, Regional, and Bilateral Trade-Policy Options for the United States and Japan," *The World Economy* 26, no. 6 (2003): 803–828; Sebastian Hess and Stephan von Cramon-Taubadel, "A Meta-Analysis of General and Partial Equilibrium Simulations of Trade Liberalisation under the Doha Development Agenda," *The World Economy* 31, no. 6 (2008): 804–840; Sandra Polaski, *Winners and Losers: Impact of the Doha Round on Developing Countries* (Washington, DC: Carnegie Endowment for International Peace, 2006). Technically some of these employ partial rather than general equilibrium models, but for ease of exposition the term "CGE" is used in this paper to refer to all simulation exercises.

7 See, for example, Clive George, *The Truth About Trade: The Real Impact of Liberalization* (London and New York: Zed Books, 2010); Faizel Ismail, *Reforming the World Trade Organization: Developing countries in the Doha Round* (Jaipur: CUTS International and Friedrich Ebert Stiftung, 2009); Donna Lee, "The Cotton Club: The African Group in the Doha Development Agenda," in *The WTO after Hong Kong: Progress in, and Prospects for, the Doha Development Agenda*, ed. Donna Lee and Rorden Wilkinson (London: Routledge, 2007), 137–154; Fatoumata Jawara and Aileen Kwa, *Behind the Scenes at the WTO: The Real World of International Trade Negotiations* (London: Zed Books, 2003); and James Scott and Rorden Wilkinson, "What Happened to Doha in Geneva? Re-engineering the WTO's Image while Missing Key Opportunities," *European Journal of Development Research* 22, no. 2 (2010): 141–153.

8 William R. Cline, *Trade Negotiations in the Tokyo Round: A Quantitative Assessment* (Washington, DC: Brookings Institute, 1978).

9 Hess and von Cramon-Taubadel, "A Meta-Analysis."

10 James Scott, "The Use and Misuse of Negotiation Simulations," *Journal of World Trade* 42, no. 1 (2008): 87–104.

11 See Frank Ackerman, "The Shrinking Gains from Trade: A Critical Assessment of Doha Round Projections," Working Paper No. 05–01, Global Development and Environment Institute (Medford, MA: Tufts University, 2005); Hess and von Cramon-Taubadel, "A Meta-Analysis."

12 Brown, Deardorff, and Stern, "Multilateral"; Joseph François, Hans van Meijl, and Frank van Tongeren, "Trade Liberalization and Developing Countries under the Doha Round," CEPR Discussion Paper 4032, 2003. The reason for the disparity lies principally with the inclusion in the Brown,

Deardorff, and Stern study of estimates relating to liberalization of foreign direct investment flows.

13 Glenn W. Harrison, Thomas F. Rutherford, David G. Tarr, and Angelo Gurgel, "Regional, Multilateral and Unilateral Trade Policies on MERCOSUR for Growth and Poverty Reduction in Brazil," mimeo (Washington, DC: World Bank, 2003); Kym Anderson and Will Martin, "Agricultural Trade Reform and the Doha Development Agenda," *The World Economy* 28, no. 9 (2005): 1301–1327.

14 For more details, see Ackerman, "The Shrinking Gains from Trade."

15 Ernesto Valenzuela, Kym Anderson, and Thomas Hertel, "Impacts of Trade Reform: Sensitivity of Model Results to Key Assumptions," *International Economics and Economic Policy* 4, no. 4 (2008): 404–407.

16 Specifically, they are taken from Thomas Hertel, David Hummels, Maros Ivanic, and Roman Keeney, "How Confident can we be of CGE-based Assessments of Free Trade Agreements?" *Economic Modelling* 24, no. 4 (2007): 611–635.

17 See P.J. Lloyd and Xiao-guang Zhang, "The Armington Model," Staff Working Paper (Melbourne: Productivity Commission, 2006); Valenzuela, Anderson, and Hertel, "Impacts."

18 Lance Taylor and Rudiger Von Armin, *Modelling the Impact of Trade Liberalisation: A Critique of Computable General Equilibrium Models* (Oxford: Oxfam International, 2006), 41.

19 Rob Vos, "What We Do and Don't Know About Trade Liberalization and Poverty Reduction," DESA Working Paper 50 (New York: DESA, 2007), 7–8.

20 See James Scott, "Squeezing the state: tariff revenue, state capacity and the WTO's Doha Round," BWPI Working Paper No. 169 (Manchester: University of Manchester, 2012). The developed countries do not face this problem because tariff revenue is a very small percentage of total taxes, and because any tax falls are counterbalanced by the reduction in agricultural subsidies.

21 Valenzuela, Anderson, and Hertel, "Impacts," 402–403.

22 Ackerman, "The Shrinking Gains from Trade," 19–22; Joseph Stiglitz and Andrew H. Charlton, "A Development-Friendly Prioritization of Doha Round Proposals," IPD Working Paper (New York and Oxford: Initiative for Policy Dialogue, 2004), 7.

23 For example, Polaski, *Winners and Losers.*

24 George, *The Truth About Trade*, 58–60.

25 Ha-Joon Chang, *Kicking Away the Ladder: Development Strategy in Historical Perspective* (London: Anthem, 2002).

26 See Ackerman, "The Shrinking Gains from Trade," 3.

27 Frank Ackerman and Kevin P. Gallagher, "The Shrinking Gains from Global Trade Liberalization in Computable General Equilibrium Models: A Critical Assessment," *International Journal of Political Economy* 37, no. 1 (2008): 50–77.

28 See Ismail, *Reforming the World Trade Organization.*

29 For an unpacking of the range of developing country views on the launch of a new round, see Rorden Wilkinson, "A Tale of Four Ministerials: The WTO and the Rise and Demise of the Trade-labour Standards Debate," *IPEG Papers in Global Political Economy*, No. 3, 2002.

30 WTO, "Statement by H.E. Mr Murasoli Maran, Seattle Ministerial Conference," WT/MIN(99)/ST/17, 1999.

31 WTO, "Doha Ministerial Declaration," (Geneva: WTO, 2001), WT/MIN (01)/DEC/1, 2001.

32 See Arvind Panagariya, "Developing Countries at Doha: A Political Economy Analysis," *The World Economy* 25, no. 9 (2002): 1219.

33 Laura Baughman, Rolf Mirus, Morris E. Morkre and Dean Spinanger, "Of Tyre Cords, Ties and Tents: Window-Dressing in the ATC?" *The World Economy* 20, no. 4 (1997): 407–434; J. Michael Finger and Julio J. Nogues, "The Unbalanced Uruguay Round Outcome: The New Areas in Future WTO Negotiations," *The World Economy* 25, no. 3 (2002): 321–340.

34 Munir Akram, "Implementation Concerns – A Developing Country Perspective," *South Bulletin* 6 (2001): 1–4, www.southcentre.org; WTO, "Preparations for the 1999 Ministerial Conference, Ministerial Text: Revised Draft," JOB(99)/5868/Rev.1, 1999.

35 *Bridges Weekly Trade News Digest*, "Singapore 'Mini-Ministerial' Moves Doha Agenda Forward," 5, no. 35 (2001).

36 See WTO, "General Council Implementation-Related Issues and Concerns, Decision of 15 December 2000," WT/L/384, 2000; and WTO, "Implementation-related Issues and Concerns: Decision of 14 November 2001," WT/MIN(01)/17, 2001. Such best endeavor clauses have a long history in the GATT and WTO, are little more than cosmetic, and have been almost universally ignored.

37 Panagariya, "Developing Countries"; WTO, "Implementation-related Issues and Concerns," paragraph 7.1.

38 See Amrita Narlikar and Rorden Wilkinson, "Collapse at the WTO: A Cancún Post-Mortem," *Third World Quarterly* 25, no. 3 (2004): 447–460.

39 *Bridges Weekly Trade News Digest*, "S&D Review Coming Down to the Wire – Meeting Almost Daily," 6, no. 41 (2002).

40 WTO, "Ministerial Declaration: Adopted on 18 December 2005," WT/MIN(05)/DEC, 2005, paragraph 39; Rorden Wilkinson, "The WTO in Hong Kong: What it Really Means for the Doha Development Agenda," *New Political Economy* 11, no. 2 (2006): 291–303.

41 WTO, "ACP Ministerial Communiqué to the Seventh Session of the WTO Ministerial Conference and ACP Declaration on the Seventh Session of the WTO Ministerial Conference," WT/MIN(09)/7, 2009; Scott and Wilkinson, "What Happened to Doha in Geneva?"

42 Sylvia Ostry, "The Uruguay Round North-South Grand Bargain: Implications for Future Negotiations," paper presented at the conference The Political Economy of International Trade Law, University of Minnesota, 2000, www.utoronto.ca/cis/ostry/docs_pdf/Minnesota.pdf.

43 WTO, "Doha Ministerial Declaration," WT/MIN(01)/DEC/1, 2001, paragraph 13.

44 The AMS is the total quantity of support given to farmers, minus exempt payments.

45 For background and discussion, see Kym Anderson and Will Martin, "Agricultural Trade Reform and the Doha Development Agenda," *The World Economy* 28, no. 9 (2005): 1301–1327; Oxfam, *Analysis of Recent Proposals in WTO Agricultural Negotiations*, Media Brief, 2005, www.oxfam.org.uk.

46 See WTO, "Revised Draft Modalities for Agriculture," Committee on Agriculture, TN/A/W/4/Rev.3, 2008, paragraph 35.

47 WTO, "Revised Draft Modalities for Agriculture," TN/AG/W/4/Rev.4, 2008, Annex 1.
48 UNCTAD, *Green Box Subsidies: A Theoretical and Empirical Assessment* (Delhi: UNCTAD India, 2007); Ricardo Meléndez-Ortiz, Christophe Bellmann, and Jonathan Hepburn, *Agricultural Subsidies in the WTO Green Box: Ensuring Coherence with Sustainable Development Goals* (Cambridge: Cambridge University Press, 2009); Oxfam, *A Round for Free: How Rich Countries are Getting a Free Ride on Agricultural Subsidies at the WTO,* Oxfam Briefing Paper No. 76 (Oxford: Oxfam, 2005).
49 Oxfam, *A Round for Free,* 24–26.
50 See Lee, "The Cotton Club"; and Chapter 4 of this volume.
51 WTO, "Doha Work Programme: Decision Adopted by the General Council on 1 August 2004," WT/L/579, 2004.
52 WTO, "Revised Draft Modalities for Agriculture," TN/AG/W/4/Rev.4, 2008.
53 Fairtrade Foundation, *The Great Cotton Stitch-up* (London: Fairtrade Foundation, 2010).
54 See, for example, WTO, "Remarks of United States Trade Representative Ron Kirk at the Opening Plenary of the 7th Session of the WTO Ministerial Conference November 30, 2009 – Geneva, Switzerland," 2009, www.wto.org/english/thewto_e/minist_e/min09_e/min09_statements_e.htm.
55 WTO, "Doha Ministerial Declaration," paragraph 16.
56 Ha-Joon Chang, *Why Developing Countries Need Tariffs: How WTO NAMA Negotiations Could Deny Developing Countries' Right to a Future* (Geneva: South Centre, 2005); George, *The Truth About Trade,* 31–50.
57 WTO, "Doha Ministerial Declaration."
58 Oxfam, *What Happened in Hong Kong? Initial Analysis of the WTO Ministerial,* Oxfam Briefing Paper No. 85 (Oxford: Oxfam, 2005).

2 The Doha Development Agenda 10 years on

What next?

Bernard Hoekman

The Doha Development Agenda (DDA) negotiations have now been underway for more than 10 years. The outline of what has emerged as a result of a decade of deliberations is the subject of widespread criticism. The Doha round is in a state of paralysis as a result of major disagreements between the major players on the extent and depth of new market access liberalization commitments, especially for non-agricultural products. Assessments of the market access dimension of what has been negotiated suggest that the DDA could generate a global welfare (real income) boost of some US$160 billion.[1] Whatever one's normative view of what the DDA should deliver, from a positive perspective this is not insignificant and compares well with what was achieved in previous rounds.[2] Moreover, such quantitative assessments of the economic impact of a DDA deal neglect important dimensions of what is (and what could be) on the table.[3] They also ignore the potential downsides of a "no Doha" scenario for the trading system: the negative knock-on effects of a collapse of the talks on the prospects for multilateral cooperation in new trade-related areas and continued implementation of World Trade Organization (WTO) rules and commitments by members. The inability to conclude Doha is costly for the trading system because it implies that the WTO is not delivering on its "legislative" function—the development of new global rules of the game for trade-related policies that give rise to negative pecuniary spillovers.

In what follows I argue that there are three preconditions for concluding the talks. The first of these is an acceptance and recognition that Doha (and the WTO more generally) should *not* be assessed primarily on the basis of the extent to which it results in agreements to reduce *applied* levels of protection. The WTO is not just a marketplace in which countries exchange liberalization commitments: it is also a vehicle through which governments agree on rules of the game for policies, and the institution through which implementation is monitored and negotiated rules and commitments are enforced. These rule-setting and enforcement dimensions of the WTO are very important for firms engaged in trade because they reduce uncertainty regarding the "conditions of competition" they will confront in export markets. Uncertainty can be an important source of market entry and operating costs.

An agreement to lower the applied tariff from 10 to 8 percent for a product will be beneficial to an exporter. Getting the importing country to lower the tariff further to 7 percent will raise the payoff to that exporter, but this marginal improvement in effective market access is likely to be less beneficial than knowing with certainty that the tariff in that market can never exceed 8 percent. Any assessment of the outcome of WTO market access talks therefore needs to include consideration of the value to firms (and consumers) of the reduction in uncertainty that is associated with such "ceiling" tariff bindings. If, in the example just given, the current ceiling binding is 25 percent, an outcome that brings the ceiling binding down to 8 percent therefore has a value that is greater than the 2 percentage point decline in the applied tariff (from 10 to 8 percent). The associated reduction in uncertainty as to what the applied tariff might be in the future is an important dimension of what the WTO process is designed to deliver.

The same argument applies to access to services or government procurement markets: even if governments today have a liberal stance and do not impose discriminatory treatment on foreign suppliers, if this has not been bound in the WTO, there is no constraint on the imposition of discriminatory measures in the future. Thus, commitments to lock-in prevailing policies have value even if there is no liberalization involved at all.

The market access dimension of the DDA extends beyond import tariffs and policies affecting the ability of firms to enter and contest services markets. Some of the areas of negotiation aim to lower the costs associated with satisfying tax and regulatory compliance procedures at borders. A prominent example is the negotiation on trade facilitation, which aims at agreement among countries to apply certain procedures and good practices to transit trade and border clearance processes. Such an agreement will not only lower costs directly but also reduce uncertainty for firms regarding the associated procedures and thus the timeliness of consignments. The "uncertainty reduction" dimension of market access negotiations in the WTO tends to be ignored in the rhetoric and media communication strategies employed by governments and the business community.[4]

A second precondition is recognition that the source of the deadlock that has prevailed since 2008 is disagreement among a small number of large players on market access. This is not something smaller countries can do much about. What is needed is that a "critical mass" of the larger protagonists improve their offers on market access—defined both as reductions in applied barriers to trade and ceiling-binding commitments. The evolution of the Doha negotiations since 2001 has implied that to a larger extent than originally envisaged by some of the major players the talks have revolved around a rather traditional market access agenda: reducing tariffs and agricultural support. The way the negotiations were structured—the main focal point being agreement on "modalities" (formulae) for tariff-cutting and agricultural support-reduction—resulted in protracted negotiations on what could be excluded from the application of formulae (sensitive and special products, exceptions for some countries, flexibilities for others, and the like). This, in turn, created much less clarity regarding what was effectively being offered by a given country than would have resulted from the request-offer modalities used in the Uruguay round. Whatever the role that negotiating modalities played in slowing down progress in "getting to yes," insofar as the results of the 2008 framework of modalities (the formulae and exceptions) are unacceptable to some major players, more will need to be put on the table. This could entail additional liberalization of applied policies, but it could also revolve around greater ambition in terms of locking in current policies (additional policy bindings for goods and services), or the introduction of additional issues on the table.

Third, WTO members need to identify a forward-looking process and work program as part of a Doha deal. Many observers have noted that much has changed during the decade in which the Doha talks have been held. For example, financial market developments, policies to promote the use of bio-fuels, and sustained high economic growth rates in large emerging markets—most notably China—have had impacts on global commodity and food markets. Instead of a situation characterized by low food prices, we now have a situation where prices are expected to remain substantially higher on average than they have been during recent decades, as well as more volatile. Greater demand for food and natural resources and the prospect of more activist use of trade-related policies that have negative pecuniary spillovers on trading partners call for multilateral cooperation to determine rules of the game for food, resource, and climate-related trade policies.

Some of the relevant policies are not part of the Doha agenda; others are in principle but have been excluded or resisted by some WTO members. In addition to the need to address these "new issues," it has become clear that for some subjects that are centrally on the table in Doha the preconditions for a comprehensive multilateral agreement covering all members have not been satisfied—in part because of a lack of common understanding on how to design rules in a way that countries can be assured that there are benefits from participating.

Insofar as the market access deadlock continues through the 2012–2013 period because of electoral cycles, there is a window to launch a process of discussion of some of these issues in working groups under the auspices of existing WTO committees. These deliberations could feed into an eventual Doha round conclusion but more realistically would aim to define an agreed set of follow-on activities that would be pursued under WTO auspices.

These three preconditions do not include a fundamental change in the operating principles of WTO negotiations: that commitments made by members benefit all members (the non-discrimination principle) and that decision-making is based on consensus. While these norms have often been criticized as factors holding up forward progress, there are strong reasons why these practices have become core WTO operating principles, not least because they enhance the voice of developing countries. As discussed later, these core norms do not preclude the use of "critical mass" and variable geometry approaches to the negotiations under which not all members are expected to make concessions in a given area. These approaches are desirable and are already being used. The fact of the matter is that the lack of progress in concluding the Doha round reflects the assessment of major players that what has emerged on the table is not of sufficient interest to them—it is not that a subset of small developing countries are holding up a deal. As is stressed in the economic theory of trade agreements, the WTO is a self-enforcing treaty: if the large players do not see it as being in their interest to deal, changing institutional arrangements and approaches—for example, to shift to greater use of plurilateral agreements, because these can exclude those who do not participate—or to shift to a system of weighted voting and representation will not make a difference.

Moving away from the predominant "market access narrative"

The DDA started with calls by many in the trade and development community for an ambitious outcome, defined as one that would greatly reduce trade barriers and agricultural support policies in Organization for Economic Cooperation and Development (OECD) countries that constrain exports from developing countries. While the elimination of tariff peaks, disciplines on the use of farm production subsidies, and a significant liberalization of access to high-income service markets through the movement of natural persons ("Mode 4" service suppliers) would make the DDA live up to its name, it is clear that only a portion of these objectives is likely to be realized.

Negotiators have been working for almost 10 years to define a negotiating set. The contours of this set have been narrowed down over time, especially following the 2003 Cancún Ministerial Conference when potential new investment, competition, and procurement disciplines were taken off the table. Since 2004 the negotiations have centered primarily on a "traditional" market access and rules agenda (including disciplines on agricultural support policies). This agenda offers potential gains for all WTO members, both in terms of lower barriers on goods and services exports and a reduction in uncertainty regarding possible increases in levels of import protection—through greater tariff bindings, reductions in the average level of bound tariffs (the so-called ceiling tariffs that governments commit not to exceed) and specific commitments for services.

Average tariff levels today are much lower than just a decade ago and far below the averages that prevailed in the 1980s. Quantitative import restrictions have largely disappeared. The last (2008) proposals under active discussion in the DDA would reduce the world average *bound* tariff for agricultural products from 40 to 30 percent and that for non-agricultural goods from 8 to 5 percent. Average *applied* farm tariffs faced by developing country exporters would fall from 14.2 to 11.5 percent; and those on their exports of manufactures from 2.9 to 2.1 percent. The reductions in applied tariffs are beneficial to exporters and consumers, but do not appear to add up to a lot—after all, if Doha only generates less than a one percentage point cut in the average tariff on manufactures this clearly will not do much to lower prices of the goods concerned or enhance the ability of exporters to contest foreign markets.

As Scott and Wilkinson point out in the previous chapter, much attention has centered on the results of global simulation models that suggest the net real income gains from any politically feasible DDA outcome are likely to be small in the aggregate: as mentioned earlier, what was on the table in 2008 would generate "only" US$160 billion or so in additional income as a result of lower trade barriers. Whether one regards this number as significant or not, this numerical lens misconstrues a critical feature (function) of WTO negotiations. These are not primarily about reducing applied levels of protection but center to a great extent on establishing trade policy rules and reducing uncertainty (through the "locking-in" of policies and binding of tariff rates either at, or much closer to, applied levels). The benefits of this dimension of WTO negotiations are ignored in models because economists do not have the technologies to allow them to quantitatively assess these features.

The quantitative analyses also tend to underemphasize the fact that although tariffs are generally already low on average, therefore limiting the aggregate effect of further reductions, the formula-based negotiation modalities that have been developed will effectively eliminate all tariff peaks in OECD countries. The focus should not be on what happens to average tariffs, but what happens to products and sectors where tariffs are much higher than average. We are left with pockets of protectionism (tariff peaks) that are not that relevant in economy-wide terms but that do have significant impacts on the producers/consumers of the goods concerned. The same is true of agricultural support policies in OECD countries, which generate costs for consumers that are not large enough to concern them overly and that negatively affect only a relatively small proportion of economic agents in countries with a comparative advantage in specific products. However, for the affected groups, what is on the table matters much more than what is inferred from looking at the reduction in average tariffs.

Tariff bindings—and more generally negotiated disciplines and restrictions on the ability of governments to use certain policies—reduce the uncertainty that is inherently associated with engaging in international trade. Exporters confront more uncertainty than do firms that operate only in their domestic market. National transactions and contracts can be enforced in national courts; there are no borders where goods may be held up in Customs; there is no exchange rate risk to worry about; and so forth. The fixed costs of getting goods into a foreign market are higher than those associated with domestic transactions. Anything that can be done to lower the costs associated with exporting will both benefit existing exporters and, more importantly, encourage new exporters. As foreign market entry costs fall, more firms will be able to start exporting to new markets. The associated expansion of exports along this so-called extensive margin of trade will boost economic welfare and growth.[5] Trade barriers may be prohibitive for a firm—a 50 percent tariff will be hard to overcome for most firms. Negotiations that result in lower tariffs therefore matter. But if tariffs are already at 5 percent—and the average applied tariff in most countries today is often around or below that figure—variability/uncertainty in the taxes and regulatory regimes that apply in a market can be of much greater concern to firms, and have a much greater effect in impeding entry by firms into export activity and the penetration of new markets. This is a key reason why trade rules matter—even if the associated tariff and other commitments do not do anything to change actual (applied) policy in a given market.

These observations suggest that a first precondition for successful conclusion of the DDA is greater recognition and advocacy that the potential deal on the table has significant benefits, and communicating this more effectively than has been done to date. Selling or criticizing the round on the basis of simulated estimates of real income gains or export growth resulting from the application of market access formulae misses much of the story. Advocacy for the round (and the WTO more generally) needs to center more on the effects of the negotiated rules and policy disciplines. A complete ban on agricultural export subsidies would be a major step forward, for example, and one that cannot be quantified by estimating the impact of removing extant subsidies—especially in a period where high prices have greatly reduced the prevalence of their use. Such a ban is significant because if world prices fall in the future this could not trigger an increase in export subsidies. Maximum allowed levels of domestic agricultural support (subsidy ceilings) would fall by 70 percent in the European Union and 60 percent in the United States, based on the 2008 modalities. Again, instead of stressing how much a deal will reduce the actual amount of subsidization, more emphasis is needed on explaining why such ceiling bindings are valuable. Agricultural protection and subsidies in OECD countries have reduced the amount of food that is traded internationally, and led to greater instability of world prices with large negative spillover effects on developing countries, whether exporters or importers. Disciplines on the ability of governments to use import or export barriers to insulate domestic markets and hence make world markets thicker would be a major source of welfare gain for developing countries.[6]

More ambition on market access: leveraging "critical mass"

Major protagonists in the negotiations, first and foremost the United States, have stressed that more market access concessions are needed in order for any Doha deal to be acceptable. Such additional offers can be configured in a way that all WTO members will benefit more. The dire current economic context for many major OECD nations makes this more important than it was before 2009. There are significant structural adjustment challenges confronting the United States and a number of European Union countries that need to expand net exports as part of a rebalancing of their economies. Conversely, countries with large current account surpluses need to adjust as well, reducing reliance on external demand and increasing domestic consumption and investment. The DDA can be part of the solution—allowing deficit countries to expand exports to countries that have been growing rapidly and facilitating the needed shift in surplus states towards greater domestic absorption.

Most of the focus to date in the DDA has been on the agriculture and Non-Agricultural Market Access (NAMA) negotiations. Agriculture is a subject that pits countries with a comparative advantage such as Australia, New Zealand, Argentina, and Brazil against the European Union and Japan. This traditional constellation of opposing interests has been complicated by world market developments in the last five years. The United States, a major exporter of food and traditionally a strong proponent of liberalization, also has strong protectionist interests in specific crops. The implementation of bio-fuel consumption mandates and related subsidies has tilted the incentives for some farmers away from pushing for better access to export markets as domestic demand for their crop has expanded. High prices and volatility have increased the desire of many countries to maintain the possibility of (re-)imposing trade barriers and using policy to promote greater self-sufficiency. The push in the DDA by many developing countries to exempt "special" products and for a special safeguard mechanism has attenuated the interest of exporters to support what has emerged from the DDA to date, while actions by some exporting countries to restrict exports so as to limit domestic price increases have strengthened concerns in importing nations regarding their ability to rely on global markets as a source of supply of food.

The NAMA talks have revolved around "modalities": agreeing on the formula and the extent and coverage of allowable exceptions (the formula approach by its nature induces a focus on exempting "sensitive" products). While what is on the table is significant, some countries—the United States in particular—argue that greater reductions are needed in large emerging markets. While concessions that go beyond the contours of the 2008 package will be beneficial for the world economy, tariffs have already been much reduced in many countries—unilaterally. This raises the question of the value of additional liberalization at the margin as compared to binding the liberalization that has already occurred. As noted previously, bringing bound tariffs down towards applied rates is beneficial because it reduces uncertainty. A willingness by the United States and European Union to impose lower caps on agricultural support—which would also help improve fiscal positions—could be part of a quid pro quo for further reductions in applied tariffs and fewer product exceptions. Commodity prices are projected to remain substantially higher than they were during the 1990s and 2000s, providing an opportunity to substantially reduce the magnitude of subsidy programs and to lock this in. Reducing the extent of the proposed exclusion of special and sensitive products would increase the cut in average bound tariffs resulting from the agricultural formula: without the exceptions the average bound tariff would be 20 instead of 30 percent.

The contours of any deal to do more to lower applied barriers to trade and agricultural support need to be pursued by the large players on a "critical mass" basis. What small countries do in this regard is of second order importance in terms of "getting to yes," in that they can do little to help mobilize the support for a deal that is needed in the national parliaments of the large players. A key feature of critical mass agreements is that they need not involve all of the WTO membership. Instead, they imply agreement among the large players to undertake certain actions, with the associated benefits extended to all WTO members (that is, those who are not part of a deal are allowed to "free ride"). Such an approach is nothing new for the WTO; in practice, negotiations under the General Agreement on Tariffs and Trade (GATT) always were limited to those countries with the greatest interest in a particular area or set of products, with whatever was eventually agreed being extended to all members as a result of the most favored nation rule. The threshold for agreement has tended to be around 90 percent: that is, some 90 percent of the trade involved in an area or set of products needed to be between the participating countries. A recent example of a critical mass agreement is the Information Technology Agreement, but tariff negotiations in earlier GATT rounds also conform to this rule of thumb.[7]

To date, the focus of efforts to extend what is on the table on market access has centered on sectoral approaches and proposals. This has been controversial. While in principle additional sectoral commitments may result in an eventual agreement, other elements of the DDA offer significant scope for countries to expand the level of their commitments. Services are one area where much could be done. Although some increase in the offers on agriculture and NAMA will help negotiators make the case that improvements have been made on what was on the table in 2008, focusing more on complementing the NAMA-centered efforts with meaningful commitments on services offers significant prospects for doing more within the currently defined negotiating agenda. Services negotiations have been sidelined for much of the post-2001 period, in part as a result of a decision that services talks would commence in full force only *after* a deal on agricultural and NAMA modalities was concluded.

Trade and investment in services is inhibited by a range of policy barriers that are more restrictive than those applying to trade in goods, but the best offers to date are on average still twice as restrictive as actual policy.[8] This matters for a number of reasons. Most important is the development dimension. The productivity and competitiveness of both goods and services firms depends on access to low-cost and high-quality producer services such as telecommunications, transport, finance, and distribution. Telecommunications are crucial to the dissemination and diffusion of knowledge; transport services affect the cost of shipping goods and the movement of workers within and between countries; financial services influence the transformation of savings into investment and their allocation to the most productive uses; professional services such as accounting, legal, engineering, and consulting services reduce transaction costs associated with the operation of markets and are channels through which process innovations are transmitted across firms. Retail and whole-sale distribution services connect producers and consumers. Health and education services are key inputs into—and determinants of—the quality of human capital.

Services have assumed added significance in the aftermath of the 2008 financial crisis. Much of the policy debate on the need for "global reba-lancing" revolves around fiscal, monetary, and exchange rate policies. But, as services account for most non-labor costs of production, action to improve the efficiency of services must be a major focus of policy in deficit countries, complementing policies to switch the pattern of expenditure and reduce net consumption. Expanding domestic consumption and investment in surplus countries must also involve a focus on services—including the retail sector, leisure-related activities, social and health insur-ance services, pension fund/asset management, among others. Expanding the scope for international trade and investment in services can help sup-port the required structural changes by expanding the supply and quality/variety of such services in major surplus countries such as China.

A more ambitious approach to the Doha services negotiations is needed, driven by the 15–20 or so WTO members that account for the lion's share of global services production. A critical mass agreement on a package with three elements could make a big difference in support-ing an overall Doha deal. While not being overly ambitious in terms of liberalization (that is, they are consistent with the objectives agreed by WTO Ministers in Annex C of the Hong Kong declaration) and thus feasible to implement, they would help make the negotiations more relevant to the needs of business than they have been to date:[9]

- Agreement to maintain the degree of openness to trade in services embodied in current policies by undertaking to make binding com-mitments where currently applied policies are more liberal than current legal commitments under the General Agreement on Trade in Services (GATS);
- A package of liberalization commitments organized around clusters of services that are critical to business users and the smooth func-tioning of the global economy—such as logistics and supply chain management; and

- Greater freedom for the temporary movement of contractual service suppliers and independent professionals, conditional on source-country obligations related to the management of such movement, building on initiatives at the bilateral and regional levels that have already been put in place (for example, the Asia-Pacific Economic Cooperation framework for business visas).

One of the subjects on the Doha agenda that is of great potential importance from a market access perspective is trade facilitation. The costs created by inefficient trade facilitation—both monetary, and, more important, delays and uncertainty associated with clearance and regulatory compliance—can be greater than the cost of paying tariffs on the affected imports. The recent trade literature has documented the importance of trade costs as a determinant of whether firms export; that exporters tend to be among the most productive firms; and that the productivity effect of greater trade—deriving from both imports and exports—is an important driver of overall economic growth. Most firms do not export, and those that do often sell into only a few markets. Major factors explaining this include lack of information, difficulties in obtaining credit, and various costs that must be overcome in entering each new export market. Trade clearance and associated regulatory compliance assessment requirements are an element of such market entry costs that impede the participation of smaller firms in export activities.

A trade facilitation agreement that reduces such costs will expand trade along both the intensive and extensive margin. The latter is particularly important from a welfare and growth perspective because new varieties of goods and services account for a large part of the potential gains from liberalization. This is a feature of the Doha negotiating agenda that is rarely emphasized sufficiently in discussions of what is on the table. It is not only the effect of a marginal reduction in the costs that impact on existing trade flows that generates benefits; more important is the extent to which agreements that lower trade costs generate new trade.

Define the path to be pursued looking forward

There are many systemically important issues that the DDA does not address and one reason for concluding the DDA as rapidly as possible is to clear the ground for efforts to do so. Indeed, a precondition for successful conclusion of the talks is likely to be explicit agreement to engage in efforts to cooperate in areas that are currently off the table. Some of the relevant issues that arise are well known and have been giving rise to tensions and disputes. Examples include bio-fuel subsidies and other types of "green" industrial policy measures; the use of trade measures as part of domestic climate change mitigation programs motivated by competitiveness and leakage concerns; the use of export taxes on inputs to support domestic downstream industries; and the use of export restrictions on food products as part of an effort to insulate domestic markets. Others include discrimination in government procurement; restrictions on foreign ownership of assets (natural resources; real estate; enterprises in "sensitive" sectors); and allegations of exploitation of market power/anticompetitive behavior by multinationals along global value chains that have adverse effects in jurisdictions that are not able to impose corrective measures.

There is also an important agenda revolving around increasing the transparency of WTO member policies. The financial crisis revealed major gaps in the available information on trade and investment policies. WTO notification requirements are often not satisfied on a timely basis, if at all. In some areas—trade finance, for example—there are no global databases on flows and prices. Very little is known about applied government procurement practices. There are no comprehensive depositories of information on non-tariff measures applied by WTO members. Concrete actions to enhance both monitoring and analysis of trade and investment policies and their effects—including the extent to which countries discriminate in favor of some trading partners in the context of preferential trade agreements—will help the WTO fulfill its role of sustaining cooperation.

Space constraints prevent a substantive discussion of the issues that WTO members arguably need to get to grips with. The main point here is to recognize that there are various issues that concern all WTO members, and that call for multilateral cooperation and agreement on the rules of the game that should be followed to maintain an open trading system. Agreeing on a process to address these matters or, at the very least, on a process to define where and how they are best addressed will give assurances that issues of interest to all WTO members will be addressed in the future. This applies as well to defining whether issues that have been raised by some members deserve to be considered by the WTO. An example is systematic exchange rate undervaluation. This is a matter that some observers have argued needs to be addressed through WTO rules to allow the WTO dispute settlement mechanism to be used to determine instances where a member should be allowed to impose trade barriers on imports originating in a country that has been found to engage in deliberate undervaluation. At the moment the WTO does not provide this possibility. There are good conceptual and practical reasons why the WTO does not do so, and compelling arguments why efforts to go down this path are likely to do much more harm than good in terms of sustaining multilateral cooperation.[10] Whatever one's views, clarifying what are, and what are not, subject to rules and what are permissible policies to promote investment in and production of tradeables is important in defining the boundaries of the WTO.

A major element of any future-looking agenda is to further improve the coverage of the GATS and reduce barriers to trade and investment in services. Given that regulatory policies often have the effect of constraining trade, and that countries may have legitimate concerns about the effects of liberalization because of inadequate, or an absence of, regulation, the post-Doha action agenda could include putting in place "modalities" through which WTO members can engage and learn from each other as regards regulatory policies affecting the contestability of markets. In the case of both service sector policies and non-tariff barriers, the objectives underlying specific measures are often regulatory in nature, not necessarily protectionist.

The WTO does not offer very effective mechanisms through which members can learn lessons from each other on the design and implementation of regulatory systems that minimize negative impacts on trade. The prospects for liberalization of trade in services, for example, would benefit from the creation of "knowledge platforms" that bring together regulators, trade officials and stakeholders to assess current policies and options for improving regulation and trade policies; as well as to identify where cooperation between regulators could facilitate more trade. A parallel process that does *not* involve negotiations but instead focuses on the substance of regulation (or the effects of a lack of appropriate regulation) would help countries improve regulatory regimes and create the preconditions for a more open trade regime to have greater benefits for consumers. This need not be through the WTO— it may be better pursued through other fora—but it is arguably something that is missing at the moment. Creating such platforms and mechanisms for exchange and learning can help avoid a recurrence of the DDA experience with the Singapore issues and help prepare the ground for future negotiations on services.[11]

Moving forward to discuss these issues need not wait for the conclusion of the DDA. Adding some of them to the agenda may help conclude the DDA—especially if the market access components of the Doha round remain paralyzed in the coming years. Ideally the DDA would be concluded rapidly based on what is on the table—and there is arguably more than enough on the table if more is done on services and the appropriate weight is given to the value of binding policies as opposed to actual liberalization of applied policies. But if the talks continue to drag on for some time, the hiatus provides an opportunity to launch discussions in the relevant WTO committees and/or special sessions on some or all of the subjects noted earlier. Such efforts should be defined as exploratory, preparing the ground for possible future negotiations, although they may result in decisions to move forward in a given area. The main point is that the opportunity cost of waiting for Doha to come to a conclusion is increased substantially if it means that discussions are delayed on the various issues that are not on the DDA agenda and that call for cooperative solutions.

Conclusion

Concluding Doha is important in itself and even more important in sustaining the multilateral cooperation on trade that has resulted in the current open rules-based multilateral trade regime. Opinions differ on the prospects for continued implementation of the rules and disciplines that are embodied in the WTO and the functioning of the dispute settlement mechanism if there is a prolonged DDA deadlock. It may well be that "no Doha" has no major repercussions for the WTO as an institution. Even if this proves to be the case, continued paralysis is costly for the system because it prevents progress on the "legislative side"—the negotiation and agreement of rules of the game in new areas as well as old areas that matter for the operation of global markets.

In addition to its importance for continued multilateral cooperation on trade, a Doha deal is needed to support the process of global re-balancing, which in turn is part of the broader challenge of managing the transition away from the export development driven strategy that has been pursued by a number of countries, most notably and significantly by China. The needed process of structural reform and adjustment includes a major expansion of services sector activity in both the advanced and emerging markets. There is much that the WTO can and should do to support this transformation, which will inevitably take time. Services liberalization and expanding the coverage of policy commitments in the GATS is one element. More generally, the WTO offers a multilateral umbrella under which the major trading powers can agree on how to manage and support the transition that each needs to make—China towards a more domestic demand driven growth model; the United States towards expanding net exports and a decline in the current account/fiscal deficit. Using the WTO as an umbrella to map out rules of the game and deal with policy externalities is likely to be more productive than the pursuit of unilateral policies—both in terms of supporting the needed transformation and maintaining an open trading system.

As noted briefly at the outset of this chapter, moving forward on the DDA arguably does not require any fundamental change in the way that the WTO negotiating process is organized. There has been much discussion in this regard about the Single Undertaking: the notion that nothing is agreed until everything is agreed. This clearly is a factor that can slow down the process of "getting to yes." One solution that is often proposed is a greater reliance on plurilateral agreements that bind only those countries willing to sign on, who then may decide not to accord the benefits of what has been agreed to non-signatories. The main reason to consider plurilaterals is to avoid free riding—an issue that arises if some large countries do not want to join. However, this is not the source of the current deadlock—the problem is that some large countries want more than other large countries want to offer. If the demandeurs form a club that excludes those that they are seeking concessions from, this will not address the source of the problem because it will not create incentives for those excluded to join—reflecting the fact that the demandeurs have little to offer. Plurilateral agreements can only be effective instruments to address market access if those that form the club make economically meaningful concessions to each other—this is not the case in NAMA or agriculture in the Doha round.[12]

Relaxing the "single undertaking constraint" by pursuing a "partial harvest" strategy—agreeing to move forward in areas in which a deal can be done—could be beneficial. The single undertaking implies an opportunity cost if agreements in specific areas must wait for an overall deal to be agreed. If such areas also generate little in the way of "reciprocity value"—that is, the issue is not something that trading partners care much about (in that the prevailing policies that become subject to additional disciplines do not generate substantial negative pecuniary spillovers), carving them out of the single undertaking does not come at the cost of taking valuable negotiating chips off the table that could have been used to link to other issues. Alternatively, if the gains and costs of agreement in a specific area are balanced, a carve-out also comes at little cost from a linkage perspective. The best example of such an issue of the first type is duty-free quota-free access for least developed countries, because this is an action that does not entail any reciprocity by those countries. An example of the second possibility is trade facilitation—this will benefit all WTO members, both as exporters and as importers. As inefficient trade facilitation mostly generates socially wasteful costs—as opposed to rents or government revenues (terms of trade effects)—moving forward on trade facilitation is important from a trade promotion and economic welfare perspective, and would come at low cost from a "linkage foregone" perspective because most of the benefits accrue to the countries that take actions to improve facilitation. These issues and other critical areas are reflected in *The Johannesburg Statement on the DDA*.[13]

The problem with the partial harvest approach is that insofar as the area concerned requires approval by parliaments it generates political and administrative costs compared with a situation where a package agreement (the single undertaking) is put forward for approval. In an area such as trade facilitation, a more pragmatic approach seems desirable: given that most of the benefits of trade facilitation accrue to the countries that pursue reforms, governments should simply do so rather than incur the opportunity costs of waiting for a deal to be struck at the WTO.

Notes

1 David Laborde, Will Martin, and Dominique van der Mensbrugghe, "Implications of the Doha Market Access Proposals for Developing Countries," World Bank Policy Research Working Paper 5697 (Washington, DC: World Bank, 2011).

2 See Will Martin and Patrick Messerlin, "Why is it so Difficult? Trade Liberalization Under the Doha Agenda," *Oxford Review of Economic Policy* 23, no. 3 (2007): 347–366.

3 For a more extensive treatment of some of these arguments, see Bernard Hoekman, Will Martin, and Aaditya Mattoo, "Conclude Doha: It Matters!" *World Trade Review* 9, no. 3 (2010): 505–530.

4 Empirical assessments of the possible impacts of an agreement on trade facilitation suggest that the likely associated reductions in trade costs for both importers and exporters can easily generate a larger trade response than would arise from the reduction of applied tariffs generated by the proposed 2008 formulae cuts. See e.g. Bernard Hoekman and Alessandro Nicita, "Trade Policy, Trade Costs and Developing Country Trade," *World Development* 39, no. 12 (2011): 2069–2079.

5 There are a number of channels through which costs for firms can be lowered, including liberalization at home. Recent empirical work has shown that the indirect productivity effects associated with opening markets to new imported varieties of goods account for 10 to 25 percent of the typical country's per capita income growth (Christian Broda, Joshua Greenfield, and David Weinstein, "From Groundnuts to Globalization: A Structural Estimate of Trade and Growth," NBER Working Paper 12512, 2006). On the export side of the equation, the magnitude of the productivity gains from reducing trade costs come from the expansion of trade along the extensive margin—firms selling into new markets and selling new products into existing and new markets, driven by a process of intra-industry adjustment in which the less productive firms exit and the more productive ones expand. See Stephen J. Redding, "Theories of Heterogeneous Firms and Trade," 2010, for a survey of the recent literature, www.princeton.edu/~reddings/papers/hetfirmstrade_080110.pdf.

6 Will Martin and Kym Anderson, "Export Restrictions and Price Insulation During Commodity Price Booms," Policy Research Working Paper 5645 (Washington, DC: World Bank, 2011).
7 See Bernard Hoekman and Michel M. Kostecki, *The Political Economy of the World Trading System* (Oxford: Oxford University Press, 2009), 3rd edition.
8 Batshur Gootiiz and Aaditya Mattoo, "Services in Doha: What's on the Table?" *Journal of World Trade* 43, no. 5 (2009): 1013–1030.
9 Bernard Hoekman and Aaditya Mattoo, "Services Trade Liberalization and Regulatory Reform: Redesigning International Cooperation," World Bank Policy Research Working Paper 5517 (Washington, DC: World Bank, 2010).
10 WTO commitments pertain to specific policy measures—tariff bindings, etc.— and to general principles—such as most favored nation (MFN) and national treatment. Absent a system of fixed rates, the exchange rate is not a policy instrument on which a government can make specific commitments. It is generally endogenous, and will reflect a mix of fiscal and monetary policies. Assessing whether a government is engaging in deliberate undervaluation is inherently a subjective exercise that requires judgment. Even if this assessment is left to the International Monetary Fund (IMF)—as is specified in the relevant WTO provision (GATT Art. XV) dealing with exchange rates— and the IMF makes a judgment that implies deliberate manipulation, it will be very difficult to assess objectively to what extent a country is undercutting its trade policy commitments to liberalize access to its markets and/or is subsidizing its exports. This is important because there are many objectives that may underpin an active exchange rate management policy that have nothing to do with seeking to circumvent trade policy commitments. Nor is it the case that exchange rate interventions are in fact equivalent to the pursuit of a mercantilist export policy—it may in fact have no effect on trade at all. (For a detailed analysis and discussion, see Robert W. Staiger and Alan O. Sykes, "Currency Manipulation and World Trade," *World Trade Review* 9, no. 4 (2010): 583–627).
11 For an elaboration of these arguments see Hoekman and Mattoo, "Services Trade Liberalization."
12 Plurilateral agreements differ from critical mass agreements in that the latter apply on a MFN basis—i.e. they permit free riding by those that are not part of the critical mass.
13 Global Poverty Summit 2011, *The Johannesburg Statement on the Doha Development Agenda*, www.povertydialogue.org, reproduced in the appendix to this volume.

Part II
Key issues

Key Issues

3   Food security and the WTO

Jennifer Clapp

Food price volatility experienced in the 2007–2011 period has had a profound impact on food security in the world's poorest countries. The food price spikes experienced in 2007–2008 were especially stark, with the doubling of prices of key staples, such as wheat, soybeans, and corn in a short period of time. The International Monetary Fund (IMF) price index of internationally traded food commodities rose by 56 percent from January 2007 to June 2008.[1] This sharp and sudden rise put basic food staples out of the reach of many of the world's poorest people. Food price riots experienced in 2008 across the developing world were witness to this basic fact. Food prices have remained volatile since that time, with sharp ups and downs. By 2011, food prices had again reached the peaks experienced in 2008.

At the height of the 2008 food price spikes, policy briefs issued by the World Bank, the Organization for Economic Cooperation and Development (OECD), and the Food and Agriculture Organization (FAO) all called for a rapid conclusion to the Doha round of trade talks as a key policy response to address the crisis.[2] In a speech to the World Food Summit in June 2008 Pascal Lamy, Director-General of the World Trade Organization (WTO), echoed these reports: "In order to cope with soaring food prices, supply must adjust to demand. For this to happen, trade will help. Easier, more open trade can strengthen the production capacity of developing countries, rendering them less vulnerable … This is why the WTO Doha round of trade negotiations can be part of the medium-to-long term response to the food price crisis."[3]

But the WTO trade talks collapsed in July 2008, just as the impact of higher food prices was pushing ever more people in the developing world into poverty and hunger. Ironically, the cause of the trade talks' collapse was the agriculture agreement—specifically the rich countries' unwillingness to agree to robust measures that would enable poor countries to charge higher tariffs on a temporary basis on imports from rich countries when there were surges in imports of food products that were important for the livelihood of poor countries' farmers.

Although food prices fell back briefly in late 2008 and in 2009, the impact of the crisis was still felt in the world's poorest countries at this time. By early 2009, the FAO announced that over one billion people were food insecure, moving the world further from its Millennium Development Goal of halving world hunger to no more than 420 million people by 2015.[4] The number of hungry people declined slightly by early 2010, although volatility returned to food prices in 2010 and 2011. The FAO food index hit a new peak in early 2011 as wheat prices shot up sharply on news of poor harvests in Russia that was accompanied by an export ban in that country.[5] Food prices remained high throughout 2011 despite Russia's mid-year removal of its export restrictions.

Throughout this period of food price volatility and climbing hunger, calls for a rapid completion of the Doha round continued. The G-8 and G-20 leaders' meetings, for example, have not yet missed an opportunity to promote the conclusion to the round in conjunction with its statements on the need to improve global food security. But despite the pledges by WTO member states to make meaningful progress, the Doha round is still stuck in a state of stalemate.

It is important to step back and examine the linkages between the WTO's Doha agenda and food security, especially as food prices continue to fluctuate sharply and as most economists predict high and volatile food prices for the foreseeable future. In this chapter, I advance two points about the linkage between the WTO's Doha round and food security. The first is that the food crisis and episodes of price volatility are much more complex than simple supply and demand imbalances and the trade barriers that restrict the movement of food across borders. Simply facilitating more trade will not necessarily reduce food price volatility. The second is that the Doha round itself does not do a great deal to help the world's poorest countries to head off future food security crises. In fact, the measures likely to be adopted—should the current round be eventually completed—may exacerbate some of the key factors that have contributed to both volatility in prices and the vulnerability of developing countries to sharp food price shifts.

Complexity of the food crisis: it's not just a misalignment of supply and demand

There are several significant shortcomings to the argument that the completion of the Doha round—which proponents argue will better align supply and demand through enhanced trade—will resolve the problems of food price volatility and the associated rise in food insecurity. First, important factors beyond supply and demand for food were involved in the price rises on world commodity markets in the first place. Second, the vulnerability of developing countries to the suddenly higher food prices appears to be strongly linked to past movement to agricultural trade openness in developing countries as well as other factors that trade liberalization cannot address.

Price volatility

The fluctuations in food prices experienced since 2007 are best character-ized as a situation of volatility combined with gradual upward pressure on prices. Numerous forces are at play. Most of the initial analyses of the situation focused their explanation on the causes of the gradual trend of rising prices, assuming a basic mismatch of food supply with food demand. But this approach missed some key causes of the extreme vola-tility in food prices. Moreover, it was the sharp upward swings in prices that made the situation a serious crisis, not the underlying trends. Mas-sive price increases over a short period of time caused abrupt realign-ment of the poor's access to an adequate diet. It is doubtful whether "freer trade" via tariff reductions could have made much difference to the situation, at least in the short run.

A mismatch of supply and demand on world markets cannot ade-quately account for the volatility in food prices.[6] Research since the 2008 episode of extreme prices has revealed a highly complex picture in which financial and other factors played important roles. The value of the US dollar at the time was important. As the US currency's value fell on world markets, commodity prices, including food, began to rise sharply. The connection is complex, but it is increasingly understood that commodity prices tend to rise with a weak dollar because com-modities are priced in US dollars on world markets, meaning prices must rise to compensate for the weaker currency, and also because investors seek out commodity investments in such times in the hopes of improving investment returns because their prices are rising. The effect is somewhat self-reinforcing, and commodity prices tend to rise quickly in this situation.[7]

Investors moving into commodity-linked financial investments might not have contributed to such a severe price bubble if there had been strict limits on how much exposure they could gain in commodity futures markets. A series of deregulatory decisions over the course of the 1980s and 1990s, however, increased the ability of large-scale investors to pur-chase financial products linked to commodities. These decisions relaxed rules regarding how much non-commercial investors (that is, banks and investment funds that did not ever deal in the physical commodity) could invest in commodity futures markets.[8] In response, large banks and other institutional investors moved en masse into commodity market investments through instruments such as commodity index funds that track commodity prices on futures markets. Investment in commodity index funds increased 10-fold from 2003–2008, climbing from approximately US$15 billion to US$200 billion.[9] This rise in commodity index fund activity resulted in a huge increase in actual commodity futures contracts purchased on futures exchanges by financial institutions to offset their risks from selling these funds.

This increased investment in commodity futures contracts has been implicated as a factor pushing up food prices since 2007. Although the exact extent to which this massive influx of financial investment in commodity futures is responsible for food price volatility is difficult to discern with precision and is subject to debate, it is widely seen to have been at the very least an exacerbating factor in the wild price fluctuations seen in recent years.[10] These financial factors linked to the rapid food price rises show that to pin the food price crisis on supply and demand alone does not capture the entire picture of the food price crisis. Indeed, food production was at record levels in 2008 and is set again to reach a record level in 2010.

Many studies have also identified the large increase in diversion of grain for biofuels—particularly the production of corn-based ethanol in the United States—as an important driver of higher and more volatile food prices since 2007.[11] Biofuel investment affects food prices in several ways. Not only does corn-based ethanol production divert grain from the food supply, affecting the supply and demand balance, but it also spurs speculative investment in commodity markets, contributing to volatility. Blending mandates that require a certain percentage of fuel to contain renewable fuel sources in both North America and in Europe have also been linked to increased pressure on food prices because these requirements have sparked increased investment in commodity markets as well as large-scale agricultural land investments abroad.

A lubrication of international trade in food would likely not do much to curb the effects of the above causes of high and volatile food prices. But trade is not completely out of the picture when it comes to food price volatility. Some countries imposed trade restrictions—especially rules that restrict food exports—after food prices began to climb sharply.[12] Food export bans have typically been imposed by countries in response to already high and rising prices, driven by fear of national shortage in such a volatile price context. In early 2008, a number of countries around the world, including India, Vietnam, China, and Argentina, imposed food export bans in the hopes of insulating their own economies from the rapidly rising prices. As noted earlier, Russia imposed an export ban in 2010, also a time of high food prices, and in this case prompted by drought and a lower than expected harvest in that country.

Export bans have been identified in many analyses as having caused some of the food price volatility, as sudden closure of borders disrupted food trade and led to regional shortages that caused price spikes.[13] Import dependent countries and grain trading firms were forced to seek alternative sources of supply when export restrictions cut them off from suppliers. Export bans have also been important because they fuelled further financial speculation in agricultural commodity markets, which in turn drove up food prices. It is not clear that the export bans themselves were alone a primary cause or even an initial cause of food price volatility, because they tend to be imposed in contexts where food prices are already high and volatile.[14] Headey notes, for example, that even though trade factors in his view played an important role in the price rises, that "deeper non-trade factors ... probably still played an important role in creating initial pressures in grain markets, which in turn contributed to export restrictions and import surges."[15]

Given the multiple dimensions of food price outlined earlier, in which restricted international trade only plays a partial role in food price volatility, simply lubricating international trade through increased openness would not necessarily have prevented the crisis from erupting, nor would it necessarily make a dramatic difference to existing food price volatility.

Vulnerability to price shocks

Food price volatility in recent years has taken its hardest toll on the most vulnerable populations—the world's poorest people who spend 50–80 percent of their income on food. The World Bank estimated that over 130 million people were pushed into poverty by higher food prices, while the FAO estimated that an additional 75 million suffered malnutrition as a result of the crisis.[16] For countries that had become dependent on food imports over the past 40 years, including most of the least developed countries (LDCs), the rapid food price increases had a devastating impact. In the 2007–2011 period, the number of low-income food-deficit countries (LIFDCs) listed by the FAO hovered between 70 and 80. These LIFDCs, most of whom were also LDCs, had been especially vulnerable to sharp movements in international food prices. The situation became even more precarious after the food price bubble burst in fall 2008, because credit for importing poor countries dried up in the global recession that followed the financial collapse. This is precisely when the number of hungry people in the world passed the one billion mark.

It is important to examine the causes of the world's poorest countries' dependence on world markets for a significant portion of their caloric intake. These countries were not always agricultural importers, and in fact in the 1960s were on the whole agricultural exporters (see Figure 3.1). There are a host of potential explanations for this situation and indeed there has been intense debate for decades over whether the causes are primarily internal to these countries or whether external factors play the leading role.[17]

Although there are many potential forces that contributed to the negative agricultural trade balance of LDCs after the mid-1980s, it is widely agreed that declining investment in agriculture in these countries played a role. There was a rapid fall in agricultural investment by the World Bank from 30 percent of its lending in the 1980s to just 12 percent by 2007. Indeed, aid to agriculture constituted 18 percent of all official development assistance in the 1980s and fell to just 3 percent by 2007.[18] Weak and declining agricultural investment at that time was exacerbated by low prevailing world food prices over much of the 1980s–1990s, which dampened interest in promoting food production in poor countries, particularly when cheap, subsidized food imports from industrialized countries were readily available.

It is also widely understood that the situation was compounded by unbalanced liberalization of trade policies over the course of the 1980s and '90s. In this period, many developing countries opened up their

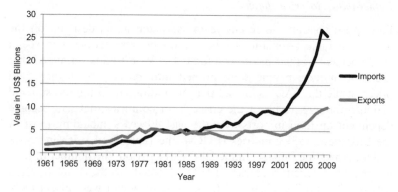

Figure 3.1 Agricultural trade balance of the least developed countries, 1961–2006
Source: FAO data.

agricultural markets as conditions for obtaining World Bank sponsored structural adjustment loans. At the same time, the rich industrialized countries continued to heavily subsidize their own domestic production and food exports, in addition to maintaining trade barriers to imports of food items from the South using mechanisms such as tariff peaks and tariff escalation.[19] These practices were institutionalized with the 1994 Uruguay round Agreement on Agriculture, which allowed rich industrialized countries to continue with high levels of subsidies to the tune of over US$300 billion per year, while also keeping out food products from the South with the use of tariff barriers. Although agricultural tariffs were reduced under the agreement in both industrialized and developing countries, there were flaws in the way this was done, and in practice the relative depth of the tariff cuts in developing countries was effectively higher than it was in the rich countries, because the poor countries had already made such substantial cuts under structural adjustment programs a decade earlier.

Many have pointed to this uneven nature of trade liberalization, where the developing countries in effect liberalized to a much greater extent than the rich countries, as contributing to the problems of import dependence that we see today in the poorest countries.[20] "Import surges" have been a particular concern of developing countries, especially when they are comprised of subsidized products from the industrialized countries that out-compete domestic production, in turn harming farmer livelihoods.[21]

A simple mismatch in the international supply and demand for food was not a major cause of the food crisis that followed the price spikes in 2007–2008. Food price volatility—itself only partially linked to trade factors—played a major role. This volatility caused crisis in those countries that were most vulnerable to the effects of the price swings: the world's poorest countries. Their vulnerability meant that suddenly higher prices immediately affected their ability to command food on world markets. Their vulnerability to this situation was the product of a long history of unbalanced trade practices between rich and poor countries that was both linked to and exacerbated by declining investment in the agricultural sector in most developing countries since the 1980s.

The implications of the proposed Doha agreement for global food security

The Doha round was launched precisely to rectify the trade imbalances that had been institutionalized in the 1994 Uruguay round Agreement on Agriculture. As noted earlier, this agreement has been widely criticized for reinforcing North-South agricultural trade imbalances by allowing rich countries to continue to heavily subsidize their own agricultural sectors while at the same time forcing open markets in developing countries. The stated aim of the Doha round was to finally bring a better balance with a deal that would be fair to developing countries. The Doha Declaration was clear that special and differential treatment was essential for rebalancing the deal:

> We agree that special and differential treatment for developing countries shall be an integral part of all elements of the negotiations and shall be embodied in the schedules of concessions and commitments and as appropriate in the rules and disciplines to be negotiated, so as to be operationally effective and to enable developing countries to effectively take account of their development needs, including food security and rural development.[22]

Given the lack of space in this chapter for a full evaluation of every aspect of the Doha agriculture negotiations and their implications for food security, the focus here is specifically on what the current draft text on agriculture means for the two key food security problems outlined earlier: food price volatility and vulnerability to sharp agricultural price swings in the world's poorest food-importing countries.

What does Doha offer for food price volatility?

The implications of the Doha agreement for food price volatility are unclear. The current draft of the Doha agriculture agreement does not specifically address the question of food price volatility and current rules may in fact restrict the ability of countries to take some measures to address it. Analysis from the Institute for Agriculture and Trade Policy (IATP) has noted that the use of national-level strategic grain reserves, including in developing countries, could help to dampen food price volatility.[23] In a recent IATP paper, Sophia Murphy points out that the existing WTO Agreement on Agriculture makes it very difficult for governments to implement and manage grain reserves, because any such program that may interfere with prices and/or production levels is considered to distort trade, and thus may be subject to severe restrictions under WTO rules.[24] There has not been talk of changing these rules as part of the Doha agreement. If anything, there has been open discouragement of the idea of establishing national grain reserves as part of countries' policy interventions to address food price volatility, as stressed in the 2011 G-20 Agriculture Ministers' Action Plan on Food Price Volatility.[25]

At the same time, another part of the Doha agenda, the negotiations on services, may be set to exacerbate food price volatility. Currently some countries, including Canada and the United States, are seeking much broader liberalization of financial services under Doha, and part of their proposal includes the opening up of developing countries to commodity exchanges and derivatives trade, which includes commodity futures and options trading. If developing countries agree to these provisions as part of a Doha deal, it could exacerbate the price volatility in these countries and also make them more vulnerable to swings in international food prices. The provisions also prevent countries from suspending agricultural commodity-linked derivatives trade, as India did during the 2008 food price crisis.[26] Such measures, if included in the Doha round, would potentially expose developing countries to yet more food price volatility that is linked with agricultural commodity speculation while taking away tools that might help smooth its local impacts.

The only direct talk about stemming food price volatility in the current Doha round—despite these obvious areas where it is relevant—is discussion of opening the agenda to allow negotiations on language to prevent members from imposing restrictions on food exports in times of high food prices. WTO rules currently do allow countries to restrict food exports. This issue has not been contentious in the past, because most of the WTO's efforts have been geared toward opening up countries to imports, rather than forcing exports. Although the issue of export bans is not part of the official Doha agenda as it was set out in 2001, Pascal Lamy has pressed this point repeatedly since the food price shocks of 2007–2008. He has urged WTO members to exploit the narrow window of opportunity to include the addition of restrictions on export bans, which in his view directly fuel land-grabbing.[27] There has been pressure at the very least to exempt the LDCs and the World Food Program from any future export restrictions. Food-exporting developing countries are not keen to give up their right to ban exports in extreme price situations, though most are likely to agree to exempt the LDCs in future bans. It is unlikely, however, that blanket rules outlawing its practice are about to be adopted anytime soon by WTO members.

Does Doha address vulnerability to food price shocks?

With respect to addressing the longer term factors that have deepened the vulnerability of developing countries in the global food economy, the agriculture agreement under the DDA is unlikely to reverse the situation. Two important weaknesses stand out in the current draft text: the lack of a robust special safeguard mechanism (SSM) to shield developing countries from unwanted and domestically damaging import surges; and the lack of sufficient cuts to domestic support subsidies in the industrialized countries. These two issues, it should be noted, are linked to one another in that rich country subsidies have been associated with lower commodity prices and import surges in developing countries.

The current Doha draft text does not include a robust enough SSM in the view of the developing countries. Import surges, which are rapid increases in imports of certain food products, have been a growing concern of developing countries since the 1980s and '90s when these surges increased dramatically. In an extensive study, the FAO found that for 23 food items in 102 developing countries, between the 1980s and 2003, there were between approximately 7,000–12,000 import surges. Looking at data from 2004 to 2007 for a group of just 56 developing countries, the South Centre identified over 9,000 import surges *per year*. These surges tended to be for staple food items, with cereals making up over 40 percent of the surges in the poorest and most vulnerable developing countries. Senegal, for example, saw its rice imports doubling and even tripling over short periods of time since the 1990s.[28]

Developing country groupings in the Doha round, particularly the Group of 33 (G-33), have argued strongly that an SSM could help to dampen these surges, and they are viewed by the group as a necessary tool to enable poor countries to provide livelihood security for their farmers. A robust SSM would allow these countries to apply higher tariff levels on goods for which imports began to surge, triggered either by suddenly lower prices for that product, or a spike in imports. The higher tariff level would only be temporary, but the idea is that it would provide protection from local farmers who would otherwise be squeezed out of domestic markets by lower priced imports.

Agricultural exporters in particular, including the United States, Canada, and Australia, argued in WTO talks that the use of an SSM for developing countries would have to be severely restricted, because otherwise it would hurt their own exports. The negotiations on the Agreement on Agriculture broke down in mid-2008 over this very issue, even in the context of soaring food prices that affected the developing countries far more than the industrialized ones. The proposal for strict restrictions on the SSM was seen by developing countries as an attempt to force them to pay for US cuts to domestic support by opening their markets to US products. This, for them, does not promote development, but rather spells disaster for millions of the world's poorest farmers. Such an outcome is clearly not in the spirit of the special and differential treatment for developing countries that was stressed in the Doha Declaration.

Regarding domestic support, the rich industrialized countries have at this point agreed to reduce their levels of trade distorting subsidies by only minimal levels. Rich country domestic subsidies are widely seen to be highly damaging to the agricultural sectors in developing countries because they effectively lower world prices for agricultural products, including for goods produced by developing countries that do not have the luxury of also subsidizing their own producers.[29] The effect of this imbalance is that farmers in poor developing countries cannot compete with subsidized goods either in global markets or in their own domestic food markets.

The draft Doha Agreement on Agriculture tabled in late 2008 indicates that the maximum domestic subsidy level agreed to by the rich countries was still above the level that was being paid out at that time, meaning in effect that no real cuts to subsidies would be achieved from the offers on the table. Martin Khor of the South Centre argues that the December 2008 draft rules, which constitute the basis for current negotiations, remain "grossly imbalanced against developing countries."[30] If there is not sufficient movement on these two points—a robust SSM and domestic support in rich countries—developing countries are very limited in what they can do to bolster their domestic food security efforts. Highly subsidized agricultural products from the rich industrialized countries will only continue to flood developing country markets, making it virtually impossible to sustain measures designed to improve domestic production incentives and in turn reduce poverty.

Conclusion

The analysis discussed earlier suggests that the Doha deal, if it is ever completed, will most likely not do much to rectify longstanding trade imbalances that have made the developing world so vulnerable to food price shocks. Nor will it do much to stem food price volatility, and it may even make matters worse on that front. The deal also does not promise much financial benefit. If the Doha round were to be completed today, the benefits are few for the world's poorest countries. The most recent estimates show that the likely "gains" for the developing world are around $16 billion, with likely gains for all developing countries related to the agriculture deal sitting at less than $9 billion. Africa as a whole will only make a one-time gain of at most US$400 million.[31] This amount is far too little to make any substantial improvements in the ability of the poor to access food.

Given these problems with the current Doha round agenda on agriculture, the question remains: is it worth an unbalanced deal in order to get a miniscule benefit without adequate protection against future food price shocks? To make a real difference in addressing food price volatility, vulnerability to price shocks and in turn potential future crises, important changes to the proposed text of the Doha Agreement on Agriculture are required, as called for in *The Johannesburg Statement on the Doha Development Agenda*.[32] It is also important to look well beyond the push to complete the Doha round if future food price crises are to be avoided.

As for the issues currently on the table, a robust SSM that fully embraces special and differential treatment for developing countries must be part of the Doha agreement. Improving the scope and depth of the SSM will assist efforts to improve agricultural production incentives in developing countries. The global community has already embraced the need to improve agricultural productivity in developing countries,[33] but this needs to go beyond simply increasing investment. It must also acknowledge the role that imbalanced trade rules have played in dampening incentives for agricultural production in poor countries. At the same time, industrialized countries must undertake meaningful agricultural subsidy cuts, to levels that are *below* current subsidy levels. Such cuts would help to ensure that food prices do not drop to levels that out-compete production in developing countries, and would help to lessen the import surges that have harmed production incentives in developing countries.

Regarding issues that should be on the table, provisions should be made to prohibit challenges against WTO members that institute national grain reserves. The use of food reserves needs be seen as a legitimate tool to smooth food price volatility, especially given the high interest in this tool among developing country governments, and their widespread past use by industrialized countries. At present, only the use of food reserves for emergency uses, and only on a pilot basis, has been widely endorsed (as is evidenced by the G-20 Agriculture Ministers' Action Plan). Further, food security concerns should be integrated into the financial services liberalization agreement, in order to ensure that developing countries in particular are not prohibited from using tools that may assist in smoothing the impact of international food price volatility. In particular, countries should be given the right to restrict and regulate agricultural derivatives trading under the financial services agreement in cases of extreme food price volatility. Finally, more discussion is required on rules regarding food export restrictions. If members can at least agree to exemptions on such restrictions for the LDCs, especially in times of high food prices, this may be a fruitful step.

Beyond the WTO, the international community could improve coordination in a number of key areas that could help to prevent and/or mitigate the impact of future food price crises. Coordination on food price volatility—for example, the adoption of global rules and standards to limit excessive speculation in agricultural commodities, stem biofuel production in times of high prices, and regulate foreign land acquisitions—could help to dampen some of the forces contributing to food price volatility. Significantly greater agricultural investment, especially in the world's poorest countries, could help to reduce vulnerability to food price shocks in food import dependent developing countries. These wider measures are currently being discussed within the G-20 and other forums such as the UN Committee on World Food Security. But without major improvements to the trade rules, as outlined earlier, these measures will only deliver partial protection against future crises. Improvements to trade rules are needed—especially those that provide the promised special and differential treatment for developing countries—in addition to these wider measures to address food price volatility and developing country vulnerability.

Notes

1 Donald Mitchell, "A Note on Rising Food Prices," Policy Research Working Paper 4682 (Washington, DC: World Bank, 2008).
2 See, for example, UN High-Level Task Force on the Global Food Security Crisis, *Comprehensive Framework for Action* (July 2008), www.un.org/issues/food/taskforce/Documentation/CFA%20Web.pdf; OECD, "Rising Agricultural Prices: Causes, Consequences and Responses," (August 2008), www.oecd.org/dataoecd/1/36/41227216.pdf; World Bank, "Rising Food Prices: Policy Options and World Bank Response," (Washington, DC: World Bank, 2008).
3 Pascal Lamy, "The Doha Round can be Part of the Answer to the Food Crisis," Speech to High Level Conference on World Food Security, Rome, 2008, www.wto.org/english/news_e/sppl_e/sppl92_e.htm.
4 FAO, "More People than Ever are Victims of Hunger," FAO Newsroom (Rome: FAO, 2009), www.fao.org/fileadmin/user_upload/newsroom/docs/Press%20release%20june-en.pdf.
5 FAO, Global Food Price Monitor (2010), www.fao.org/giews/english/gfpm/GFPM_11_2010.pdf.
6 See Jennifer Clapp, "Food Price Volatility and Vulnerability in the Global South: Considering the Global Economic Context," *Third World Quarterly* 30, no. 6 (2009): 1183–1196.
7 Philip C. Abbott, Christopher Hurt, and Wallace E. Turner, *What's Driving Food Prices?* (Oak Brook, IL: Farm Foundation, 2008).
8 Jennifer Clapp and Eric Helleiner, "Troubled Futures? The Global Food Crisis and the Politics of Agricultural Derivatives Regulation," *Review of International Political Economy* (2010), iFirst: 1–27. DOI: 10.1080/09692290.2010.514528.
9 United States Senate, *Excessive Speculation in the Wheat Market*, Majority and Minority Staff Report, Permanent Subcommittee on Investigations (Washington, DC: US Senate, 2009), 5.

10 See Institute for Agriculture and Trade Policy (IATP), "Betting Against Food Security: Futures Market Speculation" (Minneapolis: IATP, 2009), www.iatp.org/tradeobservatory/library.cfm?refID=105065; Bank for International Settlements, *81st Annual Report* (2011), www.bis.org/publ/arpdf/ar2011e.pdf. It should be noted that some economists, such as Scott Irwin and Dwight Sanders, staunchly deny that there is any connection between commodity speculation and food prices. See Dwight Sanders and Scott Irwin, "A Speculative Bubble in Commodity Futures Prices? Cross-sectional Evidence," *Agricultural Economics* 41, no. 1 (2010): 25–32.

11 For example, UNCTAD, *Price Formation in Financialized Commodity Markets: The Role of Information* (2011), www.unctad.org/en/docs/gds2011 1_en.pdf; Kimberly Ann Elliott, "US Biofuels Policy and the Global Food Price Crisis," in *The Global Food Crisis: Governance Challenges and Opportunities*, ed. Jennifer Clapp and Marc Cohen (Waterloo: Wilfrid Laurier University Press, 2009).

12 Ramesh Sharma, "Food Export Restrictions: Review of the 2007–10 Experience and Considerations for Disciplining Restrictive Measures," FAO Commodity and Trade Policy Research Working Paper 32 (2011), www. ictsd.org/downloads/2011/05/sharma-export-restrictions.pdf.

13 For example, Derek Headey, "Rethinking the Global Food Crisis: The Role of Trade Shocks," *Food Policy* 36, no. 2 (2011): 136–146.

14 See Sharma, "Food Export Restrictions," for an overview.

15 Headey, "Rethinking the Global Food Crisis," 145.

16 Cited in Headey, "Rethinking the Global Food Crisis," 136.

17 See World Bank, *World Development Report 2008: Agriculture for Development* (Washington, DC: World Bank, 2007).

18 World Bank, "Double Jeopardy: Responding to High Food and Fuel Prices" (Washington, DC, World Bank, 2008). UN High Level Task Force, *Comprehensive Framework for Action*.

19 Walden Bello, *The Food Wars* (Verso: London, 2009).

20 For example, Martin Khor, "Analysis of the Doha Negotiations and the Functioning of the WTO," (Geneva: The South Centre, 2009); Jennifer Clapp, "WTO Agriculture Negotiations: Implications for the Global South," *Third World Quarterly* 27, no. 4 (2006): 563–577.

21 South Centre, "The Extent of Agriculture Import Surges in Developing Countries: What are the Trends?" (Geneva: South Centre, 2009).

22 WTO, "Doha Ministerial Declaration" (Geneva: WTO, 2001), WT/MIN (01)/DEC/1.

23 Sophia Murphy, *Strategic Grain Reserves in an Era of Volatility* (Minneapolis, MN: IATP, 2009).

24 Sophia Murphy, "Trade and Food Reserves: What Role Does the WTO Play?" (Minneapolis: IATP, 2010).

25 G-20 Agriculture Ministers, "Action Plan on Food Price Volatility and Agriculture," (June 2011), www.G-20.utoronto.ca/2011/2011-agriculture-plan-en.pdf.

26 Myriam Vander Stitchele, "Ignoring the Crises? How Further GATS Liberalisation Impacts the Financial and Food Crises," *South Bulletin* 16 (June 2008).

27 Pascal Lamy, "The World Needs a Shared Vision on Food and Agricultural Trade Policy," speech to the International Food and Agricultural Trade Policy Council (May 10, 2009), www.wto.org/english/news_e/sppl_e/sppl124_e.htm.

28 See South Centre, "The Extent of Agricultural Import Surges."

29 For example, on the case of Mexico, see Timothy Wise, "Agricultural Dumping Under NAFTA: Estimating the Costs of U.S. Agricultural Policies to Mexican Producers," Working Paper 09–08, Global Development and Environment Institute (Medford, MA: Tufts University, 2009), www.ase. tufts.edu/gdae/Pubs/wp/09–08AgricDumping.pdf.
30 Khor, "Analysis of the Doha Negotiations."
31 Kevin Gallagher and Timothy Wise, "Back to the Drawing Board: No Basis for Concluding the Doha Round of Negotiations," RIS Policy Brief No. 36 (Delhi: RIS, 2008), www.ris.org.in/images/RIS_images/pdf/pb36.pdf.
32 Global Poverty Summit 2011, *The Johannesburg Statement on the Doha Development Agenda*, www.povertydialogue.org, reproduced in the appendix to this volume.
33 G-20 Agriculture Ministers, "Action Plan on Food Price Volatility and Agriculture."

4 Poverty and cotton in the Doha Development Agenda

Donna Lee

The singular most important recommendation to the Doha Development Agenda (DDA) that will help alleviate poverty among some of the poorest farming communities in a sustainable way is that developed country cotton subsidization, which in recent years has topped $6 billion annually, must be removed expeditiously. Numerous studies have demonstrated the direct link between these developed country subsidies and income poverty in the West and Central African farming communities;[1] it is estimated that subsidies provided by the US Congress and the European Commission reduce the annual income of francophone African cotton farmers by around $150 million, thus directly decreasing the earning power of some 40 percent of the cotton farmers of Benin, Burkina Faso, Chad, and Mali (hereafter referred to as the "Cotton Four").[2] The fact that domestic cotton subsidies primarily used by the US Congress and the European Commission have not already been removed despite the mounting evidence of their negative impact on the livelihood of some 10 million African farmers is evidence of the huge political influence of powerful cotton lobbies in Washington and Brussels, and the limitations of the influence of African countries in the DDA, as well as the World Trade Organization's (WTO) ability to regulate cotton trade policy. That said, given the weight of moral suasion in the cotton issue, the small step changes to US policy brought about by the WTO's judicial process,[3] and the reductions in European Union (EU) levels as a result of agreements reached in an intra-regional African-EU process,[4] there is some room for hope that the level of American and European subsidies will continue to decline with or without the completion of the DDA.

This chapter begins by highlighting the link between developed country cotton trade policy and poverty in West and Central Africa. It then analyses the political economy of cotton subsidies in the United States to illustrate the difficult domestic politics that are embedded in the

DDA cotton negotiations and that thwart the WTO's attempts to influence and regulate cotton trade liberalization. Finally the chapter briefly scopes the DDA cotton negotiations in order to assess the impact of African states in the WTO on cotton trade policy. In the chapter I set out two recommendations. My first recommendation calls for the elimination of cotton subsidies in line with *The Johannesburg Statement on the Doha Development Agenda*.[5] My second calls for reform of the WTO's Dispute Settlement Understanding (DSU) to compel members to provide financial compensation to injured parties in disputes. Both recommendations, if implemented, would provide liberal cotton trade policy as well as multilateral process solutions that would go a long way towards addressing the problem of income poverty in African cotton farming communities.

Cotton trade policy and poverty in West and Central Africa

West and Central African countries are heavily dependent for their income on cotton production and export. In Burkina Faso and Benin, for example, cotton provides 60 percent of foreign exchange earnings with more than 40 percent of the population in both countries dependent on cotton exports for their earning power.[6] The problem of African cotton highlights the extent to which poverty in African peasant communities is not primarily a growth issue but rather a matter of *income*. Not surprisingly, the high level of dependency on cotton production and export for household income makes African cotton farmers exceptionally vulnerable to price drops in the world cotton market. Price instability, along with several severe price drops, throughout the last 25 years have exposed this vulnerability and increased poverty among farming communities across West and Central Africa. While cotton production in these regions increased by 14 percent between 1999 and 2002, income from cotton exports dropped by 31 percent.[7]

Data in Figure 4.1 indicate that from 1996 to the launch of the DDA in 2001 the price of cotton dropped by 50 percent, from 77 cents to 35 cents per pound, drastically reducing the income of non-subsidized African cotton farmers. During the DDA negotiations price shocks in 2001–2002 and again in 2004–2005 coupled with a 50 percent increase in the price of fertilizer for African cotton farmers led to severe financial crises and increased levels of poverty among African cotton farmers during the most active period of the DDA negotiations.[8] Despite price rises in 2010 and early 2011, prices in late 2011 were once more facing downward pressures.[9]

A recent detailed study of poverty in Benin demonstrates the impact of cotton price reductions on rising poverty levels.[10] In the short term,

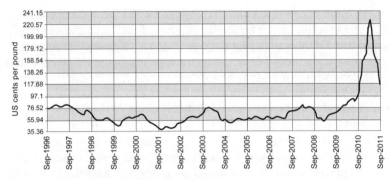

Figure 4.1 Cotton price instability 1996–2011
Source: International Monetary Fund.
Note: From Indexmundi, www.indexmundi.com.

before farmers are able to respond to price changes, the data in this study indicate that a 40 percent price reduction leads to a three-fold increase in the severity of poverty in cotton farming overall. The study calculates that 334,000 Benin farmers would fall below the poverty line following a 40 percent reduction in the world price of cotton.[11] The study finds that in the long term Benin's farmers responded to price falls by shifting production to other crops and livestock and that, while income was higher than before these shifts in production, it was lower than before the fall in cotton prices. Thus poverty among cotton farmers in Benin increased in both the short and long term as a result of the levels of price reductions experienced as the DDA negotiations kicked off.

Most West and Central African farmers are not benefiting from the 2010–2011 price hikes in cotton because of the production adjustments they made following the two periods of cotton price falls in the 2000s. In Mali, for example, cotton production dropped by 60 percent and so, despite the recent increase in cotton prices, Malian farmers remain trapped in long-term poverty. At a time when cotton prices are at their highest for 15 years, cotton production in Burkina Faso and Mali is at its lowest.[12] A key point to be made here is that African farmers, not supported by domestic cotton subsidies, are highly exposed to the bad times yet poorly placed to take advantage of the good times. For these unfortunate poor communities bad times rather than good times have prevailed in the cotton market during the DDA negotiations; and as a result severe poverty has prevailed too. Oxfam, for example, reports that almost 10 million cotton farmers in Africa are currently living in poverty because of their extreme income dependence on cotton exports.[13] Oxfam's study, written by Kevin Watkins, links the causes of income poverty among these communities to developed country trade policies; in particular Oxfam highlight the link between the very high levels of domestic subsidization of cotton production in developed countries and the downward trend in world cotton prices and African cotton production.

I now turn to an examination of the levels of developed cotton subsidies focusing on data from the United States. Although there are several developed countries that subsidize cotton production and export, I focus on the United States because it is the world's dominant player in cotton markets accounting for some 40 percent of total world exports and thus its price support mechanisms have the greatest impact on world cotton prices. Although the European Union is the key market for African cotton, and the European Commission subsidizes cotton production in Greece and Spain, European domestic support mechanisms have a much smaller impact on cotton prices compared with US subsidies.[14]

Cotton subsidies

Trade scholars have long recognized the negative impact of domestic support mechanisms. Subsidies typically include direct payments to farmers, which guarantee fixed prices no matter what the market demand or supply. These, and other subsidies such as counter-cyclical payments (which provide top ups to farmers when the global price falls below a set price), encourage over-production that causes drops in world market prices of cotton. Mário Jales' detailed report highlights the record high trade distorting domestic support in 1999 and 2001—the critical period leading into the launch of the DDA.[15] Various studies suggest that the cotton subsidies reduce world prices somewhere in the region of 6 to 10 percent, reducing African cotton farmers' revenue by as much as $150 million annually.[16] Given America's dominant position as the world's largest cotton exporter, US domestic subsidies have the greatest impact on world prices. During the 10 years of DDA negotiations American farmers have received some $26 billion in cotton subsidies from Washington. Removing these subsidies would, according to the Fairtrade Foundation, increase world prices by between 6 and 14 percent.[17]

The total spent on direct support to world cotton production in 2009–2010 as reported to the WTO reached $1.33 billion. This includes $368 million in EU subsidies, $329 million in China, and $319 million in the United States. The International Cotton Advisory Committee (a long-standing Washington-based advisory body funded by cotton producing and consuming countries) and the Environmental Working Group (an America-based non-governmental organization) report that official subsidy figures submitted to the WTO tend to be lower than actual levels. The Environmental Working Group reports, for example, that US figures for 2010–2011 exclude subsidies not directly linked to support, including the vast sums spent on counter-cyclical programs. Since 2002, these non-reported programs comprise the largest component of US domestic cotton subsidies. If these and other support mechanisms are included in the data then the total value of US cotton subsidies in 2010 was more than $835 million.[18] Figure 4.2 provides data on a decade of US cotton subsidies. Note that the drop in the level of subsidies provided in 2010 reflects the rise in cotton prices during that year that reduced the amount of price support paid to American farmers and not a change in subsidy policy in Washington.

The DDA cotton negotiations have been focused on reaching an agreement to eliminate these price distorting support mechanisms rather than on market access and tariff reduction. This is because access and tariffs are already liberalized in cotton; 84 of the 153 WTO member states—including most importantly the major importers—offer duty

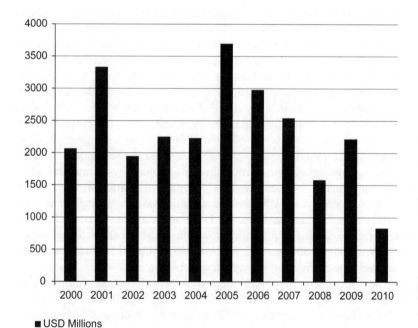

■ USD Millions

Figure 4.2 US cotton subsidies, 2000–2010
Source: Environmental Working Group.
Note: Data available at http://farm.ewg.org.

free access and tariff levels in the sector are relatively low, less than 10 percent in all but the most marginal cotton markets.[19] The entire diplomatic purpose of the cotton talks in the DDA is the removal of developed country subsidization mechanisms, primarily those decided by the law makers in Washington.

The link between domestic cotton subsidies and poverty in West and Central African cotton farming communities is empirically established. Price distorting policies in cotton drive down African farmers' incomes leading to higher levels of poverty. Relative to changes to other poverty reducing policy options (such as increased aid programs) the elimination of developed country cotton subsidies provides the most effective and sustainable means of reducing poverty. As such the completion of the DDA must entail cotton trade policy reform to end domestic support. This demand is written into *The Johannesburg Statement on the Doha Development Agenda*, the recommendations of which provide the policy purpose and analytical core of this chapter and book. In paragraph 4 *The Johannesburg Statement* calls for the negotiators to:

> Fast-track the elimination of export subsidies and trade-distorting domestic support in the developed countries on agricultural products that are of export interest to least-developed countries, particularly in the areas of sugar, groundnuts, dairy products and fish. In particular, the immediate elimination of export subsidies and domestic support that has been a major cause of the decimation of cotton farmers and a threat to livelihoods in the "cotton four" countries, Benin, Burkina Faso, Chad, and Mali needs to be addressed as a matter of urgency.[20]

How can the WTO achieve this, if at all? While the links between African poverty and developed country cotton trade policy are widely acknowledged in the WTO, its capacity to steer through a reform agenda in cotton is weak in the face of resistance by major powers, particularly the United States, to remove trade and price distorting subsidies. The inclusion of cotton in the DDA negotiations has been highly contentious and a key plank in the ensuing discord between developed and developing countries that has characterized the DDA negotiations and has come to dominate WTO proceedings.[21] The friction in cotton negotiations between the developed member states and the African Cotton Four exposes the difficult domestic politics of cotton trade liberalization. Despite widespread scholarly and elite-level criticism of cotton subsidies, the domestic political costs of discarding this support have so far prevented significant reform of US cotton trade policy. This is because, like all trade policy, cotton trade policy creates winners and losers. In the case of US cotton subsidization schemes, the overwhelming winners are the politically powerful 25,000 or so cotton businesses that have received total revenues of $2.5 billion from Washington during the DDA talks.[22] And the overwhelming losers are the politically weak African cotton farmers who have lost a total of around $1.5 billion in revenue throughout the decade of the DDA talks.[23] Before discussing the WTO cotton negotiations, I will first analyze the political economy of US cotton policy in order to highlight the redoubtable domestic forces opposing reform of farm policy in Washington and multilateral trade policy processes such as the WTO's DDA.

The re-making of US cotton trade policy

One of the most formidable political barriers to multilateral reform of cotton trade policy is the power of the US farm block within Congress. In a very detailed study of the politics of the 2008 Farm Bill, Dan Morgan highlights how the politics of agriculture in Washington helps sustain the very high levels of subsidies to farmers such that the 2008 Farm Bill "left in place, and in some cases built on, the government subsidy ... by adding more than $10 billion to the costs."[24] These increases reflected the expanded political influence of agriculture within the US polity following the 2006 elections, which left the Senate Agriculture Committee "stacked with lawmakers from states growing the staple crops that are the main beneficiaries of traditional farm programs."[25] More specifically, powerful cotton interests are well represented on the House Sub-Committee on General Farm Commodities and Risk Management, the body responsible for US cotton subsidy policy. This Committee is chaired by Congressman Mike Conaway (R-11th District) who represents Dawson County in Texas. Dawson County was the third top county in the United States to receive cotton subsidies in the period 1995–2010. The top two counties to receive cotton subsides in that period, Gains County and Hale County, are also well represented by Congressman Randy Neugebauer (R-19th District), another member of the House Sub-Committee who in 2010 was able to secure over $72 million in cotton subsidies for companies in his District. The State of Texas alone receives almost 32 percent of all US cotton subsidies.[26]

In his blow by blow account of the political battle over the 2008 Farm Bill, Morgan highlights how a bipartisan farm bloc in the House and Senate exists to resist any meaningful reduction in agricultural subsidies. This bloc prevails over minority reform interests and was also able to overturn President George Bush's veto of the 2008 Bill. The resulting $307 billion Bill passed by Congress is, Morgan argues, evidence of the "conservatism, parochialism, and change resistance" of US domestic agricultural politics during the DDA negotiations.[27] This change resistance is driven by the political reality that few, if any, US lawmakers from the Farm Belt states of the South West and the Delta would gain re-election if they were to vote for reductions in cotton subsidy programs.

Political pressure on Congress comes from the influential agricultural businesses active in Washington that spend millions of dollars lobbying lawmakers. In 2008, for example, according to the non-governmental organization, *Open Secret*, which publishes data on lobbying expenditures based on data submitted to the House and Senate, agricultural businesses spent almost $150 million lobbying Senators and Congressmen. Included in these are the top four cotton associations—the National Cotton Council, Amcot, Georgia Cotton Commission, and American Farm Bureau—that spend thousands of dollars each year in Washington.[28] An official lobbying report to the House and Senate covering the April to June 2011 period shows that the National Cotton Council (the main professional body representing cotton business) spent $100,000 on lobbying House and Senate members on cotton related legislation.[29] Lobbying activity ensures that the top 10 cotton producers in the United States receive 81 percent of all American cotton subsidies. In sum, there are powerful forces protecting the status quo in US farm policy and the few who benefit economically wield enormous political power in Congress.

Taken together, the domestic political costs of discarding farm support schemes and the extensive lobbying activities on behalf of agricultural business work to prevent notable reform of US cotton trade policy. Given the power and influence of the United States as one of the dominant powers within the WTO,[30] this domestic resistance makes the prospects of an agreement in the WTO's DDA cotton negotiations pretty bleak. Powerful bipartisan domestic pressures to promote and maintain large cotton subsidies mean that American negotiators are unwilling or unable to accede to demands by developing countries to remove domestic cotton subsidies, despite the clear link to African poverty and the strong moral argument in favor of reform. However much the Cotton Four ride shotgun at the DDA negotiations on cotton, the prospects for significant policy reform are unpromising. Yet for the Cotton Four in particular, reform of cotton trade policy is a red-letter issue for any DDA agreement. Supported by developing country coalitions such as the G-20, the G-90 and the Africa Group, they have repeatedly stated that a final DDA must contain an agreement on cotton.[31]

For 10 years now, cotton has been a predominant issue in global trade governance as the United States and the Cotton Four have locked horns over demands for, and resistance to, the removal of cotton subsidies. This stand-off is a battle over the domestic political economy of cotton in the South West and Delta states of America, and the development needs and ambitions of farmers in Benin, Burkina Faso, Chad, and Mali, with no noteworthy concessions by either side seemingly possible. Many informed commentators from the trade community think the DDA cannot be completed and many also believe that the conflicts in the WTO reflect unresolved domestic conflicts.[32] In what follows I will briefly highlight and discuss the unfolding of the cotton issue in the WTO in order to draw attention to the difficulties least developed countries (LDCs) face in securing multilateral trade policy reform.

Growing the cotton dispute in the WTO

The campaign by developing countries to liberalize cotton in the WTO has been waged on two fronts. On one front, African states and their developing country allies have used the DDA negotiations to demand the removal of domestic subsidies.[33] On another front, Brazil, supported by other member states, mounted a successful legal challenge to US uplands cotton subsidies through the WTO's Dispute Settlement Mechanism (DSM).[34] In what now follows, I will highlight how pushing for redress over US cotton trade policy in the judicial process has proven to be more productive for Brazil than negotiating for redress and reform by the African states in the Doha round. This comparative success demonstrates, among other things, the continued prevalence of market power within the WTO regime and the need to militate against this where possible.[35]

The DDA cotton negotiations

Cotton has been in the spotlight of the DDA negotiations since 2003 when four of the poorest African countries, the Cotton Four, submitted a 'cotton initiative' to the WTO ahead of the Cancún ministerial meeting that appealed for the liberalization of cotton trade.[36] The title *Poverty Reduction: Sectoral Initiative in Favour of Cotton* highlighted the link between developed country subsidies and high levels of income poverty among cotton farming communities in West and Central Africa and as such the cotton initiative quickly became a focal point for the pro-development lobby both within and outside the WTO. The cotton initiative sought two things: one, the removal of domestic cotton subsidies;

and two, emergency financial compensation for African cotton farmers to offset financial losses until such time that subsidies were eliminated. During the last eight years, the cotton negotiations have produced fairly meager results in terms of policy reform as a number of recent studies have already pointed out.[37] That said, some concessions on cotton have been made—for example, on export subsidies—and there is certainly a higher level of accountability and transparency in multilateral trade policy making as I discuss later. These small steps pave the way for the enhanced possibility of significant trade reform, or at least preventing the continuing asymmetrical decision-making that so characterized policy-making in the General Agreement on Tariffs and Trade.[38]

There have been three notable and complementary elements to the DDA cotton negotiations. First has been the sustained assertiveness in the talks of the Cotton Four in seeking the elimination of cotton subsidies. The period 2003–2006 marked a hiatus of African activism that produced some progress on the cotton issue in the DDA. During these three years the Cotton Four were able to force their agenda of policy reform and financial compensation measures onto the DDA. These included reform of the European Union's Common Agricultural Policy in 2003–2004, which replaced the guaranteed minimum fixed price for cotton to a mix of coupled and decoupled payments. Specific proposals on cotton, for example, were included in the Cancún Ministerial Declaration, known as the Derbez Text,[39] the 2004 July Framework for Establishing Modalities in Agriculture[40] and the 2005 Hong Kong Ministerial Declaration.[41] These included the elimination of export subsidies by 2006, quota-free and duty-free access for LDC cotton exports to developed country markets, and a commitment to reduce cotton subsidies more "ambitiously" and more "expeditiously" than other agricultural subsidies. The 2004 July Framework package set out a two-pronged approach to negotiate the two aspects of the cotton initiative that would create a separate negotiating process for the trade aspects and the development assistance aspects. The trade related aspects would be discussed in the new Cotton Sub-Committee (CSC) and the assistance aspects would be addressed in a new Consultative Framework Mechanism on Cotton within that Sub-Committee.[42]

From 2006 onwards the cotton negotiations were embroiled in the near paralysis of the DDA negotiations as a whole and, as such, talks in the CSC produced little of note. Throughout this period the Cotton Four were unable to effectively engage the subsidizing member states, particularly their chief protagonists in the cotton negotiations, the United States. For two years the talks languished. At the July 2008 Ministerial Meeting cotton was largely ignored. Later that summer, however, the major players in the cotton negotiations, the United States, the European Union, Brazil, and the Cotton Four engaged in active consultation so that cotton was included in the December 2008 Revised Draft Modalities on Agriculture.[43] Nothing of note has been agreed in the CSC or the Agriculture Committee since. The cotton negotiations are stalled while members await the submission of tangible counter-proposals from the main subsidizers.

With no cotton agreement in sight and no progress on other agricultural issues the DDA has been in stalemate for much of the time since 2008. A quick stocktake of what has been achieved in the CSC talks reveals some minor concessions on cotton trade policy have been secured—the removal of all developed country export subsidies and the decoupling of 65 percent of European domestic cotton. By 2011, however, the vast majority of domestic subsidy measures remain in place and price distorting levels continue at some 90 percent of their previous value.[44] The more positive elements registered in the early phase of the cotton negotiations have not progressed beyond repeated collective statements underlining *intentions* to eliminate subsidies, and the setting of new deadlines for this by African members of the Committee. Minutes of the CSC show that a major stumbling block to an agreement to eliminate cotton subsidies is the insistence by the American negotiators on a "single undertaking" approach to the talks. From day one, as minutes of the CSC show, the American negotiators have argued that an agreement on cotton cannot be separated from an overall agreement on agriculture. As Richard Mills, spokesman for the US Trade Representative, stated at the onset of the cotton negotiations, "For us this is not just about one commodity. We have been pushing for broad agricultural reform."[45]

Despite this stalemate, the CSC has managed to create greater transparency in cotton trade policy by requesting members to disclose details of their domestic subsidies. Although a fairly small concession, public disclosure of the data does at least provide ammunition for the reformers in their struggle to secure the elimination of these subsidies. This name and shame process puts the subsidizers on the back foot in the cotton negotiations since it makes them fully accountable for their protectionist trade policies. This has been an important element in securing widespread condemnation and criticism of domestic subsidies in cotton both within and outside the WTO.[46] Exposure of the high levels of cotton subsidization has also meant that the discussions on development assistance in the Consultative Framework Mechanism on Cotton meetings have been fully informed of the huge injury caused to African cotton producers. Discussion at these meetings has readily delivered annual increases in development assistance to African cotton farmers and progress in this area has been quite easy to secure compared with agreement on the trade policy aspects of cotton. Major countries such as the United States, the European Union, Canada, Brazil, as well as the African Development Bank, United Nations Industrial Development Organization, and the International Monetary Fund have contributed around $136 million to poor cotton farmers in 2009 in order to address the problems of poverty in farming communities.[47]

In sum, the cotton issue has remained prominent in the DDA since the launch of the Cotton Initiative in 2003, and some concessions have been achieved. But they fall very short of African demands as set out in the Cotton Initiative and reiterated throughout the negotiations.[48] If the DDA is to be completed cotton must be addressed in a way that satisfies the Africans. Discussions ahead of the December 2011 Ministerial Conference in Geneva centered on the possibility of agreeing a limited Doha package—a so-called "Doha Light"—designed to provide trade benefits for LDCs, with a clear work program to deal with outstanding DDA issues. This would involve an "early harvest," that is, implementation of agreements already reached in the DDA. It would, however, exclude agriculture and, as yet, there is no agreement to include cotton either.[49] In the absence of these red-letter issues for developing countries in any Doha Light package, the DDA is likely to remain in deadlock.

Cotton in the DSM

During a time when the stalemate in the DDA negotiations seemingly played into the hands of American lawmakers' reluctance to reform cotton trade policy, Brazil was attacking US subsidies from another front, using the WTO's judicial process to dispute American cotton subsidies. It is interesting that the four African countries chose to push for cotton trade reforms through the negotiating process rather than seek change through the WTO's judicial negotiation process, a decision that has produced fairly thin results after eight years of deliberation and robustly stated African demands in the CSC. Brazil, by contrast, has achieved spectacular results in the WTO's DSM in its quest to force change in US cotton policy. Following a sustained campaign fought through the WTO's Dispute Settlement Body (DSB), Brazil and the United States reached a bilateral agreement in April 2010 whereby the Americans agreed to pay Brazil $147.3 million annually until such time as US cotton subsidies are reduced. In all likelihood, these payments will run until at least 2012 when the Americans are next due to revise their Farm Bill.[50]

In 2004 the WTO's DSB judged US cotton subsidies to be unlawful following a complaint submitted by Brazil in 2002.[51] Two of the Cotton Four members, Benin and Chad, were third parties to the complaint along with 14 other countries.[52] The Brazilian complaint was that US subsidies caused overproduction in the United States and that this seriously prejudiced Brazilian farmers. Although the United States appealed this decision, the ensuing 2005 Appellate Body Report supported this initial ruling finding US subsidies illegal and instructing the Americans to comply with the ruling by removing the subsidy programs.[53] In 2007 Brazil returned to the DSB to make further complaints against the United States for foot dragging on eliminating its cotton subsidies. Again the complaint was upheld by the WTO. Although the United States administration did eliminate some subsidies in 2007, these were later restored with the passage of the 2008 US Farm Bill. Following yet further Brazilian appeals, the WTO ruled in 2009 that Brazil was entitled to $295 million, and $147 million each year afterwards from the US until the illegal subsidies were eliminated.[54] The newly empowered Brazilians then launched an offensive against the United States, threatening to impose $830 million in trade sanctions on American exports. The sizable market power that the Brazilians now have as an emerging market provides Brasilia with leverage to take effective countermeasures. Faced with Brazilian sanctions against powerful trade interests in the motor vehicle, wheat, medical instruments, and pharmaceutical industries, the United States reached an agreement with Brazil to pay compensation to their cotton farmers.[55] This bilateral agreement has led to an overall increase in domestic subsidies because Washington is now paying subsidies to Brazilian cotton farmers in addition to American farmers. Ironically, the $147 million payment is about the same amount as the loss of income to African cotton farmers from US cotton subsidies. This bilateral agreement highlights the extent to which current institutional rules and processes in the WTO produce unintended results—in this case more injury to African farmers rather than the intended elimination of US subsidies. It also highlights the inability of the WTO to ensure compliance with its trade disciplines; at the end of the day, the Brazilian-US cotton agreement preserves the most injurious US cotton subsidization policies.

The African decision to address the matter of cotton subsidies through WTO negotiation processes rather than the WTO litigation processes has, in hindsight, proved to be a mistake. That said, given the failings of the WTO's DSM in relation to LDCs it was perhaps the only choice. Evidence clearly shows that the DSM, as currently configured, only provides redress for member states with significant market power and the dominant political powers within the WTO. The DSM seems incapable of enabling LDCs to assert their rights in global trade and this is a key reason why no African country has ever initiated a dispute (though they have signed up as third parties and did so in the Brazilian complaint against US cotton subsidies as well as the EU-sugar subsidies dispute).[56] The costs of initiating a complaint are too prohibitive and least developed states have insufficient legal resources and capacity to engage with the DSM. While the WTO funds an international law advisory center in Geneva to support LDCs in the dispute settlement system, African countries tend to seek advice here on policy initiatives rather than litigation initiatives from its staff.[57]

The compensatory measures provided by the dispute settlement process (Article 22 of the DSU) involve trade concessions rather than monetary rewards and as such the process can only work for states that have a semblance of market power. As Evans and Schaffer argue, "countries with larger economies and larger trade flows are better able to access the DSU in large part because they have the resources and market incentives to invest in deploying it."[58] LDCs lack market power, and so any ruling in their favor would be economically meaningless since they would not be able to take any countermeasures. What would be the point of winning the right to impose tariffs on US exports to Africa? Trade flow volumes between the United States and Africa are too small to offer any kind of economic or political leverage. Moreover, African countries are exposed to bilateral pressures from the United States and other developed states because of existing preferential trade agreements and a range of aid and finance programs. The Brazilian success in the *US Uplands Cotton* case was built on its ability, as an emerging economy and rising market power, to take serious retaliation measures against US exports to Brazil. Least developed African countries lack the volume in trade flows with any country to retaliate; their markets are just too small to be of much concern to developed country exporters. As such the DSU must be revised to provide for financial compensation for member states when rulings find in their favor. Although this would be second best to a system that could force compliance, it is certainly preferable to the current retaliation-based system. I therefore recommend a revision of Article 22 of the DSU to establish a monetary compensation mechanism for LDCs unable to use retaliatory trade measures.

Conclusion

Cotton is a focal point for poverty eradication and development advocacy in the DDA negotiations. For the 10 million cotton farmers in West and Central Africa the WTO's failure to secure reform of protectionist cotton trade policies of the major player in international cotton trade, the United States, is a tragedy because it is a major cause of poverty in these communities. The Cotton Four, supported by developing country coalitions such as the G-20 and the Africa Group, have strived for a development outcome in the DDA negotiations. They have insisted on the liberalization of cotton trade. As the Presidents of Mali and Burkina Faso stated in 2003 as they began their campaign against cotton subsidies, "Our demand is simple: apply free trade rules not only to those products that are of interest to the rich and powerful, but also to those products where poor countries have a proven comparative advantage."[59] If cotton production and trade were left to the free market then many African countries would enjoy sustained economic growth and millions of African cotton farmers would be hoisted out of their poverty. But in the cotton sector protectionist policies prevail. The world's biggest exporter of cotton, the United States, subsidizes its farmers at eye-watering levels. These subsidies drive up production and drive down global market prices. With low world prices, African farmers are pushed into debt and out of cotton production because of falling incomes from their only cash-crop. In debt, African farmers cannot afford to pay for health care and food for their families, or for their children to attend school.

During eight years of the DDA negotiations, the Cotton Four have put forward clear proposals for the liberalization of the cotton sector, have insisted on public disclosure of the levels of cotton protectionism in developed states, and have continued to push for development assistance to their cotton farmers to offset the long-term income losses. Despite active engagement in the DDA talks, domestic subsidies in developed states remain at high levels. Indeed the recent United States-Brazil agreement penalizes the Africans further because it provides for new subsidies for Brazilian cotton farmers rather than complying with WTO disciplines and reducing subsidies to its own farmers. Powerful domestic parties with cotton interests in the United States have learnt that they can ignore WTO disciplines without severe penalty while the rest of us have learnt that the WTO is in its present form a clumsy institution, incapable of driving through a fairer trade system for the poorest and most needy of its members.

The WTO and its members have failed to resolve the kernel of the cotton dispute—price distorting subsidies—either by negotiation or by judicial rulings. In light of these failings this chapter has put forward two recommendations. The first recommendation, which is also written into *The Johannesburg Statement*, calls for the immediate elimination of domestic cotton subsidies. If subsidies are ditched, cotton prices would rise and so would African cotton farmers' income. The second recommendation calls for the reform of the DSU to enable LDCs to claim financial compensation following WTO rulings in their favor. This shift would be a small step in rebalancing power within the WTO's DSM away from the large market powers such as the United States and Brazil and towards least developed members such as Benin and Chad, which have no market power. It would at least encourage least developed member states to make more use of the DSM and therefore have a more influential role in trade policy making, or at least be able to claim compensation when their trade partners drag their feet in reforming illegal trade practices. Together, both recommendations would make the WTO that little bit more philosophically consistent with the development aspirations written into the DDA. Eliminating subsidies would create trade development opportunities and reforming the DSM would better safeguard these opportunities.

Notes

1 See Kym Anderson and Ernesto Valenzuela, "The World Trade Organization's Doha Cotton Initiative: A Tale of Two Issues," World Bank Policy Research Working Paper 3918 (Washington, DC: World Bank, 2006); John Baffes, "Cotton Subsidies, the WTO, and the 'Cotton Problem'," World Bank Policy Research Working Paper 5663 (Washington, DC: World Bank, 2011); Felix G. Baquedano, John H. Sanders, and Jeffrey Vitale, "Increasing Incomes of Malian Cotton Farmers: Is Elimination of US Subsidies the Only Solution?" *Agricultural Systems* 103, no. 7 (2010): 418–432; Fairtrade Foundation, "The Great Cotton Stitch-Up," A Fairtrade Foundation Report (London: Fairtrade Foundation, 2010); Ian Gillson, Colin Poulton, Kelvin Balcombe, and Sheila Page, "Understanding the Impact of Cotton Subsidies on Developing Countries," Overseas Development Institute Working Paper (London: ODI, 2004), www.odi.org.uk/resources/download/3608.pdf; Louis Goreux, "Prejudice Caused by Industrialized Countries' Subsidies to Cotton Sectors in Western and Central Africa," (2004), paper prepared for the Food and Agriculture Organization, www.fao.org/es/esc/common/ecg/306/en/Goreux_Prejudicef.pdf; Mário Jales, "How Would a Trade Deal on Cotton Affect Exporting and Importing Countries?," International Centre for Trade and Sustainable Development (ICTSD), Issue Paper No. 26 (Geneva: ICTSD, 2010); Adam Sneyd, *Governing Cotton: Globalization and Poverty in Africa* (Houndmills, Basingstoke: Palgrave Macmillan, 2011); Daniel Sumner, "Reducing Cotton Subsidies: The DDA Cotton Initiative," in *Agricultural Trade Reform and The Doha Development Agenda,* ed. Kym Anderson and Will Martin (Washington, DC: World Bank, 2006); Kevin Watkins, "Cultivating Poverty: The Impact of US Subsidies on Africa," Oxfam International Briefing Paper No. 30 (Oxford: Oxfam, 2002).
2 Fairtrade Foundation, "The Great Cotton Stitch-Up."
3 See Dan Morgan, "The Farm Bill and Beyond," Economic Policy Paper Series (Washington, DC: The German Marshall Fund of the United States, 2010).

4 See European Union, "Update Relating to the European Union-Africa Partnership on Cotton," (Brussels: EU, 2010), www.coton-acp.org/docs/acpue/ Update_July_2010_EU-Africa%20Cotton%20Partnership_EN_Finalx.pdf.

5 Global Poverty Summit 2011, "*The Johannesburg Statement on the Doha Development Agenda*", www.povertydialogue.org, reproduced in the appendix to this volume.

6 Fairtrade Foundation, "The Great Cotton Stitch-Up."

7 WTO, "Poverty Reduction: Sectoral Initiative in Favour of Cotton," Joint Proposal by Benin, Burkina Faso, Chad, and Mali, TN/AG/GEN/4, 16 May 2003.

8 European Union, "Update Relating to the European Union-Africa Partnership on Cotton," 14.

9 Up-to-date data on cotton prices available at Cotton Outlook, www. cotlook.com.

10 Nicholas Minot and Lisa Daniels, "Impact of Global Cotton Markets on Rural Poverty in Benin," paper presented at the Northeast Universities Development Consortium Conference Program, 25–27 October 2002, Williams College, Williamstown, Massachusetts.

11 Minot and Daniels, "Impact of Global Cotton Markets," 9.

12 Elizabeth Day, "The Desperate Plight of Africa's Cotton Farmers," *The Observer*, 14 November 2010.

13 Watkins, "Cultivating Poverty."

14 Donna Lee, "The Cotton Club: The Africa Group in the Doha Development Agenda," in *The WTO After Hong Kong: Progress in, and Prospects for, the Doha Development Agenda,* ed. Donna Lee and Rorden Wilkinson (London: Routledge, 2007), 142.

15 Jales, "How Would a Trade Deal on Cotton Affect Exporting and Importing Countries."

16 See endnote 1.

17 Fairtrade Foundation, "The Great Cotton Stitch-Up," 14.

18 Environmental Working Group, "Despite Claims of Reform, Subsidy Band Marches On," News Release, 23 June, 2011, http://ewg.org/node/29072/print.

19 Jales, "How Would a Trade Deal," 16.

20 Global Poverty Summit, "The Johannesburg Statement."

21 For a detailed discussion of the cotton dispute in the context of the DDA negotiations more generally, see Donna Lee, "Global Trade Governance and the Challenges of African Activism in the Doha Development Agenda Negotiations," *Global Society* 26, no. 1 (2012), 83–101.

22 Data from Environmental Working Group web pages, http://farm.ewg.org.

23 Fairtrade Foundation, "The Great Cotton Stitch Up."

24 Morgan, "The Farm Bill and Beyond," 4.

25 Morgan, "The Farm Bill and Beyond," 32.

26 Data from Environmental Working Group web pages, http://farm.ewg.org, and US government web pages, http://ag.senate.gov and http://agriculture. house.gov.

27 Morgan, "The Farm Bill and Beyond."

28 See data available at www.opensecrets.org/lobby/indus.php?id=A&year=a.

29 The report is available at http://soprweb.senate.gov/index.cfm?event=getFili ngDetails&filingID=48631BDE-F962-499E-B8DE-F02322C0BFD1.

30 For a detailed discussion of the dominant power of the United States in the WTO process, see Fatoumata Jawara and Aileen Kwa, *Behind the Scenes at*

the WTO: The Real World of International Trade Negotiations: The Lessons of Cancún, updated edition (London: Zed Books, 2003); and Rorden Wilkinson, *The WTO: Crisis and Governance of Global Trade* (London: Routledge, 2006).

31 For evidence of developing country solidarity on cotton, see the minutes of the Sub-Committee on Cotton in the WTO document series TN/AG/SCC.

32 Patrick Messerlin and Erik van der Marel, "Polly Wants a Doha Deal: What Does the Trade Community Think?" *World Trade Review* 10, no. 4 (2011): 551–555.

33 For a more detailed discussion of the African challenge in the cotton negotiations, see Lee, "The Cotton Club."

34 For a more detailed discussion of the WTO US Uplands Cotton Case, see Karen H. Cross, "King Cotton, Developing Countries and the 'Peace Clause': The WTO's US Cotton Subsidies Decision," *Journal of International Economic Law* 9, no. 1 (2006): 149–195; Elinor L. Heinisch, "West Africa versus the United States on Cotton Subsidies: How, Why and What Next," *The Journal of Modern African Studies* 44, no. 2 (2006): 251–274; Hilton Zunckel, "The African Awakening in United States–Upland Cotton," *Journal of World Trade* 39, no. 6 (2005): 1071–1093.

35 For a discussion of the exercise of market power in the WTO, see Lee, "Global Trade Governance."

36 WTO, "Poverty Reduction."

37 Baffes, "Cotton Subsidies, the WTO, and the 'Cotton Problem'"; Lee, "Global Trade Governance"; Sneyd, *Governing Cotton.*

38 For a detailed discussion of decision-making in the GATT, see Rorden Wilkinson, *Multilateralism and the World Trade Organisation: The Architecture and Extension of International Trade Regulation* (London: Routledge, 2000).

39 WTO, "Draft Cancún Ministerial Text, Second Revision," JOB/(03)/150/REV.2, 13 September 2003.

40 WTO, "Doha Work Programme: Decision Adopted by the General Council on 1 August 2004," WT/L/579, 2004.

41 WTO, "Doha Work Programme – Ministerial Declaration Adopted 18 December, 2005," WT/MIN(05)/Dec, 2005.

42 WTO, "Sub-Committee on Cotton, Director-General's Consultative Framework Mechanism on Cotton, High-Level Session, 15–16 March 2007, Director General's Summary Remarks," TN/AG/SCC/W/7, 2007.

43 WTO, "Revised Draft Modalities on Agriculture, Committee on Agriculture Special Session," TN/AG/W/4/Rev.4, 6 December 2008.

44 *Bridges Weekly Trade News Digest,* 20 February 2008, cited in Sneyd, *Governing Cotton,* 69.

45 Quoted in Elizabeth Becker, "US Subsidizes Companies to Buy Subsidized Cotton," *The New York Times,* 4 November 2003.

46 For a detailed discussion of this internal and external condemnation of cotton subsidies, see Donna Lee and Nicki Smith, "Small State Discourses in the International Political Economy," *Third World Quarterly* 31, no. 7 (2010): 1091–1105.

47 WTO, "Sub-Committee on Cotton, Update on the Development Aspects of the Cotton–Secretariat Progress Report," WT/CFMC/23, 7 September 2009; and "Secretariat Progress Report," WT/CFMC/28, 21 May 2010; and "Secretariat Progress Report," WT/CFMC/32, 14 July 2011.

48 See, for example WTO, "Ouagadougou Declaration on the Sectoral Initiative in Favour of Cotton; Communication from Burkina Faso," TN/AG/SCC/GEN/7, 12 January 2007.
49 ICTSD, "'Doha Light' Takes Shape as WTO Members Lower Ambitions," *Bridges Weekly Trade News Digest* 15, no. 20, 1 June 2011. See also WTO News, "Members to think about 'what next for Doha, WTO' for December meeting," 26 July 2011.
50 ICTSD, "US, Brazil Agree to Negotiate End to Cotton Dispute," *Bridges Weekly Trade News Digest* 14, no. 13, 14 April 2010.
51 WTO, "United States – Subsidies in Upland Cotton. Report of the Panel," WT/DS267/R, 8 September 2004.
52 Argentina, Australia, Benin, Bolivia, Canada, Chad, China, the European Union, India, Japan, New Zealand, Pakistan, Paraguay, Taipei, Thailand, and Venezuela.
53 WTO, "United States – Subsidies in Upland Cotton. Report of the Appellate Body," WT/DS267/AB/R, 3 March 2005.
54 WTO, "United States – Subsidies in Upland Cotton. Decision of the Arbitrator," WT/DS267/ARB1, 31 August 2009.
55 Michael Grunwald, "Why the US is also giving Brazilians Farm Subsidies," *Time*, 9 April 2010, www.time.com/time/printout/0,8816,1978963,00.html.
56 For a detailed discussion of the experiences of developing countries in the DSM, see Chad P. Bown and Bernard M. Hoekman, "Developing Countries and Enforcement of Trade Agreements: Why Dispute Settlement is Not Enough," World Bank Policy Research Working Paper 4450 (Washington, DC: World Bank, 2007); Gregory C. Shaffer and Ricardo Meléndez-Ortiz (eds) *Dispute Settlement at the WTO: Developing Country Experience* (Cambridge: Cambridge University Press, 2010).
57 Lee, "Governing Global Trade."
58 David Evans and Gregory C. Shaffer, "Conclusion," in Shaffer and Meléndez-Ortiz, *Dispute Settlement at the WTO*, 342.
59 Amadou Toumani Touré and Blaise Compaoré, "Your Farm Subsidies are Strangling Us," *The New York Times*, 11 July 2003.

Part III

The view from inside

Part III

The view from inside

5 The changing global economy, Africa and the Doha Development Agenda

Ujal Singh Bhatia

The World Trade Organization's (WTO) Doha round of trade negotiations was launched in the shadow of the horrific events of 11 September 2001 to demonstrate global solidarity and to highlight global cooperation in meeting global challenges. To enhance its appeal among a large number of developing countries that remained sceptical about the need for such an enterprise, it was billed a Development round, a round which would address the imbalances of the past and give due importance to the special needs of developing countries. The Ministerial Declaration adopted at Doha on 14 November 2001 is replete with references to the role of international trade in promoting development and alleviating poverty. It makes a special reference to the vulnerabilities of the least developed countries (LDCs) and commits itself to addressing their marginalization in international trade and to improving their effective participation in the multilateral trading system.

More than 10 years down the line, these intentions are nowhere near being realized, as WTO members seek to come to terms with the dramatic changes in the global economy. The impasse in the Doha round has many facets—at one level, it is the result of a dispute between the United States and the emerging economies about their respective contributions to the final outcome. At another level, it represents the deep structural changes taking place in the global economy that have altered the political economy of the negotiations in the WTO. At yet another level, it reflects the deep crisis in multilateralism brought about by the changes in the global economy. But a preoccupation with the macro aspects of this unfortunate stalemate tends to conceal the identity of its real victims—the poorest and small economies in the world. The focus of this chapter is on the implications of these developments on such developing countries, especially those in Africa, as well as the role the multilateral process in general and the WTO in particular can play in assisting these countries in addressing their challenges.

A changing world

The financial crisis that erupted in 2008 has served to highlight the deep structural changes that have taken place in the global economy over the last two decades. Economic interdependence is the key feature of an increasingly globalized economy. In such a scenario, seamless commerce is critical for competitiveness, especially in the context of the unbundling of global manufacturing and the consequential emergence of international production networks based on trade in intermediates. Countries that have leveraged the opportunities offered by globalization are producing a new paradigm of growth in the twenty-first century based on interdependence and economic integration.

The WTO's 2011 *World Trade Report*[1] highlights the remarkable acceleration in the execution of Preferential Trade Agreements (PTAs) in recent years. There are at present around 300 active agreements. However, what *is* really remarkable is not the tariff preferences they confer on the participants but the other benefits of deep integration. The *Report* points out that only 16 percent of global trade is preferential and for the bulk of such preferential trade the margins of preference are no more than 2 percent. About half of global trade is carried out at zero most favored nation (MFN) rates. We therefore have to look beyond the issue of tariff advantages to understand the rationale of PTAs. The analysis of the deep integration taking place through PTAs in the 2011 *World Trade Report* reveals how pervasive rule-making is in PTAs. It is this growing network of rules that binds the participants closer and provides them with some insurance of inclusion in international production networks.

The dynamic changes in the Asia Pacific region have served to highlight the remarkable improvements in competitiveness achieved by countries that have been quick to take advantage of the opportunities presented by globalization. The rapid proliferation of international production networks as well as the spate of new PTAs in the region have served to fuel deeper integration in the participating economies. An important feature of the new PTAs is the emphasis on behind-the-border regulatory coherence. PTAs increasingly include rules on a range of economic and social issues—investment, competition policy, supply chain management, standards, intellectual property rights, labor, environment, and so on. This is leading to an unprecedented level of integration among the participating economies that has deep political, strategic, and economic implications. It will also have implications for the premier role that the General Agreement on Tariffs and Trade and subsequently the WTO have so far played in rule-setting for the global trading system.

The frenetic churning in the global economy is also changing attitudes to globalization. Most developed economies are still in the process of an uncertain recovery from the financial crisis and are in no position to push for further liberalization of the global economy. On the contrary, in many of these countries, there is a resurgence of protectionism, especially because of high (and rising) unemployment levels. On the other hand, emerging economies that have benefited from greater openness are still in the process of consolidation. They remain fearful of the threat of contagion and of uncertainty about the recovery of the global economy, preferring to respond to new economic challenges by focusing on domestic policy and regional liberalization. The resulting vacuum in global leadership helps to explain the Doha round impasse. It also helps to explain the paralysis in the multilateral process in other areas like the climate change negotiations as well as the less than decisive role being played by the G-20.

The changing world and Africa

These developments have implications for Africa's participation in the global economy in a number of ways. The changes in the way global manufacturing is now organized have largely bypassed Africa. The international production networks involving cross-border supply chains and trade in intermediates do not traverse the African continent. Africa has also largely remained outside the process of deep integration that has spread throughout the Asia Pacific region. The continent has witnessed very little regional integration so far. African countries average only 0.4 PTAs per country. Their cross regional average (0.5 per country) is significantly lower than almost all other regions.[2] What little regional or cross regional integration that has taken place is quite shallow and covers a small portion of trade. This is despite initiatives to revitalize existing regional groupings and to form new ones. The important initiatives have been the Common Market for Eastern and Southern Africa, the East African Community, the Economic Community of West African States and the Southern African Development Community. These initiatives were launched with the objective of "accelerating industrialization, diversifying economies, developing regional infrastructure, encouraging the adoption of common negotiating positions, and promoting peace and security."[3] There are many reasons for the poor progress of Africa towards these objectives—poor physical infrastructure across the continent, political differences, an unpredictable investment climate, lack of processing capacity, little by way of an efficient trade facilitation network, shortage of skilled labor, among others.

A major portion of Africa's exports are covered by preferences, especially to developed countries. For instance, the European Union's (EU) "Everything but Arms" scheme for the LDCs, a part of its Generalized System of Preferences, which has been operational since March 2001, provides duty-free access for LDCs for all products except armaments. Similarly, the members of the African, Caribbean, and Pacific group have signed Economic Partnership Agreements with the EU to obtain preferential access for their exports. The United States provides duty-free access to the US market for a large number of products exported from more than 40 eligible sub-Saharan African countries, including South Africa, under Africa's Growth and Opportunity Act. Similar initiatives have been announced by other countries including developing countries like India. India announced its Duty Free Tariff Preferences Scheme in 2008. It provides tariff preferences to all LDCs (most of which are in Africa) on 94 percent of tariff lines.

However, because of autonomous tariff liberalization in a large number of countries, as well as the consequence of the proliferation of PTAs, margins of tariff preferences are being rapidly eroded. For most African countries, especially the LDCs, erosion of preferences means a decline of their export competitiveness. The fact that preferences cannot prevent a decline in export competitiveness is highlighted by the case of the textiles and clothing sector. After the phase out of the Multi Fibre Arrangement, the share of Africa in the global market has plummeted. The biggest gainers have been China and other Asian countries. Even though the DDA is seeking to address this issue, to a large extent the erosion of preferences is an inevitable development arising from the dynamics of global economic change.

Of the various economic challenges confronting African countries, one of the most daunting is that of food security, an issue highlighted by food crises in a large number of African countries in the last few years. Food shortages and the increased volatility of food prices in recent years have caused great hardship to the poor in these countries. While structural imbalances in demand and supply of key food crops are an important factor, sharply increased speculative activity in agricultural commodity markets has also contributed. Eighty-five percent of trade in agricultural products is controlled by five large transnational companies.[4] Export restrictions imposed by food exporters have further exacerbated the problem. The only reliable hedge against such uncertainty is greater food self-sufficiency. This means that poor countries have to put agricultural development at the top of their development strategies. It also means that a vigorous multilateral process is required to address the issue holistically. Elements in such a process would include speculative investments by large hedge funds and others in acquiring agricultural lands, especially in Africa, similar investments by sovereign entities for producing food for export to home countries, diversion of agricultural lands to energy crops and the provision of subsidies by several governments for such production, the role of oligopolistic cartels in cornering food stocks and driving up food prices, the issue of export restrictions, among others. The G-20 has taken the lead in initiating this process but the WTO will have an important role to play in making the rules that allow the affected countries to address the problem.

An important development in recent years has been the volatility and secular rise of prices of natural resources. Trade in natural resources (fish, forestry, fuels, mining products) constituted 24 percent of global trade in 2008 and has been growing at around 20 percent annually in value terms over the last decade.[5] Africa is rich in natural resources, but has not been able to use its natural resource endowments as policy leverage to move up the value chain. There are various reasons for this, including governance issues, tariff escalation issues, and non-availability of a stable investment environment in many African countries. But the sustained rise in demand for natural resources, especially from emerging economies, provides an excellent opportunity for resource endowed African countries to use these endowments as an instrument for their development.

To summarize, the remarkable changes in the global economy over the last two decades have created new challenges as well as opportunities for Africa in its quest for development. The challenges are quite daunting. The new wave of deep integration PTAs is changing the dynamic of global trade and threatening to create a two-tier world trading order. The threat that these developments pose to the non-discrimination principle is real and Africa will be among the regions in the world that will be most affected. The WTO, because of its preoccupation with the Doha round, is unable to address this issue head on. Similarly, the erosion of tariff preferences can have a serious impact on Africa's export competitiveness. Food security has emerged as a major public policy issue for the multilateral process and most African countries that are net food importers will need to work hard to keep this on the multilateral agenda so that global solutions can be found. The sustained rise of prices of natural resources offers a possible opportunity for many African countries to leverage their resource endowments to meet their development objectives. To address these challenges in an integrated manner, African countries will need not only to work on a positive agenda in multilateral fora, but also to revisit many policy frameworks and craft a new set of public policies. The issue of agricultural development is one example of an area where a new policy approach is necessary.

Africa and the DDA

An assessment of whether African countries stand to gain or lose from a completion of the Doha round has to be based on its impact on these challenges and opportunities. The discussion that follows highlights the state of play in the key areas of importance in the DDA negotiations from an African perspective.

Agriculture is indisputably the most important sector in the negotiations from a development perspective. The outcomes achieved so far in the subsidies negotiations are clearly sub-optimal from the viewpoint of the long-term objective of the Agreement on Agriculture "to establish a fair and market-oriented trading system through a programme of fundamental reform encompassing strengthened rules and specific commitments on support and protection in order to correct and prevent restrictions and distortions in world agricultural markets."[6] The reductions proposed in trade distorting support do not generally have an impact on current support levels in the major subsidizing countries and do not, therefore, satisfy the mandate for "substantial reductions in trade-distorting domestic support."[7] Substantially higher ambition in tackling such subsidies is required, including by further tightening the "green box" disciplines, which in their present form would allow some trade distorting subsidies to be shifted to the green box.

Some of the most problematic of such subsidies are the cotton subsidies in the United States. No commitments have yet been given by the United States to deliver on the mandate for addressing cotton "ambitiously, expeditiously and specifically, within the agriculture negotiations in relation to all trade-distorting policies affecting the sector in all three pillars of market access, domestic support and export competition."[8] This is a major issue affecting farmers in several African countries and requires an outcome that is faithful to the mandate.

Within the market access pillar of the agriculture negotiations, the issues that have a direct connection with food security are special products and the special safeguard mechanism (SSM). The categorization of products as "special products" would enable them to avoid tariff cuts or to undertake minimal cuts. Developing countries, especially those with subsistence agriculture, need an easy to use SSM to protect themselves against import surges and sharp price declines. While the issue of special products has been broadly stabilized, the SSM issue remains unresolved. A consensus on how to design such an instrument, while keeping its potential for abuse to the minimum, has so far eluded the negotiators.

In other areas of agricultural market access, there are a number of provisions in the draft text issued in 2008,[9] that will help African producers to export their products and to mitigate the effects of preference erosion. For products subject to tariff escalation, deeper tariff cuts have been provided. Similar treatment has been proposed for tropical products. On the issue of preferences, the proposals involve a longer time frame for effecting the tariff reductions. The LDCs are not required to make any reductions in their bound duties.

In the Non-Agricultural Market Access (NAMA—industrial goods) negotiations, a number of carve outs have been proposed to benefit the smallest and poorest countries. The small and vulnerable economies are required to undertake lower tariff reduction commitments. The LDCs are exempt from reductions from their bound rates. Duty-free quota-free treatment is required to be extended to the products of LDCs by developed countries and "developing countries declaring themselves in a position to do so."[10] Special treatment, in terms of an extended schedule for making tariff reductions, has been proposed for products identified as preference products.

In the context of the deep integration being brought about by the new PTAs, the issue of standards has become increasingly important for ensuring market access. A major objective of the twin agreements on Technical Barriers to Trade and Sanitary and Phytosanitary Measures is to encourage harmonization of standards across the world. For this it is important that international standards are recognized and adhered to by all countries. However, this is far from being the case. In the NAMA negotiations, proposals for greater cooperation between standard-setting bodies and the WTO have been discussed. The issue of better participation of developing country representatives in international standard-setting bodies is also vital in ensuring that the standards reflect the situations of all countries. Overall, progress on this critical area has been below expectations.

In services, the waiver instrument that would enable special preferences to be given to LDCs without extending them to others, remains to be finalized. The finalization of this instrument, while essential, cannot be the end objective. It must be followed by specific market access commitments for LDCs as an integral part of the outcome.

It is generally agreed that some of the biggest gains from the Doha round will come from an ambitious outcome in trade facilitation. To enable developing countries to undertake such commitments, it was agreed at the 2005 Hong Kong Ministerial Conference that support would be provided by members, in particular developed ones, "in a comprehensive manner and on a long-term and sustainable basis, backed by secure funding."[11] There have been few indications of this support in subsequent discussions. In order to ensure an ambitious outcome, it is important that these commitments are honored.

The work on fisheries subsidies so far has inadequately recognized the development aspects of the issue. Overfishing has not been caused by poor fishermen operating largely in coastal waters but by the organized, mechanized fleets from developed countries. The livelihood aspects of poor fishermen in developing countries have to be recognized to ensure a balanced outcome.

The debate on the public health aspects of Trade-Related Intellectual Property Rights (TRIPs) is far from over. The Public Health Declaration of 2001 and the 2003 Decision on the Interpretation of Paragraph 6 affirmed the flexibilities available under TRIPs to member states seeking to protect public health. Despite these clarifications, the actual implementation of these measures to improve access to medicines is far from satisfactory. The TRIPs-plus measures being incorporated in many regional and bilateral trade agreements are further undermining the capacity of the poor in developing countries to access affordable medicines.

The discussion on the relationship between the TRIPs Agreement and the Convention on Bio Diversity continues to be hampered by differences over the mandate. In the meantime, bio-piracy is rampant and developing countries that are home to the bulk of the world's bio-diversity continue to suffer its consequences. Ideally, the Doha round outcome should include a decision to amend the TRIPs Agreement to include a mandatory requirement for the disclosure of the source of (or country providing) the genetic resources and/or associated traditional knowledge in patent applications. The decision should also cover the issues of Prior Informed Consent and Access and Benefit Sharing. However, there are serious differences on this issue and a definitive outcome is unlikely.

Perhaps the most important inputs to enable developing countries in Africa to take advantage of new opportunities in the global economy are improvements in supply capacity, development of skills, enhancement of knowledge base, and the like, along with appropriate interventions to improve the physical infrastructure. Similar interventions are required to improve the quality of decision-making and implementation in governments. This involves an integrated and sustained program of external assistance. The WTO's aid for trade initiative can play an important role in designing such an integrated intervention. However, given the size and nature of the problem, the WTO can at best play a catalytic role in pushing for such an intervention. It is essential that the efforts of various development institutions and bilateral and other donors are coordinated to ensure the best results.

Conclusion

The last two decades have been a period of unprecedented economic change, with significant knock-on effects on the global trading system. Many conventional wisdoms have been toppled in the process. The post-World War Two leaders of the global economy are facing new challenges to their pre-eminence, with the new challengers emerging from the ranks of the developing countries. The so-called emerging economies (a term widely used, but never clearly defined), especially those in Asia, are redefining the way manufacturing is organized and trade is done. International production networks are leading to a new push for PTAs that are focusing on "deep integration," that is, behind the border regulatory coherence. The aggressive rule-making in the PTAs raises a number of issues—the role of the WTO, the threat to the non-discrimination principle and the consequences for those excluded from such PTAs. Most African countries are not participants in such PTAs and international production networks have largely bypassed Africa.

Much of African competitiveness is derived from tariff preferences; and it is because of the general downslide in applied tariffs that pre-ferences are being significantly eroded. Moreover, the general stagnation of demand in developed country markets as a result of the current economic crisis is ensuring that African countries have to look elsewhere for their trade growth. This is already happening and South-South trade is growing rapidly.

Food security has emerged as a major development challenge for Africa. The problem has been exacerbated by faulty policy advice from international financial institutions and donors leading to sustained underinvestment in food crops. A fresh policy approach is necessary to improve food security in Africa. The surge in natural resource prices and demand, largely the result of increased demand in emerging econo-mies, offers an opportunity for resource rich African countries to leverage this development for achieving their development objectives.

The stalemate in the Doha round is bad news for Africa. The issue is not so much the trade gains for Africa, which by all accounts will be fairly modest, but the implications this has for the multilateral process in general, and the capacity of the WTO to intervene on behalf of the poorest and smallest countries in the world. The WTO treats all members equally and therefore provides a voice to the poorest and smallest devel-oping countries while taking decisions. It is essential that the Doha stalemate is broken quickly so that the WTO can move on to address the new challenges in the global trading system.

Notes

1 WTO, *World Trade Report 2011* (Geneva: WTO, 2011).
2 WTO, *World Trade Report 2011*, 57.
3 WTO, *World Trade Report 2011*, 53.
4 Raymond Saner, "The Planet Earth-Agriculture and Food Security," in the report *Más Allá de la Crisis: El Futuro del Sistema Multilateral* (Madrid: Fundación Ramón Areces, 2010).
5 WTO, *World Trade Report 2011*.
6 WTO, "Doha Ministerial Declaration" (Geneva: WTO, 2001) WT/MIN (01)/DEC/1, paragraph 13.
7 WTO, "Doha Ministerial Declaration."
8 WTO, "Doha Work Programme: Ministerial Declaration", Hong Kong Ministerial Conference, WT/MIN(05)/DEC, 22 December 2005, paragraph 11.
9 WTO, "Revised Draft Modalities for Agriculture," TN/AG/W/4/Rev.4, 6 December 2008.
10 WTO, "Negotiating Group on Market Access – Fourth Revision of Draft Modalities for Non-Agricultural Market Access – Revision," TN/MA/W/ 103/Rev.3, 6 December 2008.
11 WTO, "Doha Work Programme," paragraph 6 of Annex E.

6 Mandela's way

Reflections on South Africa's role in the multilateral trading system

Faizel Ismail and Brendan Vickers

Multilateralism and the promotion of a fairer, more balanced and inclusive system of global governance have formed the cornerstones of South Africa's post-Apartheid foreign policy. Inspired by this vision, South Africa has played a leading role in advancing the trade and development objectives of the Doha Development Agenda (DDA), as well as championing greater influence and participation by developing countries in shaping a new paradigm for global trade governance. Central to this paradigm is transforming the World Trade Organization (WTO) from a mercantilist institution that serves narrow commercial interests to an organization that promotes the objective of "sustainable development," as outlined in the Preamble to the 1994 Marrakesh Agreement establishing the WTO.[1] That would ensure that trade opportunities are made available to developing countries on a more equitable basis and that trade rules do not subvert their development prospects.[2]

However, the current playing field in world trade is still highly uneven and biased against developing countries' interests. This "asymmetry of economic opportunity" favoring rich countries was established during previous rounds of the General Agreement on Tariffs and Trade (GATT), and continues into the current Doha round given the onerous demands on developing countries, including South Africa.[3] Developed countries continue to have a strong market opening agenda directed at the emerging economies in the areas of industrial tariffs and services, while seeking greater flexibility that would maintain high levels of protection for their farmers. Indeed, persistent agricultural protection in the United States, the European Union (EU) and other developed countries continues to undermine the agricultural development and food security concerns of a large number of developing countries, many of which are in sub-Saharan Africa, the poorest region in the world. The high cotton subsidies that continue to threaten millions of agricultural jobs and livelihoods in West Africa, notably Benin, Burkina Faso, Chad, and Mali, are stark reminders of the inequity of the current regime.[4] Meanwhile, the world's least developed countries (LDCs) still wait patiently for some dividends from the Doha round, especially for the agreement reached at the December 2005 Hong Kong Ministerial Conference to create new opportunities for their development by providing them with duty-free quota-free (DFQF) market access. Although the launch of the WTO's Doha round in November 2001 had promised to correct these historical imbalances and place the needs and interests of developing countries at the heart of the Doha Work Programme, the negotiations have been at an impasse since the July 2008 Ministerial Meetings in Geneva.

This chapter explores the role of democratic South Africa in the WTO, specifically as a "norm entrepreneur" that has actively sought to advance the DDA's trade and development objectives and promote systemic reform. We argue that South Africa's participation in the WTO has been informed by its own domestic development challenges, as well as the values derived from the long struggle against Apartheid and the transition to a new constitutional democracy. The country's political leadership in the Doha negotiations has been strengthened too by its deep democratic institutions and consultative processes at home. South Africa's values, as articulated by the country's first black president, Nelson Mandela, reflect a deep commitment to multilateralism and consensus-building; fairness and justice; inclusiveness; and a concern to support and promote development, within South Africa, but also in developing countries of the South, especially the African continent. For these reasons, South Africa has been widely recognized and respected as a middle power "facilitator" or "mediator" between the industrialized and developing worlds in the WTO, a familiar motif in the country's broader post-Apartheid international relations.[5] As this chapter demonstrates, South Africa has at critical junctures exercised leadership to broker common ground on key trade and development aspects of the Doha Agenda.

This understanding of South Africa's role, interests, and identity in the WTO, especially the country's commitment to global governance reform, underscores the importance of its recent membership of the systemically significant "BRICS" formation, which includes Brazil, Russia, India and China. Coined over a decade ago by Jim O'Neill, then the chief economist of Goldman Sachs, today the BRICS are among the fastest growing, largest emerging economies and at the forefront of reshaping the global economy and the emerging architecture of twenty-first century global governance. South Africa's Minister of International Relations and Cooperation noted that the inclusion of South Africa in the BRICS quintet recognized the role it was playing in

"advancing the restructuring of the global political, economic and financial architecture into one that is more equitable, balanced and rests on the
important pillar of multilateralism."[6] This is particularly the case for
the global trading system.

The chapter is divided into three sections. In the first section, we
discuss the principles and approaches that have guided South Africa's
negotiators in the WTO since the birth of its new democracy in 1994.
Drawn from South Africa's heroic struggle for freedom, democracy, and
human dignity, and the example of its leaders, these principles and
approaches contributed to building South Africa's credibility and influence in the multilateral trading regime. Section two then explores South
Africa's role and participation in the WTO's Doha round in five negotiating areas: the launching of the Doha round; Trade-Related Intellectual Property Rights (TRIPs) and Public Health; the formation of
the Group of 20 (G-20) developing country alliance demanding fairer
global agricultural trade; the negotiations on special and differential
treatment (SDT) for developing countries; and the Non-Agricultural
Market Access coalition (NAMA-11), which continues to champion
developing countries' right to policy space for industrial development.
The chapter concludes with South Africa's perspective on how to
ensure a fair and balanced conclusion to the Doha round, on the basis
of its development mandate, and drawing on the aspirational values
espoused by Nelson Mandela.

Principles and approaches guiding South Africa's role in the multilateral trading system

In Mandela's first major statement on foreign policy, he argued that
the new democratic South Africa should base its foreign policy on six
principles, namely: human rights, justice and respect for international
law, peace, the interests of Africa, and international cooperation on
economic development.[7] In setting out the "new" South Africa's foreign
policy in this way, Mandela was to embed South Africa's international
relations in the best tradition of idealism, reflecting democratic South
Africa's "own collective self-concept"[8] and the sanguine zeitgeist of the
early post-Cold War years.

The perspective that Mandela advanced was not only personal but
deeply embedded in the struggle for freedom, democracy, and justice
waged by the people of South Africa against an unjust Apartheid regime.
In his seminal paper on foreign policy, Mandela argued that the new
South Africa's policies should be based on the principles, approaches,
and lessons learnt from the struggle against Apartheid and oppression.

Thus Mandela argued that the new South Africa could not be indifferent to the rights of others and boldly asserted that "human rights will be the light that guides our foreign affairs." He argued too that "only true democracy can guarantee rights" and that "respect for diversity" should be promoted in international institutions. He declared that South Africa's relations with the continent of Africa should be based on the "principles of equity, mutual benefit and peaceful cooperation" and he committed the new South Africa to taking responsibility for the Southern African region "not in a spirit of paternalism or dominance but mutual cooperation and respect."[9]

These values were developed within the liberation movement and the crucible of the South African struggle for freedom, democracy, and human dignity. The African National Congress (ANC) in exile, led by Oliver Tambo, had worked tirelessly to obtain the support of the international community to isolate the Apartheid regime. It took many years of dedicated and relentless work to persuade the overwhelming majority of members of the United Nations (UN) to vote in support of resolutions that denounced Apartheid as a crime against humanity and eventually to support sanctions against the Apartheid regime.[10] The ANC in turn too was influenced by the values of the international community reflected in the UN Universal Declaration of Human Rights.

In the first few years of his Presidency, Mandela expressed his commitment to the multilateral system, reminding his audience that although South Africa had been a member of the GATT since its inception when "the vast majority of South Africans had no vote" South Africa was committed to "vastly improve on the management of the world trading system to the mutual benefit of all nations and people."[11] He therefore committed South Africa to work for a rules-based multilateral trading system that was fair, balanced, and inclusive, and addressed the needs and interests of the developing countries.[12] These principles were to guide South Africa's trade negotiators in the WTO since 1994.

Beyond these aspirational values, South Africa also evolved its own negotiating approach, informed by the need to take into account the interests of "both" South Africa and others, especially the African continent; the capacity to listen to different sides of an argument; consultations with constituencies at home; balancing the country's principles with its capacity to implement; and adhering to "principles" while being pragmatic on "strategy." In advancing South Africa's foreign policy principles, Mandela was also cognizant of the vast reconstruction and development challenges that lay ahead for the country. He stated clearly that, when considering the balance between these issues, the reality of

South Africa's own development challenges and interests had to be considered and not undermined.

In his book *Mandela's Way*, Richard Stengel argues that "Mandela is a man of principle—exactly one: Equal rights for all, regardless of race, class or gender. Pretty much everything else is a tactic."[13] He goes on to argue that "Mandela is a thorough-going pragmatist who is willing to compromise, change, adapt, and refine his strategy as long as it got him the promised land." Stengel argues that Mandela learnt to examine these principles against changing conditions. Thus for Mandela, "when conditions change you must change your strategy and your mind." Mandela's approach can be described as a "mixed distributive strategy" in the academic discourse of trade negotiations. In an attempt to develop a theory of negotiating strategies, Odell argues that the behavior of negotiators may be described in "two polar ideal types:" a "purely distributive strategy" and a "purely integrative strategy." The first is described as "a set of tactics that are functional only for claiming value from others and defending against such claiming, when one party's goals are partly in conflict with those of the other." The second strategy is described as "a set of tactics instrumental in the attainment of goals that are not in fundamental conflict and hence can be integrated for mutual gain to some degree." Odell suggests that a "mixed-distributive strategy" can provide more gains than a purely distributive or purely integrative one.[14]

It will be argued that in the course of the Doha round negotiations South Africa's negotiators adopted different strategies and tactics at different stages of each of the negotiations as the "conditions" changed. Following Odell's conceptualization, we argue that South Africa was to use a mix of "purely distributive" and "purely integrative" strategies, depending on the nature (conditions) and the stage (time) of the negotiations. We next proceed to discuss the role of South Africa in the Doha round negotiations.

South Africa's role in the Doha round

South Africa was one of the founding members of the GATT in 1947. However, the Apartheid regime then considered South Africa to be a "developed" country. Since it mainly represented the interests of an affluent white minority, it did not argue the case for development issues to be considered centrally. In the Uruguay round (1986–1994), South Africa was therefore forced to undertake developed country commitments in key market access areas, including agriculture, industrial tariffs (NAMA), and services.[15] This "historical injustice" of South Africa's misclassification in the previous Uruguay round has become a major cri de coeur for South Africa in the DDA negotiations, since South Africa's legal commitments (that is, its bindings) in each of these areas are vastly higher than those of comparator developing countries in the WTO, including Argentina, Brazil, and India.[16] For instance, in the NAMA negotiations, the proposed Swiss formula to reduce industrial tariffs will result in South Africa and its lesser developed neighbors in the Southern African Customs Union (SACU), including one LDC, undertaking deeper and wider tariff cuts than any other WTO member, while obtaining very little new market access for their agricultural exporters. South Africa has thus made the case that a development outcome is far more important than an early conclusion of the trade round that does not deliver on the developmental mandate agreed to at Doha in 2001. South Africa's principled positions in advancing the DDA's trade and development objectives was demonstrated clearly in five areas of the Doha round.

Launching the Doha round

Starting at the Seattle Ministerial Conference in 1999, where efforts to launch the Millennium trade round collapsed dramatically, to the eventual adoption of the Doha Ministerial Declaration in 2001, South Africa played a key role in brokering consensus among the WTO members to launch a new round of negotiations. For South Africa, a new trade round offered an opportunity to correct the historical imbalances and inequities of the prevailing system, which favored rich countries. South Africa hence argued that it was the turn of the developed countries to undergo reforms, in order to allow for a structural shift of resources to developing countries. To level the playing field, South Africa called upon developed countries to open their agricultural markets and other so-called "grandfather industries," especially the highly protected sugar, cotton, textiles, and steel sectors.

South African Trade and Industry Minister, Alec Erwin, was to be appointed as a Friend of the Chair, together with five other Ministers, assisting the Chair to broker a consensus on the objectives and mandates of the round. South Africa also played an instrumental role in ensuring that the final text that did eventually emerge as the Doha Ministerial Declaration (later called the DDA) contained various commitments to prioritize the development needs and interests of poorer countries.

The Doha Ministerial Conference and its outcomes were very controversial. South Africa's role was criticized by many non-governmental organizations (NGOs) that were opposed to the launching of a new round at Doha. South Africa's approach, as some observers have argued, may have been "too accommodating" of the demands of developed countries. Erwin himself was criticized for privileging "trade-offs" rather than "stand-offs" with the North, and for colluding with the "undemocratic" modalities of the WTO, thereby promoting and legitimizing the WTO's liberalization agenda and its neoclassical model of development.[17] Other writers have argued that "South Africa's support before and during the Doha Conference helped the developed countries to achieve their 'success' in Doha."[18]

However, South Africa's negotiators at the time were attempting to contribute to redressing the existing imbalances in the multilateral trading system and to the creation of a fairer, more balanced, and development-oriented WTO. The accommodating approach adopted by South Africa's negotiators to the interests of developed countries was possibly a result of their lack of experience and naïve belief that the developed countries would deliver on their promises to place the needs and interests of developing countries at the heart of the Doha Work Programme. South Africa was to heed this criticism of its approach during subsequent years of the Doha negotiations.

Reforming TRIPs and Public Health

One of South Africa's first major achievements in the Doha round was to help facilitate an agreement in the TRIPs and Public Health negotiations for establishing a mechanism that would allow countries with no or insufficient manufacturing capacity to import medicines for public health reasons under compulsory license.

The TRIPs Agreement was one of the most controversial outcomes of the previous Uruguay round. Policy-makers in both developed and developing countries continued to debate how to create an optimum balance between the wider interests of society; how best to use patents (that is, market exclusivity) as an incentive for pharmaceutical companies to invest in research and development, so that new drugs can be developed to combat diseases; and the need to ensure that this exclusivity does not make these drugs unaffordable for the majority of people, particularly in poor developing countries. The TRIPs Agreement contained some flexibility (in terms of compulsory licences and parallel imports) to prevent abuse by patent owners. However, this flexibility was contested by the US pharmaceutical industry, specifically in the case of South Africa.

In 1998, 39 pharmaceutical companies launched a case against the South African Medicines Act after failing to persuade the South African government to withdraw or modify the provisions of Article 15(c) of the South African Medicines and Related Substances Act of 1965. The United States believed that this legal provision was "inconsistent with South Africa's obligations and commitments under the WTO TRIPs Agreement."[19]

Thus, there was increased public pressure by developing countries and NGOs in the United States and Europe for the WTO, at Doha, to re-affirm the right of governments to act in the interests of public health. In addition, there was recognition that many developing countries were unable to use the compulsory licence mechanism provided by the TRIPs Agreement to access affordable drugs, since they did not have the capacity to manufacture pharmaceuticals. Ministers in Doha thus instructed the WTO, in paragraph 6 of the Doha Ministerial Declaration, to develop a legal mechanism before the end of December 2002 that would enable those countries that did not have sufficient manufacturing capacity to produce these life-saving drugs. In the subsequent negotiations in the WTO, South Africa was to make a significant contribution at each stage of these negotiations.

Notwithstanding the criticisms of several NGOs that the agreement was too leaky, WTO members and other expert observers of the negotiations hailed the agreement on TRIPs and Public Health as a major victory for social justice and consensus-building in the WTO.[20] South Africa had played a very significant role in this success. Thus early in its active participation in the WTO, South Africa had built respect among its developed country trading partners for its tenacity and steadfastness, and credibility among developing countries for the leadership role it played in building convergence among the various developing country groups. This experience served to erase much of the suspicion and criticisms of NGOs and some developing countries for its role in launching the Doha round. These criticisms were also to fade as South Africa joined Brazil, India, China, and Argentina in the formation of one of the most formidable developing country alliances in the WTO—the G-20.

The G-20 and fairer global farm trade

The role of developing countries in the Doha round has been unprecedented, with the building of powerful coalitions and issue-based alliances. South Africa has played a central role in many of these new alliances. Galvanized by the formation of the G-20 in agricultural trade, these coalitions have for the first time shifted the negotiating dynamic in multilateral trade negotiations in favor of developing countries.[21]

The Doha mandate envisaged agreement on modalities for the agriculture negotiations by March 2003. However, in the lead up to the Cancún Ministerial Conference, the European Union failed to table any proposal that would meaningfully meet its Doha commitment. The March 2003 deadline for the establishment of a methodology for agriculture negotiations was thus missed. As Cancún drew closer, the United States and the European Union shifted to a strategy of bilateral engagement. The product of these intense bilateral discussions between the European Union and the United States was an accommodation of each others' trade-distorting farm support policies. In return for protecting payments under the Farm Bill, the United States reduced its ambition to open European markets and fully eliminate the European Union's destructive export subsidies. The EU-US Joint Text tabled on 13 August 2003 galvanized developing countries into action to prevent another "Blair House" type agreement, which would accommodate the interests of the European Union and the United States and reduce the ambition of the round once again.[22] The text was vociferously challenged by a range of countries, including Australia, Brazil, Argentina, South Africa, and many other former US allies, which had coalesced around the common objective of securing freer global agriculture markets.[23] Developing countries, led by Brazil, India, China, South Africa, Argentina, and several others, established a broad-based alliance that grew into the G-20. The formation of this group was based on the need for developing countries to advance liberalization and reform of agriculture in the developed world, with social justice and development in developing countries.

As a small but competitive agricultural exporter, South Africa's interests were more aligned to the Cairns Group of agricultural exporters. However, because of its internal concerns to obtain more policy space for small emerging farmers, and the need to support its African neighbors' development, South Africa was able and willing to champion the concerns of the more defensive countries, including India, China, and most of Africa. South Africa thus began to provide a natural bridge in the debate on finding the appropriate balance between the various interests. Once Brazil and India were able to find a compromise, South Africa became the next country to join this emerging new alliance—the G-20. This provided the impetus for other African members, including Egypt, Nigeria, Zimbabwe. and Tanzania, to join the G-20.

The G-20 has continued to play a leading role in the agriculture negotiations, emerging as the most important developing country interlocutor with the major developed countries in the agriculture negotiations. South Africa furthermore assisted the G-20 to forge consensus on a range of issues of interest to the small and vulnerable economies (SVEs), including market access into developing countries, preference erosion, food aid, special products (that is, new provisions for developing countries to protect agricultural products for food security and rural development reasons), and the special safeguard mechanism (SSM) (that is, a new trade remedy to protect developing countries from subsidized agricultural imports). But there has been a wider strategic objective too. At the 2005 Hong Kong Ministerial Conference, South Africa, together with Brazil and India, played an instrumental role in building an united platform for all developing country coalitions to champion the DDA's trade and development objectives—the Group of 110 (G-110).[24] It was this bridge-building capacity that led South Africa to play an important role in advancing the SDT negotiations in the WTO.

Championing the interests of LDCs and SVEs

South Africa was nominated to chair the WTO's Committee on Trade and Development Special Session (CTDSS) from 2004 to 2006, which placed the country in a prominent position to shape the Doha round's "development" discourse and architecture. In the debate on how to address the unique concerns of SVEs, South Africa was able to build compromise between the larger developing countries, which feared their opportunistic "graduation" and loss of SDT flexibilities, and the smaller developing countries, mostly from Africa. As Chair of the CTDSS, South Africa's contribution was threefold. The first was the evolution of the concept of "situational flexibility," which sought to address the concerns of the small and vulnerable developing country economies. Second, South Africa facilitated the negotiations and drafting of a compromise text on the concept of "small and vulnerable economies" during the July 2004 Framework Agreement negotiations. Third, as the Chair of the CTDSS, South Africa facilitated the process of evolving a positive outcome for LDCs at the Hong Kong Ministerial Conference.[25] It was because of this experience and reputation that South Africa was entrusted to coordinate another important developing country alliance, the NAMA-11, which was to play a crucial role in the industrial tariff negotiations.

The NAMA-11 and "reclaiming" policy space

Ahead of the Hong Kong Ministerial Conference in December 2005, a group of developing countries began to work closely together on NAMA and produced a critique of the EU and other developed countries' emerging approach to the Doha round negotiations.[26] In a paper submitted to the WTO Committee on Trade and Development, appropriately titled "Reclaiming Development in the WTO Doha Development Round," this group of countries argued that developing countries "cannot be expected to pay for the much-needed reforms in the agriculture sectors of developed countries ... by overly ambitious requests on them in industrial tariffs that do not take into account the realities of their levels of economic development and their adjustment needs."[27] The group called for the "development content of the round to be reclaimed" and united around their common concerns in the NAMA negotiations, opposing the EU's aggressive approach for formula-based tariff cuts and defending the flexibilities contained in the July 2004 Framework Agreement.[28]

It was because of their collective bargaining power that the NAMA-11 was able to achieve three important victories at Hong Kong. First, the coalition successfully resisted the attempts by developed countries to force a premature agreement on modalities in NAMA ahead of any significant agreement on the main issues in agriculture. Second, these developing countries were able to confirm that the principle of "less than full reciprocity" would be adhered to when making reduction commitments, and appropriate flexibilities would be provided to them in order to preserve their domestic policy space. Third, the group was also able to establish a strong link in the final text of the Hong Kong Ministerial Declaration between the level of ambition in NAMA and the level of ambition in agriculture.[29]

Coordinated by South Africa, the NAMA-11 developed a negotiating posture of engagement and pragmatism on the formula and flexibilities, while maintaining a steadfast and resolute approach on the principles of equity and proportionality of contributions by developed countries. Its members also provided leadership and support to other developing country groups in the WTO, including the LDCs and SVEs. At the Hong Kong Ministerial Conference, "developing countries in a position to do so" pledged to provide DFQF market access to all LDCs. The NAMA-11 also agreed that the SVEs should be treated differently and be provided with greater flexibilities.

South Africa's "norm entrepreneurship" in these five areas of the Doha negotiations demonstrates South Africa's strong commitment to the principles of equity, fairness, and a strengthened, more balanced, and development-oriented multilateral trading system.[30] On each issue, South Africa was resolute and remained steadfast on these principles, while being willing to engage with its trading partners and search for pragmatic solutions. Its negotiating approach changed when the conditions changed. At the launch of the Doha round, South Africa was willing to "accommodate" the interests of industrialized countries when developing the negotiating mandate. In the course of the negotiations on agriculture, when the EU-US alliance threatened to undermine the promise of a development outcome, South Africa joined Brazil and India in building the formidable G-20 alliance. The emergence of the G-20 was an important moral and political victory for developing countries: not only did it significantly strengthen developing countries' bargaining power, but it fundamentally shifted the terms and terrain of the farm trade negotiations, which subsequently stabilized around the G-20's "middle" ground position. Similarly, when South Africa was thrust into the leadership of the TRIPs and Public Health negotiations for cheaper and more affordable medicines, it played this role with a deep sense of commitment. When later requested to chair the negotiations on how to address the unique concerns of SVEs, South Africa was again willing and able to facilitate a compromise among developing countries. And when there was the threat of onerous obligations being imposed on developing countries to reduce their industrial tariffs, thereby undermining their industrial policies, South Africa played an effective role in leading the NAMA-11.

In each of these cases, the effectiveness of South Africa's leadership role was assisted by its own experiences in building compromises at home, to correct the inherited inequities and injustices from its Apartheid past. South Africa also had good experience in building consensus among its domestic constituencies through a well-developed institution for social dialogue, the National Economic Development and Labour Council (NEDLAC). NEDLAC was established in 1995 as a statutory body drawing together government, organized labor, business, and community organizations to develop consensus around key areas of economic, trade, labor, and development policy-making. This consultative framework provides a great deal of discipline to the positions of government negotiators in bilateral, regional, and multilateral trade negotiations. It also drew on its commitment to support the development of its neighbors in the African continent. This willingness to recognize its responsibilities vis-à-vis the smaller and more vulnerable economies from its own continent helped South Africa to facilitate consensus and compromise within and between the various developing country groups in the WTO.

South Africa's unique value system has enabled the country to play a significant role in the Doha round. The experiences of South Africa in the multilateral trading system have been inspired by the idealist and aspirational vision and principles set out by Nelson Mandela, rather than simply the narrow interest-driven discourse of realism. As we now

conclude, it is this same vision and set of values that should guide negotiators during Doha's endgame to deliver a fairer, more balanced, and
development-friendly system of global trade governance.

Conclusion

The WTO's maiden trade round, the DDA, is today the longest running
trade round in the history of multilateral trade negotiations. Nonetheless,
South Africa remains committed to concluding the round, albeit on the
developmental terms and mandate originally agreed at Doha in 2001.
It is important to appreciate that the current stasis in the DDA is the
direct result of fundamental political and policy differences between
the major economies in the WTO, which no procedural panacea (such
as informal small groups that meet in various "G" configurations, thereby
eroding multilateralism and further marginalizing Africa's interests)[31]
is likely to resolve. These differences are largely the result of the mercantilist objectives of the major developed countries that seek greater
commercial access to the markets of developing countries, beyond the
agreements reached in 2008 and the Doha mandate. The only way out
of the current impasse in the Doha round is for the developed countries
to moderate their demands and honor the multilateral convergences
reached in the July and December 2008 Texts, respect the DDA's development mandate, and be more realistic about what can be achieved
during the ongoing Great Recession and high unemployment in many
countries around the world, including South Africa.

Given these realities, a new "culture" that breaks with the mercantilist tradition of previous GATT negotiations is a necessary condition
for a breakthrough in the current impasse. As a first step, this requires
that all members should recognize, respect, and indeed mainstream the
WTO's development dimension. The Preamble to the 1994 Marrakesh
Agreement establishing the WTO set out the objective of "sustainable
development" and expressly referred to the need for "positive efforts to
ensure that developing countries secure a share in the growth of international trade commensurate with the needs of their economic development." A second step is to ensure greater inclusiveness of developing
countries in decision-making, so that trade opportunities are made available to all members on a more equitable basis and that trade rules do
not subvert their development prospects.

We offer four observations on the way forward, each of which features
prominently in *The Johannesburg Statement on the Doha Development
Agenda*,[32] to ensure developmental dividends from the Doha round
and the broader WTO architecture.

First, it is important that WTO members respect and reaffirm the DDA mandate, which remains as relevant today as it was 10 years ago. The Doha round placed agriculture at the center of the negotiations. The level of ambition in NAMA and other negotiating areas were to be proportionate to the level of ambition that developed countries were prepared to undertake in agriculture. However, there has been little progress in this regard, reflected in persistent agricultural protectionism, most egregiously cotton, and the modest levels of ambition contained in the July and December 2008 Texts on agriculture. The removal of distortions in global agricultural trade is therefore the core issue in the Doha round and is a litmus test for a development outcome.

In addition, it is imperative to address the imbalance between excessive demands on NAMA and diminished ambition to reform agriculture. The formula adopted for NAMA (that is, the Swiss formula) is onerous compared with the more lenient linear formula adopted for tariff cuts in agriculture. The relatively wide range of flexibilities insisted on by the developed countries to protect their sensitive agriculture products has been contrasted with the relatively narrow set of flexibilities they were willing to provide developing countries in NAMA for their sensitive sectors. Thus the current demands by the major developed countries for more market access from developing countries in NAMA and services are unfair. They will tilt the current imbalance in the trading system and the July and December 2008 Texts even more against developing countries. It is indeed a damning indictment on the WTO that a development round is giving way to mercantilist market access objectives of some major players.

Second, the promise made to deliver to the poorest countries, in particular the LDCs and the SVEs, must be fulfilled. The LDC package that WTO members failed to agree in July 2011 must be delivered, as a matter of priority; the issues included DFQF, Rules of Origin, an LDC services waiver, and cotton. The current decision agreed at the Hong Kong Ministerial Conference only provides 97 percent DFQF market access to LDCs and will only be implemented at the conclusion of the Doha round. Developing countries in a position to do so should also provide such access and support in accordance with their capacity.

It will also be vital to facilitate imports of LDCs and other small, weak, and vulnerable economies' services into developed country markets. This should include providing better access for the temporary movement of workers and for outsourcing in various areas, including health, education, and call-centers from these economies. The potential benefits of Mode 4 liberalization by developed countries could dwarf the benefits gained by developing countries from openings in the traditional goods sectors.

Third, the so-called "new approaches" being sought by some developed countries are nothing more than a disguised attempt to substantially raise their current level of market access into developing countries. The protagonists of these so-called new approaches are seeking a new mandate to create plurilateral approaches, which will undermine the principles of multilateralism and inclusiveness. These new approaches will lead to the further marginalization of developing countries by seeking non-most favored nation plurilaterals that prefer the most advanced and powerful economies and marginalize the weak and poor. They will perpetuate the discredited "principal supplier" approach last used in the Tokyo round (1973–1979), where developing countries were simply onlookers and excluded from most of the agreements reached among the major developed countries.[33]

Finally, some developed countries have called for so-called "new issues"—or "new global challenges"—to be discussed, with a view to their negotiation at some future date. However, it is not reasonable to expect developing countries to seriously discuss these so-called new twenty-first century issues when the issues that are of interest to developing countries, and especially the poorest, are still twentieth century issues begging to be resolved.

The recent demands by the United States and the European Union for the world's emerging economies, especially China, Brazil, and India, to take equal responsibility as developed countries in the WTO's Doha round of negotiations and in the climate change negotiations fail to recognize that these economies are still poor and their development challenges large. About 150 million people in China still live on under US$1 per day. The United States remains the world's largest economy, with a per capita income 15 times that of China and 47 times that of India.[34] It will take at least 50 years before the United States can demand to put these economies on the same playing field as its own. Some recent scenarios of global growth project that while China will become the world's largest economy by 2050 and India will be the world's third largest economy after the United States, US per capita gross domestic product will still be three times that of China and over eight times that of India in 2050.[35]

A stable and strengthened rules-based system is a vital component of multilateralism and the system of global governance. A failure to conclude the Doha round on the basis of its development mandate, and in a way that is fair and balanced, will have serious systemic implications for global governance more generally. The United States and the European Union are the largest beneficiaries of the rules-based multilateral trading system.[36] Demanding mercantilist gains at the expense of their trading partners, especially poorer developing countries, will delay the conclusion of the Doha round and undermine the stability of the rules-based system. Developed countries thus have a responsibility to provide the requisite leadership to transform the WTO into a global public good for all its members or, in the words of WTO Director-General Pascal Lamy, into an institution that is " ... more development-friendly, more user-friendly, so that its benefits are felt by all, large and small, rich and poor, strong and weak."[37]

Notes

1 The WTO still lacks clarity as to its *main goals and objectives*, which are often confused with its *main functions* (i.e. trade opening and rules creation). Given its historical failure to address the concerns of developing countries, which today constitute the overwhelming majority of its membership, the WTO needs to declare its mission to be that of advancing the development interests and concerns of the majority of its members. This will not turn the WTO into a "development agency" or "institution," as some critics of this argument suggest. Rather, it will clarify the overall high-level principles and objectives that should guide the WTO in executing its functions.

2 See Faizel Ismail, "Mainstreaming Development in the World Trade Organization," *Journal of World Trade* 39, no. 1 (2005): 11–21; Asif. H. Qureshi, "International Trade for Development: The WTO as a Development Institution?" *Journal of World Trade* 43, no. 1 (2009): 173–188; and Carolyn Deere Birkbeck, ed., *Making Global Trade Governance Work for Development* (Cambridge: Cambridge University Press, 2011).

3 Rorden Wilkinson, *The WTO: Crisis and the Governance of Global Trade* (London: Routledge, 2006).

4 See Donna Lee, "The Cotton Club: The Africa Group in the Doha Development Agenda," in *The WTO After Hong Kong*, eds, Donna Lee and Rorden Wilkinson (London: Routledge, 2007), 137–154. See also Chapter 4 of this volume.

5 See Walter Carlsnaes and Philip Nel, eds, *In Full Flight. South African Foreign Policy after Apartheid* (Johannesburg: Institute for Global Dialogue, 2006).

6 See "South Africa's Full Membership of BRICS," *The Diplomat*, December 2010, internal newsletter of the Department of International Relations and Cooperation, South Africa.

7 Nelson Mandela, "South Africa's Future Foreign Policy," *Foreign Affairs* 72, no. 5 (1993): 86–97.

8 John G. Ruggie, "Third Try at World Order? America and Multilateralism after the Cold War," *Political Science Quarterly* 109, no. 4 (1994): 533–570.

9 Mandela, "South Africa's Future Foreign Policy."

10 Luli Callinicos, *Oliver Tambo. Beyond the Engeli Mountains* (Cape Town: David Philip, 2004).

11 *Statement by Nelson Mandela, President of South Africa at the 50th Anniversary of the Multilateral Trading System*, Geneva, May 1998.

12 Mandela, "South Africa's Future Foreign Policy."

13 Richard Stengel, *Mandela's Way: Lessons on Life* (London: Virgin Books, 2010).
14 John Odell, *Negotiating the World Economy* (Ithaca and London: Cornell University Press, 2000).
15 During the 1960s, when the GATT allowed differentiation between developed and developing countries to permit the latter to receive more gentle treatment, South Africa did not consider changing its status. According to Hirsch, "Its white rulers believed they lived like wealthy western European or American societies, and would have seen developing country status as an insult." In 1993, towards the end of the Uruguay round, South Africa sought to change its status to "developing country," but this was opposed by the United States, European Union, and Japan, who insisted that South Africa would be entitled to more lenient treatment similar to the economies in transition. See Trevor Bell, "Trade Policy," in *The Political Economy of South Africa's Transition*, eds, Jonathan Michie and Vishnu Padayachee (London: Dryden Press, 1997); and Alan Hirsch, *Season of Hope: Economic Reform Under Mandela and Mbeki* (Scottsville and Ottawa: University of KwaZulu-Natal Press and International Development Research Centre, 2005).
16 This challenge not only applies to South Africa, but also to SACU through its common external tariff. SACU is the world's oldest functioning customs union, formed in 1910, and consists of one developing country (South Africa), three small and vulnerable economies (Botswana, Namibia, and Swaziland), and an LDC (Lesotho). As a result of the Uruguay round, SACU's bound tariff rates (17 percent) are today almost half the average for comparable developing countries such as Argentina and Brazil (30 percent) as well as India (40 percent).
17 Brendan Vickers, "'Reclaiming Development' in Multilateral Trade: South Africa and the Doha Development Agenda," in *Leadership and Change in the Multilateral Trading System*, eds. Amrita Narlikar and Brendan Vickers (Republic of Letters/Martinus Nijhoff: Dordrecht, 2009), 149–180.
18 Fatoumata Jawara and Aileen Kwa, *Behind the Scenes at the WTO: The Real World of International Trade Negotiations* (London: Zed Books, 2003).
19 See Carolyn Deere, *The Implementation Game: The TRIPS Agreement and the Global Politics of Intellectual Property Reform in Developing Countries* (Oxford: Oxford University Press, 2009).
20 See Frederick M. Abbott, "The WTO Medicines Decision: World Pharmaceuticals Trade and the Protection of Public Health," *The American Journal of International Law* 99, no. 317 (2005): 317–358.
21 Amrita Narlikar and Diana Tussie, "The G-20 at the Cancún Ministerial: Developing Countries and Their Evolving Coalitions in the WTO," *The World Economy* 27, no. 7 (2004): 947–966.
22 See J. Wiener, *Making Rules in the Uruguay Round of the GATT* (Aldershot: Dartmouth Publishing Company, 1995), 191–215, for a discussion of the "Blair House" agreement of the Uruguay round.
23 Faizel Ismail, "Agricultural Trade Liberalization and the Poor: A Development Perspective on Cancún," *Bridges Weekly Trade News Digest* 8, no. 1 (2004): 4–5.
24 Faizel Ismail, "The G-20 and the NAMA 11: Perspectives Revisited," *The Indian Journal of International Economic Law*, Inaugural Issue 1, no. 1 (2008).

25 See Faizel Ismail, "How Can Least Developed Countries and Other Small, Weak and Vulnerable Economies Also Gain from the Doha Development Agenda on the Road to Hong Kong?" *Journal of World Trade* 40, no. 1 (2006): 37–68.

26 See *Statement by South Africa to the 55th session of the Committee on Trade and Development on behalf of Argentina, Brazil, India, Indonesia, Namibia, the Philippines and Venezuela*, 28 November 2005.

27 See *Submission by Argentina, Brazil, India, Indonesia, Namibia, Pakistan, the Philippines, South Africa and Venezuela to the Committee on Trade and Development on "Reclaiming Development in the WTO Doha Development Round"* (WT/COMTD/W/145), 1 December 2005.

28 See *Communication from Argentina, Bolivarian Republic of Venezuela, Brazil, China, Egypt, India, Indonesia, Namibia, Pakistan, Philippines and South Africa on "Market Access for Non-Agricultural Products. Flexibilities for Developing Countries"* (TN/MA/W/65), 8 November 2005.

29 Hong Kong Ministerial Declaration (WT/MIN (05)/DEC), paragraph 24.

30 On norm entrepreneurs see Martha Finnemore and Kathryn Sikkink, "International Norm Dynamics and Political Change," *International Organization* 52, no. 4 (1998): 887–91.

31 In recent years, a few of the major players have regularly convened as informal small groups in an effort to make a breakthrough in the negotiations; these include the G-4, G-5/Five Interested Parties, G-6, G-7, and G-11. The formation of the G-7 at the July 2008 negotiations in Geneva did not include any representative from Africa, the poorest region in the world.

32 Global Poverty Summit, "*The Johannesburg Statement on the Doha Development Agenda*," (GPS/DDA/TF/5/1), 19 January 2011, reproduced in the appendix to this volume.

33 Faizel Ismail and Brendan Vickers, "Towards Fair and Inclusive Decision-making in WTO Negotiations," in *Making Global Trade Governance Work for Development*, ed., Carolyn Deere Birkbeck (Cambridge: Cambridge University Press, 2011), 461–485.

34 World Bank, *World Development Report 2010* (Washington, DC: World Bank, 2010).

35 Uri Dadush and Bennett Stancil, "The World Order in 2050," Carnegie Endowment for International Peace Policy Outlook (February 2010). See also Uri Dadush and William Shaw, *Juggernaut. How Emerging Markets are Reshaping Globalization* (Washington, DC: Carnegie Endowment for International Peace, 2011).

36 Fred Bergsten, "Obama needs to be bold on trade," *Financial Times*, 24 June 2009.

37 WTO, "Appointment of the Director-General. Statement of the Director-General," General Council, JOB(09)/39, 29 April 2009.

7 Africa and the promise of the Doha round

Yonov Frederick Agah

Attempts to launch a new round of multilateral trade negotiations after the Uruguay round did not enjoy much support from the developing world, including Africa for several reasons. Many developing countries were of the view that the new rules arising from the Uruguay round should be fully implemented before any new round of multilateral trade negotiations could be embarked upon. This means that, according to these countries, the future activities of the World Trade Organization (WTO) should rather focus on the "built-in agenda," brought forward from the Uruguay round, as well as address the inherent iniquities in the existing agreements. In Africa, most countries considered their increasing marginalization in the international trade arena largely as a result of unfair trade rules and the fragile prices of their export commodities. In this context, they were concerned that any new set of rules from a new round of trade negotiations could further hinder rather than promote the growth and development of their national economies.[1] It was therefore this cautious environment and perception that prevailed at the WTO Ministerial Conferences before Doha, particularly Singapore in 1996, Geneva in 1998, and Seattle in 1999.

In spite of the reluctance of Africa and other developing countries to engage in any new round of multilateral trade negotiations, they subsequently compromised and agreed to the launching of the Doha round in 2001, when the "rich countries promised them that this would be different: the Doha 'Development Round' would focus on the reform of WTO rules, with the specific aim of boosting the participation of poor countries in international trade."[2] In fact, given the strong belief on the part of developing countries that they were short-changed during the Uruguay round, the explicit goal of the Doha round was to pay special attention to correcting past mistakes and to target reform of the multilateral trading system on development problems.[3] Against this background, the Doha round of multilateral trade negotiations was expected to produce deeper market access in goods and services, as well as a new universal framework of rules on trade reform measures. The need to address the implementation concerns of developing countries was another key pillar of the negotiations. Indeed, the Doha round has been described as a "development round" because of its focus on the trade and development needs of developing countries. However, the state of play in the Doha round negotiations since 2001 has led to growing concerns that the development mandate of the round is being sidelined. Apart from many missed deadlines for the successful conclusion of the Doha Development Agenda (DDA), the negotiations are presently experiencing such a major stalemate that the prospects for any meaningful multilateral compromises have become increasingly difficult, because the selective sectoral interests of some members appear to have taken the negotiations hostage. Thus, rather than address the priority ambition to straighten out some of the kinks in agricultural trade,[4] the powerful trading nations, while minimizing their own commitments to reform, have continued to seek tariff cuts and the reduction of trade distorting support to improve their market access.[5] In spite of several pronouncements by world leaders at the G-20 Summits, substantial progress is yet to be made towards successfully concluding the DDA negotiations in a manner that would remove trade barriers against the world's poorest and most vulnerable.

The prevailing stalemate in the DDA negotiations has been so protracted that even instructions by the G-20 political leaders to "negotiators to engage in across-the-board negotiations to promptly bring the Doha Development Round to a successful, ambitious, comprehensive, and balanced conclusion consistent with the mandate of the Doha Development Round and built on progress achieved"[6] have not been able to significantly influence any change in positions, or the exercise of the requisite flexibilities that are needed for a major breakthrough in the negotiations. Despite intensified efforts by members in the negotiations, even the window of opportunity identified by the G-20 political leaders to successfully conclude the Doha round in 2011 could not be realized. Even attempts to focus on a few core deliverables for the least developed countries (LDCs) at the 8th WTO Ministerial Conference (MC8) in December 2011 ran into a gridlock, due to the seeking of concessions and trade-offs by the major players over such a package. Interestingly, the identified issues of interest to LDCs, including duty-free quota-free (DFQF) market access, a services waiver, simplified rules of origin, and the elimination of the distortions caused by cotton subsidies, had all been agreed to at the Hong Kong Ministerial Conference in December 2005.

In that context, it is important to recall the conclusions and outcome of the first session of the Global Poverty Summit, held at Johannesburg,

South Africa, from 17–19 January 2011. The *Johannesburg Statement on the Doha Development Agenda*, issued at the end of the Summit, recognized that the almost decade old negotiations "have yet to yield an outcome that contributes meaningfully to the alleviation of poverty and the promotion of economic development."[7] The *Statement* specifically drew attention to those issues that need to be addressed, in order to ensure that an equitable and opportune outcome of the negotiations is realized. It encouraged WTO members urgently to reach agreement on, inter alia, an "early harvest" for LDCs; capacity building and aid for trade; non-agricultural market access; policy space and balanced rules; intellectual poverty rights; and agriculture and food security.

In terms of an "early harvest" for LDCs, six key areas were identified by the *Johannesburg Statement*. First, agreement and implementation of DFQF access for all products originating from the LDCs into the markets of all developed WTO members and those developing country members in a position to do so, prior to the conclusion of the DDA. Second, establishment of an annual reporting mechanism on the implementation of DFQF market access that goes beyond the current annual reporting mechanism under the Committee on Trade and Development (CTD) to include the implementation of legally binding commitments. Third, simplified and liberalized rules of origin, which reduce bureaucratic burdens and allow LDCs and their firms to import inputs from the most efficient suppliers, in order to enhance their competitiveness and enable them to take full advantage of trade opportunities arising from DFQF market access. Fourth, fast-tracking of the elimination of export subsidies and trade-distorting domestic support measures in developed countries, particularly the immediate elimination of those on cotton, which have caused the decimation of cotton farmers and threatened livelihoods in the "Cotton Four" countries (Benin, Burkina Faso, Chad, and Mali). Fifth, substantial improvements in market access for services exports of LDCs under Mode 4 of the General Agreement on Trade in Services (GATS), particularly temporary movement of persons and outsourcing in various sectors such as health, education, and call centers. Finally, reform and acceleration of the accession process for LDCs to ensure that acceding LDCs are not required to undertake commitments beyond those of existing WTO members at the same level of development.

On capacity building and aid for trade, the *Johannesburg Statement* called for adjustments to be made to address any erosion of preferences resulting from the conclusion of the DDA for LDCs and small and vulnerable economies (SVEs) through the provision of effective financial and technical cooperation by developed countries, as well as realistic transition time-frames for adjustment to encourage sustainable diversification and to mitigate any negative effects of the reform process. The *Statement* emphasized the need for substantial and predictable aid for trade, which should not be linked to the negotiations to remove trade barriers and other distortions. While calling for the early implementation and full utilization of technical assistance and capacity building programs under the proposed Trade Facilitation Agreement, it urged that the WTO be mandated to monitor aid for trade commitments as well as to build this into the aid for trade global review process, starting with its July 2011 meeting.

In the Non-Agricultural Market Access (NAMA) negotiations, the *Johannesburg Statement* underscored the key elements for policy space and balanced rules to enable developing countries to adopt industrial policies to promote new industries, including the need for developing country commitments to be commensurate with their level of development; an ambitious program to address non-tariff barriers in developed country markets; and the creation of significant new market access for products of export interest to developing countries, including tariff escalation to allow for value addition. Regarding agriculture, the *Statement* emphasized the need to ensure that the outcome of the Doha round, inter alia, leads to fundamental reforms in developed country agriculture through real and effective cuts in domestic support programs; elimination of export subsidies at the end of 2013 as agreed at the Hong Kong Ministerial Conference in 2005; and the provision of adequate flexibilities for special products and the special safeguard mechanism (SSM), in order to address the rural development, food security, and livelihood concerns of developing countries. Finally, the *Statement* underscored the need to reform the Agreement on Trade-Related Aspects of Intellectual Property Rights (TRIPs) to enable developing countries to utilize the flexibilities under the TRIPs and Public Health amendments to access more affordable medicines; as well as to include a mandatory disclosure of origin requirement to prevent the bio-piracy of the genetic resources and traditional knowledge of developing countries, in accordance with the Convention on Biological Diversity.

Apart from these pronouncements by the Johannesburg Global Poverty Summit, there has also been a widespread debate on the development prospects of the current trade rules for African countries, especially with respect to poverty reduction and economic development. This debate has covered a wide variety of perspectives. One point of view, particularly within the civil society community, dwells on the usual play of power politics and perceived "underhand" negotiating tactics between developed and developing countries.[8] At the heart of this perspective are the concerns over the deep-rooted practices and pitfalls of the WTO negotiating process and allegations of divide-and-rule tactics by Brussels and Washington. Apparently, at issue also is whether the WTO is ostensibly a democratic system, where decisions taken on the basis of consensus, can actually address the interests of all members rather than just those of the rich and powerful.

In terms of substance, the debate has been mostly on what comprises a pro-development Doha round package, and whether the negotiations can actually deliver on such an outcome. In terms of the former, the various views canvassed broadly include issues such as the elimination of unfair trade practices by developed countries especially trade-distorting subsidies, export subsidies and export credits as well as a defense mechanism against subsidized exports in agriculture. There is also the element of effective market access conditions for products of export interest to developing countries in developed country markets for goods and services. The need for trade and development policy space for developing countries with respect to their agricultural, industrial, services, and intellectual property sectors has also been emphasized. Other elements of a pro-development Doha outcome that are being canvassed in the discussions relate to special and differential treatment (SDT); non-tariff barriers; the relationship between regional trade agreements and WTO provisions; trade and non-trade concerns regarding preference erosion as well as commodity issues; and technical and financial assistance to enable developing countries and LDCs to overcome those challenges relating to supply-side constraints, so as to be able to take advantage of opportunities arising from global trade liberalization.

On whether the Doha round can actually deliver on its development mandate, there are those who consider the early successful conclusion of the negotiations and implementation as the pre-requisites for the achievement of that goal. The respective responsibilities of both developed and developing countries in such a context have also been discussed.[9] Overall, various views have been expressed as to whether the DDA, within its current mandate and structure should be abandoned, or whether new issues should be introduced to address the current challenges and realities of the global economy. WTO members, under these circumstances, have also been preoccupied with the future direction of the organization, including the possibility of deliverables at the MC8 and a post-MC8 work program.

The purpose of this chapter is to contribute to this debate on the challenges facing the DDA negotiations and the implications for African countries. I express support for the position that the Doha round must be completed in accordance with its mandate. I have also tried to define the contours of the possible approaches that WTO members may need to explore, in order to reach fair, balanced, and multilaterally agreed solutions. To that end, section two reviews the key elements of the development mandate of the Doha round alongside the negotiating objectives of African countries. The state of play, including the significance and dynamics arising from the current impasse in the negotiations are discussed in section three. In section four, I present my reasons as to why the Doha round must be concluded while in section five I offer my concluding comments.

Africa's objectives and the mandate of the Doha round

Recognizing that international trade can play a major role in the promotion of economic development and alleviation of poverty, the Doha Ministerial Declaration reaffirmed the determination of the WTO members to maintain the process of reform and liberalization of trade policies to ensure that the multilateral trading system plays its full part in the achievement of these objectives. They further undertook to seek to place the needs and interests of developing countries at the heart of the Doha Work Programme by making positive efforts designed to ensure that developing countries, and especially the least developed among them, secure a share in the growth of world trade that is commensurate with the needs of their economic development.[10] However, a major contention, in both economic theory and history, has been the distribution of the gains from international trade liberalization among countries. It has also been argued that most developing countries cannot benefit from improved market access, in the immediate future, as a result of supply-side constraints and non-tariff barriers. Thus, at the end of the Uruguay round, estimates by the United Nations Development Programme (UNDP) and the Organization for Economic Cooperation and Development (OECD) showed that within six years global income would grow by US$200–500 billion as a result of the round. However, it was found that all these gains would go to the industrialized countries. In sharp contrast, LDCs and sub-Saharan Africa were predicted to lose US$600 million and US$1.2 billion respectively, even before implementation had started.[11]

In respect of the Doha round, forecasts by the World Bank's *Global Economic Prospects 2002* showed a rise of US$355 billion in global income by 2015, as a result of the new round of international trade liberalization. It was, however, predicted that the greatest income gains would accrue to the industrialized countries while the developing countries' share would only be about 50 percent of the extra income. World

Bank predictions also showed that both sub-Saharan Africa and South Asia would experience minimal net gains, which in both cases would also be lower than aggregate losses resulting from displacement due to trade liberalization. The implication here is that some significant resources were required and steps needed to be taken under the Doha round negotiations to enhance the prospects of developing countries obtaining their fair share of global prosperity, in order to fulfill the development mandate of the round.

For their part, African countries have generally articulated their interests and needs in the Doha round within the context of its development mandate. To that end, African countries have been able to submit many proposals in the various areas of the negotiations, including agriculture; NAMA; services; TRIPs; trade facilitation; SDT; commodities; and rules (regional trade agreements and fisheries subsidies).[12] While most of these proposals have been submitted by African countries as a group, many of them have been tabled either by individual African countries, or jointly with some developed countries, other African countries and other developing countries, especially within the framework of LDCs and the Africa, Caribbean, and Pacific (ACP) group or G-90.[13]

The proposals tabled by African countries, like all other proposals in the WTO, largely reflect their offensive and defensive interests, which are aimed at achieving those negotiating outcomes that would positively contribute to the attainment of their development aspirations in the context of a development round. These proposals also highlight some of the African perspectives regarding the critical benchmarks for assessing the development dimension of the Doha round. Proposals by African countries in all areas of the negotiations stress the need for SDT in their commitments and the provision of technical assistance and capacity building to facilitate compliance with the agreements. Another cross-cutting aspect of the proposals relates to preference erosion concerns in agriculture and NAMA.

In the agricultural trade negotiations, proposals by African countries cover all the three pillars of the negotiations.[14] In the domestic support pillar, the focus is on the need to address the imbalances in agricultural trade arising from trade-distorting subsidies by developed countries, including a review of the use of "green box" and "blue box" measures. In the market access pillar, inputs from African countries include issues such as tariff reductions to a maximum of 12 percent; phase-out of tariff quotas; substantial reduction of tariff peaks; and tariff-capping; as well as tariff reductions by developed countries that contribute to substantial improvements in market access for all products, in an effective and measurable way. With respect to export competition, the common positions of African countries include the abolition of export subsidies, and establishment of disciplines for export credits; flexibility for LDCs to allow their greater use of export subsidies; safeguarding food security, especially the food procurement capacity of LDCs and net food importing developing countries.

African countries have also been generally supportive of proposals tabled by the G-20 and G-33 in the negotiations on agriculture.[15] The G-20 comprises countries that have adopted offensive interests in the agricultural trade liberalization negotiations. By way of contribution, the dynamics of the interplay within the G-20 membership has led to the reduction of ambition in market access issues and the adoption of the principle of proportionality in the negotiations, where developing countries are expected to pay less than the developed ones. This approach has led to middle ground positions in the dual objectives of reducing trade-distorting policies in agriculture and for the opening of developed country markets. The special needs and interests of developing countries with large populations and rural development priorities are also being taken into account by the G-20. On the other hand, the major objective of the G-33 in the agriculture negotiations is to ensure special rules that allow developing countries to continue to restrict access to their agricultural markets, with a view to meeting their food security, livelihood security, and rural development needs. To that end, G-33 proposals have focused on the designation of special products and the introduction of an SSM in favor of developing countries. There are also the proposals relating to the sectoral initiative in favor of cotton as submitted by the Cotton Four,[16] which are aimed at phasing out cotton subsidies because of their severe adverse implications for the economic activities and social lives of several African countries.

In the negotiations on NAMA, proposals by African countries while supporting the adoption of the cocktail approach in deciding modalities, have further sought, inter alia, to address concerns relating to improvements in, or an extension of, existing preferences to ensure that no single country is worse off after the negotiations; elimination of non-tariff barriers in developed country markets; and flexibilities in market access commitments that are consistent with the imperatives of Paragraph 16 of the Doha Ministerial Declaration, which states that "the objectives of the negotiations on market access for non-agricultural products should, therefore, be to facilitate and enable the development and industrialization processes in developing countries."[17] In this respect, some of the proposals are about the specific flexibilities for individual, or groups of, African countries like the development needs of countries with low tariff-bindings as well as different levels of reduction commitments under the formula that addresses regional integration concerns and/or enhances competition, promotes the development of global trade and strengthens the integration of developing countries into the multilateral trading system. African countries have also made substantive contributions to the discussions on non-reciprocal preferences and the interpretation of the Technical Barriers to Trade Agreement with respect to labeling of textiles, clothing, footwear, and travel goods as well as remanufactured goods.

On services, proposals by African countries focus on issues relating to modalities for SDT for LDCs; assessment of trade in services (overall balance of rights and obligations for all WTO members); the treatment of autonomous liberalization; guidelines and procedures for the negotiation on trade in services; liberalization of domestic services; and the needs of small economies and small suppliers of services.[18] It is obvious that all these proposals, on the whole, also aim to respond to the specific difficulties of individual and groups of African countries, given that the adoption of a one-size-fits-all approach in the services negotiations would not necessarily address the vulnerabilities of these countries at different levels of development.

Most of the proposals by African countries in the negotiations on TRIPs relate to the establishment of a multilateral system of notifications and registration of geographical indications; the Declaration on TRIPs and Public Health (paragraph 17 of the Doha Ministerial Declaration); monitoring and full implementation of the obligations under Article 66.2 of the TRIPs Agreement; amendment of Article 31 of the TRIPs Agreement (based on paragraph 11 of the 30 August Decision); and the relationship between the TRIPs Agreement and the Convention on Biological Diversity.[19] Indeed, the proposals of African countries on the issue of TRIPs and Public Health significantly contributed to the final amendment and implementation of paragraph 17 of the Doha Ministerial Declaration. However, negotiations on the other areas like the establishment of the multilateral register and the relationship between the TRIPs Agreement and the Convention on Biological Diversity, including disclosure and benefit sharing, remain part of the ongoing work program.

Under trade facilitation, issues of interest to African countries include consularization and improvement of elements relating to transit and the promotion of developing countries' interests and objectives in the negotiations in areas such as SDT, operationalizing technical assistance and capacity building based on identified needs and priorities, and expediting the movement of goods in transit (especially for landlocked countries).[20]

African countries have also submitted some proposals on commodities[21] and rules. In the area of commodities, African countries have articulated the actions that are required to address the crises faced by commodity dependent African countries from the decline in prices of primary commodities, particularly their trade and development prospects as well as their ability to service and pay foreign debts. In the rules negotiations, African countries have tabled proposals calling for SDT in WTO rules, as well as those clarifications and improvements in the developmental aspects of regional trade agreements (RTAs), to provide a multilateral framework that, in the context of RTAs between developed and developing countries, supports the regional integration strategies of developing countries.

As already indicated, although the negotiations on SDT are cross-cutting, African proposals are seeking to strengthen such provisions by making them more precise, effective, and operational.[22] In that respect, in addition to the agreement-specific proposals in the Agreement on Sanitary and Phytosanitary Measures, Agreement on Technical Barriers to Trade, Settlement of Disputes, GATS, Trade-related Investment Measures (TRIMs) Agreement and the Agreement on Subsidies and Countervailing Measures, there is a proposal on the monitoring mechanism for SDT provisions to ensure compliance with implementation, training programs, mandatory provisions, and coherence with obligations in international organizations.

State of play in the Doha round negotiations

The mandated negotiations under the Doha round have continued to experience various challenges, which have severally and collectively affected the overall progress and successful conclusion of the work program. The negotiations have generally been characterized by missed deadlines and experimentation with different configurations and approaches in the negotiating process. The first significant signal of the persisting challenges in the negotiations emerged when the fifth WTO Ministerial Conference at Cancún in 2003 ended in a failure due to the lack of agreement on the contentious new issues, also known as the "Singapore Issues," namely investment, competition, government procurement, and trade facilitation. However, on 1 August 2004, taking into account the Ministerial Statement adopted at Cancún, the General Council reaffirmed the Ministerial Declarations and Decisions adopted at Doha as well as the commitment of all members to give effect to them. Members also agreed to a work program containing frameworks and other agreements designed to focus the negotiations and raise them to a new level. The General Council Decision further emphasized members' resolve to complete the work program in full and to conclude successfully the negotiations launched at Doha.

Further agreements on the work program were reached at the 2005 Hong Kong Ministerial Conference, including a new deadline to successfully conclude the round in 2006. The Hong Kong Ministerial Declaration also emphasized the central importance of the development dimension in every aspect of the work program, and members recommitted themselves to making this a meaningful reality, in terms of the negotiations in the post-Hong Kong period. Despite the suspension of negotiations and missing of the 2006 deadline, a small group of Ministers met in Geneva from 21 to 30 July 2008 to consider and settle a range of issues in the context of the July 2008 package, as a stepping stone on the way to concluding the round. This effort also ended in a failure due to sharp disagreement between members on the modalities for the SSM for developing countries in agriculture. In spite of this major setback, draft revised versions of the modalities texts were further released in December 2008, as an improvement on the 2008 package and as a sort of blueprint for the final deal.

The global economic and financial crisis that ensued in the aftermath of the failure of the July 2008 mini-Ministerial further created a prevailing state of paralysis in the negotiations on the Doha Work Programme. It was in that context that Ministers at the seventh WTO Ministerial Conference in 2009, rather than address the issues in the round, merely underlined their commitment to conclude the DDA; and called for an interim stocktaking in the first quarter of 2010. Although this exercise too did not produce any major breakthrough, the commitment to the round and its conclusion was still re-emphasized, thus setting the stage for the commencement of the "cocktail approach" that involved intensified small group brainstorming sessions among Ambassadors in all the negotiating groups. Amid this process, the G-20 political leaders in November 2010 identified 2011 as the critical window of opportunity for the conclusion of the round, and accordingly gave instructions to that effect. On the basis of those instructions, members as from January 2011 embarked on an intensified work program, with a sequence of work that identified April 2011 as the timeline for evaluating and capturing the progress so far made.

The April 2011 "Easter package" that emerged from that process largely reflected the product of all the work that had been done in all areas of the DDA since 2001—that is, the entire market access and regulatory areas. Overall, the Easter package highlighted the value of what was on the table as well as those issues that still divided members and put the successful conclusion of the round at risk. In particular, it was revealed that "the differences among key countries in the World Trade Organization's Doha trade talks are so wide as to be unbridgeable in at least one major area (NAMA sectorals)."[23] The conclusion reached from this reality is that the DDA negotiations have missed yet another deadline; and would not be concluded in 2011 as directed by political leaders. Given the political developments in some member countries, the assessment by some is that it would be impossible to reach a deal, such that the negotiations may not be concluded in 2012 or beyond.

Efforts after this realization were focused on prioritizing LDC issues (DFQF, rules of origin, LDC services waiver, and cotton) as possible deliverables at the MC8 in December 2011. However, the acceptability of an LDC alone package was also called into question when some members wanted some "plus" elements (trade facilitation, SDT monitoring mechanism, export competition, environmental goods and services, and fisheries subsidies). Progress on the LDC plus package was also frustrated by members' linkages with other areas of the negotiations to the extent that by July 2011 it became clear that the focus since then had shifted to exploring the case elements for the political guidance by Ministers at MC8 in December 2011.

As reported by the WTO Director-General, Pascal Lamy, at the 21 October 2011 meeting of the Trade Negotiation Committee, there is a common understanding within the membership that the Doha round negotiations remain at an impasse; and it is unlikely that all the elements would be concluded in the near future as originally intended. Although all members remain committed to delivery on the Doha mandate, there is now a recognition that new approaches would need to be explored in order to advance pragmatically in areas where progress can be achieved, including the use of paragraph 47 of the Doha Ministerial Declaration to reach agreements on a definitive or provisional basis, as a step towards delivering on the entire DDA agenda. To that end, there is a convergence that work will continue on the basis of progress made, and development would remain a central theme. There is further agreement to intensify efforts towards devising pathways that allow for engagement in areas where substantial differences still persist.[24]

Why must the Doha round be concluded?

The protracted stalemate in the Doha round negotiations has given rise to an intense debate that aims at not only identifying the causes of the impasse, but also at evolving those creative approaches that would enable WTO members collectively to find sustainable solutions to the prevailing challenges. However, the unbridgeable differences within the membership have also been a major obstacle to reaching a shared under-standing of the causes and possible solutions to the successful conclu-sion of the negotiations. Different perspectives are easily discernible regarding this state of affairs.

There are those who hold the view that the Doha round cannot be successfully concluded in its present shape and form, and as such "it is time for the international community to recognize that the Round is doomed."[25] The failure of the Doha round can be traced to its outdated structure and negotiating dynamic where, even with the best of inten-tions, every negotiator's concessions are more clear than their potential gains; and the bipolar division between developed and developing countries has shortchanged most in the developing world.[26] The con-clusion under these circumstances is that it is time to give up on trying to "save" Doha. But the risk in this argument is that it ignores the fact that negotiations are principally about confidence and trust among the partners. Thus, as a prerequisite to successfully concluding the DDA members must work very hard to rebuild confidence and trust, not just about the priority attached to its development mandate but also in the negotiating process and the multilateral trading system as a whole.

On the negotiating mandate, the key challenge is for members to ensure that the excessive level of ambition by some players does not turn a development round into a market access round. The negotiating mandate, as enunciated in the Doha and Hong Kong Ministerial Declara-tions as well as the July 2004 Framework, must be respected by ensuring that development remains at the heart of the negotiations, particularly in areas such as SDT across all pillars of the negotiations, including respect for the principle of "less than full reciprocity."

In terms of the negotiating process, the real challenge is to ensure the full ownership of any negotiating outcome by the entire membership. While recognizing that members may choose to negotiate in various for-mats or configurations, it is highly essential that the multilateral character of the negotiating process, led by the chairs of the negotiating groups, must be fully preserved. This can be achieved through information sharing in inclusive and open-ended meetings. Nevertheless, the small groups should also not replace the multilateral process; and peer pressure should be used to ensure that members engaged in bilaterals do not necessarily take the negotiations hostage, or comfort themselves by not making the requisite trade-offs. The scheduling of small group meetings should also fully accommodate the concerns of small delegations.

An interesting dimension in the debate over the challenges facing the successful conclusion of the Doha round is the perception that the negotiations, per se, possess flaws that are preventing members from closing the deal. It has therefore been observed that "world leaders are frustrated that their mandates to negotiators have failed to translate into a successful conclusion to the round."[27] The disconnection between the repeated pronouncements by political leaders and the actual negotiations largely means that those directives have never been truly accompanied by those real and firm instructions that would enable negotiators to exercise the necessary flexibilities that would move the negotiations forward. This situation has been further complicated by the position of some members that the G-20, for example, is not synonymous with the WTO, which has 153 members. The resolve to ensure that any final Doha agreement must increase market access opportunities, particularly in high-potential, high-growth emerging economies has also introduced an unhelpful geo-political debate, more so as consensus is required to declare that the dichotomy between developed and developing countries in the WTO and its negotiating structures is outdated and obsolete. The policy harmonization or equalization between developed and developing countries inherent in this argument is also problematic. Greater political will is therefore required to address issues like these, which prevent a successful conclusion of the Doha round negotiations.

There is also the challenge arising from the perception that the continuing impasse in the negotiations can easily be due to a single issue like NAMA sectorals where the United States is requiring that the major emerging economies (Brazil, China and India) mandatorily cut their tariffs in three sectors (chemicals, electronics and industrial machinery) to zero or near zero. However, the reality is that there are several other difficult areas in the negotiations that may easily become deal breakers. While the SSM for developing countries in agriculture was blamed for the breakdown in 2008, the potential of increased market access demands on developing countries in agriculture and services by developed countries blocking any deal in the future is real. It may be argued that the tendency for some members to continuously "shop for deal breaking issues" is a smokescreen for their inability or unwillingness to exercise those flexibilities that are required to conclude the Doha round. There are also those who argue that the negotiations have been taken hostage by political developments like the electoral cycles in some member countries, and the expiration of the Trade Promotion Authority or fast-track negotiating authority in the United States, which allows the US President to negotiate trade agreements that Congress can approve or disapprove but cannot amend or "filibuster." The last fast-track negotiating authority granted to the US President by Congress expired on 1 July 2007.

In spite of all the challenges facing the Doha round, there appears to be very broad support for preserving the progress that has so far been made in the negotiations. Therefore, in order to retain what is already on the table and avoid unraveling the current package, negotiations would need to focus on narrowing differences on a few key areas through suitable incremental adjustments. This will not only ensure the successful conclusion of the round but also avoid the danger of losing what has been achieved in the past 10 years of negotiations.

As a corollary to building on the progress made so far, members would need to consider adopting a sequencing approach that takes into account, in a horizontal manner, the trade-offs possible in all areas. This is based on the understanding that in the context of the "single undertaking," every issue can be a deal breaker. This is more so as the concessions for a final deal would largely depend on cross-linkages and trade-offs in various areas, including agriculture, industrial products, services, intellectual property, and rules. In view of the risk of a wave of protectionism due to economic nationalism arising from the current global economic environment, it is critical that all members should be able to see where they stand in the face of a final agreement.

Against this background, if the Doha round is to deliver on its development mandate, it is important that substantial progress be made towards its successful conclusion in a manner that would remove trade barriers against developing countries, in particular LDCs and SVEs. An "early harvest," particularly with respect to cotton, DFQF market access, and the services waiver would significantly enhance the credibility of the multilateral trading system. Other key areas that would ensure a development outcome for not just African countries but other developing countries too are as follows.

1. *LDC rules of origin.* Since complex rules of origin negate DFQF market access due to bureaucratic barriers, it is important that they are simplified and harmonized for LDCs.
2. *The principle of less than full reciprocity.* African countries should ensure that the commitments they make fully take into account all issues relating to SDT treatment and non-trade concerns based on their development needs and capacities. This will assure their development policy space and options.
3. *Reduction or removal of export and domestic subsidies, which undermine poor African countries' ability to compete.* Special attention should be given to WTO rules on anti-dumping and subsidies. In particular, agricultural trade liberalization should remain at the heart of the DDA negotiations, to reduce the negative impact of

the influx of imported subsidized products on food security, health, and livelihoods in African countries. A simple and effective SSM should therefore remain a priority in the agriculture dossier of the DDA negotiations, which should also include the elimination of cotton subsidies.

4. *DFQF market access.* Developed countries and emerging economies must open their markets unconditionally to all the poorest countries. DFQF market access for LDCs must be made fully operational and effective, along with the liberalization of services sectors and modes of special interest to them, particularly Mode 4. Moreover, LDC share in the total trade of the major developed and emerging markets in 2009, as shown in Table 7.1, is clearly below 2 percent if oil imports are excluded.

5. *Article XXIV of GATT 1994.* In view of the growing proliferation of regional trade agreements, Africa would need to ensure that contentious issues like the meaning of "substantially all trade" are clarified to provide legal certainty and avoid making commitments beyond their rights and obligations under the WTO agreements, including the ability to promote South-South trade.

6. *Quality and technical standards.* Both public and private standards in developed-country markets constitute major barriers to the exports of developing countries. The DDA negotiations should address all concerns in this area, along with adequate technical assistance and capacity building.

7. *Preference erosion.* Africa would need to ensure that trade and non-trade solutions are found for any preference erosion arising from trade liberalization under the Doha round, including long implementation periods that would allow for the necessary policy adjustments.

Table 7.1 Share of LDCs' trade in major markets in 2009 (US$ million and percentages)

Member	Total imports	Imports from LDCs	LDCs' share in total imports	LDCs' share in total imports excluding LDCs' oil imports	Duty Free imports
US	1,484,075	20,661.5	1.39	0.56	73.4
EU	1,516,545	26,022.1	1.72	1.15	98.3
Brazil	126,695	504.1	0.40	0.16	78.4
China	1,002,618	27,482.7	2.74	0.57	96.4
India	311,821	6,620.6	2.12	1.21	5.7

8. *WTO accessions.* Acceding developing and least developed countries should not be required to undertake commitments beyond those that are currently enjoyed by existing WTO members, who are at the same level of development. Commitments by acceding developing and least developed countries should also be consistent with their development needs and capacities. And since the WTO is essentially a commercial organization, both in nature and character, extraneous consideration must be fully delinked from the accession process.

In addition to these expected development-oriented outcomes for the Doha round, it would be critical for African countries, at the national level, to take steps to address some key policy issues. First is the role of government in economic policy making. Based on recent experience from the global economic and financial crisis, there is a need for greater political commitment, globally, to achieve a DDA outcome that allows for policy interventions that better regulate global markets in a manner that ensures that those in the greatest need benefit from trade. Second, African countries would need to ensure improvements in roads, ports, and administrative infrastructure. In this respect, aid for trade should provide additional resources for investment in roads and ports as well as institutional and administrative structures that would make trade possible and easier.

Conclusion

Taking into account the different views on the main reasons and issues responsible for the current impasse in the DDA negotiations, what is most important now is for WTO members to commit themselves to ensuring that the round is successfully concluded based on its mandate. For the purpose of trust and confidence building among the membership, it is further desirable that the interests of developing countries, and in particular the LDCs, are prioritized for any early agreement and implementation on a provisional and/or definitive basis. It is conceivable that any introduction of new issues in the negotiations would complicate the negotiating agenda rather than facilitate the needed multilateral convergence on concluding the negotiations as soon as possible. This is more so as the enlargement of the negotiating basket under the "built-in agenda" has contributed to the present challenges.

It would also be in the interest of the multilateral trading system and the WTO that any new approaches aimed at resolving the existing challenges in some areas of the negotiations should not lead to any new sets of plurilateral agreements in the WTO, even if the liberalization results from those efforts are extended to other members on a "most favored nation" basis.

Finally, it should be recognized that the WTO remains an important forum for members to initiate discussions and/or negotiations on any trade issues of interest to them, based on convergence, particularly in the context of the work of the regular bodies under the covered Agreements. This should provide comfort that the Organization would continue to positively respond to emerging challenges in the global economy. In doing this, the key approach should remain multilateral convergence based on transparent, all-inclusive, and bottom-up processes.

Notes

1 Oxfam, "Africa and the Doha Round," Oxfam Briefing Paper No. 80 (Oxford: Oxfam, 2005).
2 Oxfam, "Africa and the Doha Round."
3 Michael Friis Jensen and Peter Gibbon, "Africa and the WTO Doha Round: An Overview," *Development Policy Review* 25, no. 1 (2007): 5–24.
4 *The Economist*, "The Doha Round... and Round... and Round," 31 July 2008, www.economist.com/node/11848592/point.
5 Mareike Meyu, "The WTO Round Impasse: Implications for Africa," Overseas Development Institute Briefing Paper No. 41 (London: ODI, 2008).
6 G-20, *The Seoul Summit Document*, 11–12 November 2010, 2.
7 Global Poverty Summit, *The Johannesburg Statement on the Doha Development Agenda*, (GPS/DDA/TF/5/1), 19 January 2011, reproduced in the appendix to this volume.
8 Oxfam, "Africa and the Doha Round"; Action Aid, *The Doha Deception Round: How the US and EU Cheated Developing Countries at the WTO Hong Kong Ministerial* (London: Action Aid, 2006).
9 Faizel Ismail, "Trade, Development and Aid: Some Misconceptions and Myths," CUTS Briefing Paper TDP3/2007 (Jaipur: CUTS International, 2007), 3–4.
10 WTO, *Doha Declarations*, (Geneva: 2005), 2.
11 Joint statement by CAFOD, Save the Children, Oxfam, Action Aid, World Vision, Christian Aid, Fairtrade Foundation, Traidcraft, ITDG and World Development Movement, "A Genuine Development Agenda for the Doha Round of WTO Negotiations," London, 28 January 2002, 2.
12 For a full compilation of African Group proposals, see Joseph Senona, *Compilation of Formal African Proposals to the WTO* (Harare and Midrand: SEATINI and Institute for Global Dialogue, 2005).
13 The G-90 comprises the African Group, ACP and LDCs: Angola, Antigua and Barbuda, Bangladesh, Barbados, Belize, Benin, Botswana, Burkina Faso, Burundi, Cambodia, Cameroon, Central African Republic, Chad, Republic of Congo, Cote d'Ivoire, Cuba, Democratic Republic of the Congo, Djibouti, Dominica, Dominican Republic, Egypt, Fiji, Gabon, Gambia, Ghana, Grenada, Guinea (Conakry), Guinea Bissau, Guyana, Haiti, Jamaica, Kenya,

Lesotho, Madagascar, Malawi, Maldives, Mali, Mauritania, Mauritius, Morocco, Mozambique, Myanmar, Namibia, Nepal, Niger, Nigeria, Papua New Guinea, Rwanda, Saint Kitts and Nevis, Saint Lucia, Saint Vincent and the Grenadines, Senegal, Sierra Leone, Solomon Islands, South Africa, Suriname, Swaziland, Tanzania, Togo, Trinidad and Tobago, Tunisia, Uganda, Zambia, and Zimbabwe.

14 See, in particular, common positions of the member states of the West African Economic Monetary Union in the multilateral trade negotiation on agriculture (G/AG/NG/W/188, 26 September 2002); negotiating proposal on market access and domestic support: specific input by Barbados, Fiji, Guyana, Madagascar, Mauritius, Swaziland, Trinidad and Tobago (JOB(02)/16, 14 November 2002); special and differential treatment for developing countries: specific input by the African Group (JOB(02)/187, 20 November 2002); proposals on cotton issues relating to the sectoral initiative in favor of cotton (TN/AG/GEN/4, 16 May 2003; TN/AG/GEN/6, 4 August 2003; JOB (04)/106, 28 July 2004; TN/AG/SCC/GEN/1, 7 April 2005; and TN/AG/SCC/2, 22 April 2005); and special products: contribution by the G-33 (JOB(05)/230, 12 October 2005, and JOB/AG/17, 24 March 2011).

15 Note that the G-20 here does not refer to the Group of 20 Finance Ministers. It is the coalition of developing countries that was formed in the run-up to the Cancún Ministerial Conference. The G-20 members are Argentina, Bolivia, Brazil, Chile, China, Cuba, Ecuador, Egypt, Guatemala, India, Indonesia, Mexico, Nigeria, Pakistan, Paraguay, Peru, Philippines, South Africa, Tanzania, Thailand, Uruguay, Venezuela and Zimbabwe. The G-33 members are Antigua and Barbuda, Barbados, Belize, Benin, Botswana, China, Cote d'Ivoire, Cuba, Democratic Republic of the Congo, Dominican Republic, El Salvador, Grenada, Guyana, Guatemala, Haiti, Honduras, India, Indonesia, Jamaica, Kenya, Laos, Mauritius, Madagascar, Mongolia, Mozambique, Nicaragua, Nigeria, Pakistan, Panama, Peru, Philippines, Saint Kitts and Nevis, Saint Lucia, Saint Vincent and the Grenadines, Senegal, South Korea, Sri Lanka, Suriname, Tanzania, Trinidad and Tobago, Turkey, Uganda, Venezuela, Zambia, and Zimbabwe.

16 The Cotton Four comprises Benin, Burkina Faso, Chad, and Mali.

17 Some African proposals on market access for non-agricultural products: TN/MA/W/2, 7 January 2003; TN/MA/W/22, 8 January 2003; TN/MA/27, 18 February 2003; TA/MA/W/31, 25 March 2003; TN/MA/W/34, 9 May 2003; TN/MA/W/40, 11 August 2003; TN/MA/W/42, 13 August 2003; TN/MA/W/47, 30 March 2004; TN/MA/W/49, 21 February 2005; TN/MA/W/57, 29 June 2005; and TN/MA/W/65, 8 November.

18 Some of the African proposals for the services negotiation: JOB (02)/30, 2 March 2002; TN/S/W/3, 10 June 2004; JOB (02) 77, 5 July 2002; TN/S/W/8, 28 October 2002; TN/S/W/13, 7 May 2003; TN/S/W/16, 25 July 2003; TN/S/W/19, 31 March 2004; JOB (05) 114, 17 June 2005; and TN/S/W/34, 18 February 2005.

19 African Group TRIPs proposals include documents TN/IP/W/3, 24 June 2002; IP/C/W/351, 24 June 2002; IP/C/W/357, 5 July 2002; JOB (02)/156, 5 November 2002; IP/C/W/389, 14 November 2002; IP/C/W/390, 26 November 2002; IP/C/W/401, 28 May 2003; IP/C/W/404, 26 June 2003; TN/C/4, 13 July 2004; WT/GC/W/540 TN/C/W/21, 10 December 2004; IP/C/W/437, 10 December 2004; IP/C/W/440, 1 March 2005; and IP/C/W/445, 6 April 2005.

20 Trade facilitation proposed by African countries can be found in documents: TN/TF/W/22, 21 March 2005; TN/TF/W/33, 28 April 2005; TN/TF/W/39, 2 May 2005; TN/TF/W/69, 24 October 2005; TN/TF/W/73, 10 November 2005; and JOB (05)/110, 15 June 2005.
21 Documents WT/COMTD/W/113, 19 May 2003, and JOB (05)/113, 16 June 2005.
22 See documents TN/CTD/W/1, 14 May 2002; TN/CTD/W/2, 14 May 2002; TN/CTD/W/3, 24 May 2002; TN/CTD/W/4, 24 May 2002; TN/CTD/W/23, 11 December 2002; and JOB(05)/151, 13 July 2005.
23 South Centre, "Present Situation of the WTO Doha Talks and Comments on the 21 April Documents," Analytical Note (Geneva: South Centre, 2011), 2.
24 Susan C. Schwab, "After Doha: Why the Negotiations Are Doomed and What We Should Do About It," *Foreign Affairs* 90, no. 3 (2011): 2.
25 Schwab, "After Doha," 3.
26 Schwab, "After Doha," 3.
27 Schwab, "After Doha," 5.

8 The Doha round and the future of the WTO

Sun Zhenyu

It is already 10 years since the start of the Doha Development Agenda (DDA) in November 2001. Over the past 10 years, many deadlines have been missed and the tremendous efforts made by a group of Trade Ministers in Geneva in July 2008 ultimately failed. Is the Doha round already dead as some scholars have declared? Is there still a chance to re-invigorate the negotiations? Is it possible to have an early harvest before the end of the negotiations? And if not, what will the future look like for the World Trade Organization (WTO)?

It may not be appropriate to declare the Doha round dead right now and no member of the WTO has openly said so. At the same time it does not appear that anything could be achieved in the near term. This chapter considers what has been achieved in the round so far and explores what this will mean for the future of the WTO.

An assessment of what is already on the table

After 10 years of good faith negotiations we have now two Chairs' texts on Agriculture and Non-Agricultural Market Access (NAMA) on the table as well as texts by other Chairs on other issues. In July 2008, ministers spent 10 days in Geneva and made a real effort to try to make a deal at least on agriculture and NAMA. The effort failed, but the result was later reflected in the two Chairs' renewed texts. While most members made it clear that they were not satisfied with the results, they agreed that if all other members could accept the texts they could form the basis of an agreement. Unfortunately, one of the key players, the United States, could not get onboard. The US argument was simple: there was not enough market access for the United States on agriculture, NAMA, and services. Although the United States was not going to re-do the whole negotiation, it needed more to conclude the deal and sell it domestically. It also targeted India, China, Brazil, and other emerging economies and asked them to make extra efforts to meet US requirements, particularly on NAMA, sectorals, and services.

The question is how much more do they want? Is it a little bit more or a lot more? Are they ready to pay in return for any further improvement in market access? If it is only a little bit more, and if they are ready to make compensatory concessions for the extra efforts, it might not be too difficult to resolve at the final stage of the negotiations. But if it is a lot more and without much to offer in return, it would clearly go against the Doha mandate and re-open the whole negotiations. In that case, there would be no hope for any possible conclusion of the round anytime soon.

The atmosphere in Geneva is, I am sorry to say, more pessimistic than optimistic on the future of the Doha round. But that does not give people enough reason to announce that the Doha round is dead because the overall political situation may change and there might be a narrow window of opportunity sometime in the future. Besides, people have to develop a clear idea of what they are going to do post-Doha. Will there be future rounds or will there be no round at all?

If we look carefully at what is already on the table we can discover great value in the package. Pascal Lamy, the Director-General of the WTO, has said on many occasions that what is on the table is already twice or three times more ambitious than the previous rounds. It is also true that the contributions from the developing countries are already quite impressive in the package.

On agriculture

According to the text of the Chair of the Agriculture negotiations,[1] the developing countries are committed to cut their tariffs by up to 36 percent by applying the tiered formula, which aims at deeper cuts on higher tariffs. The tariff cut by developing members was 24 percent on average during the last round. Some may argue that there is too much "water" in developing members' schedules (that is, the gap between bound and applied tariff rates) and that there are loopholes in the flexibilities of special products for them. But these people should also remember that there are a lot of flexibilities and loopholes for the developed members as well in their cut on overall trade-distorting domestic support (OTDS— the overall level of agricultural subsidies), particularly for the United States. The current US commitment to their OTDS upper limit is $14.5 billion, while their actual spending over the past few years was no more than $8–10 billion annually. Unfortunately there is not much real cut in this round on the actual spending in the case of US agricultural subsidies and the new "blue box" designed meticulously by the United States and for the United States is another big loophole. On top of that the high number of sensitive products, new tariff rate quotas, and complex tariffs allowed for the developed members will not help improve market access from developing countries into the developed market.

On NAMA

In the draft text by the Chair of the NAMA negotiations, the developing members have made great concessions by accepting a line-by-line formula cut for the first time in the history of the General Agreement on Tariffs and Trade (GATT) and WTO.[2] The developing members will apply the Swiss formula, which cuts high tariffs much deeper than lower tariffs, and they are cutting more of their tariffs than the developed countries. As a result, in spite of the principle of less than full reciprocity and special and differential treatment (SDT) for the developing countries in the Doha mandate, the developing countries will have an average cut of around 60 percent on their tariffs, while the developed countries will have an average cut of around 40 percent only. Of course some developed members may argue that since there is a lot of water between bound and applied tariffs in the developing countries, they are not cutting too much into their applied rates. The irony is that many developed members are not cutting their actual spending of agricultural subsidies at all—that is, they are not cutting beyond the water into applied rates of agricultural subsidies while demanding that developing members do precisely that in NAMA. Thus, while the developed members have been claiming that since they are cutting a lot of their agricultural subsidies the developing members should pay them back by cutting their NAMA tariffs, the actual situation does not support their claim. On top of that, during the recent financial and economic crisis, people must have realized the value of the cut on water (bound rates), which could provide great certainty for future trade. It is only the self-restraint of most of the developing countries that helped prevent massive increases in their tariffs during the financial and economic crisis.

It is worthwhile mentioning that China's bound and applied tariffs are roughly the same as a result of its accession negotiations. There is almost no water between them. According to the formula in the Chair's draft text, China will have a 27 percent cut on its applied rates, while the United States will only have a 24 percent cut on its applied rates. If you look at the numbers in absolute terms, China's contribution to market opening in the NAMA negotiations is even more impressive than that of many developed members.

Sectorals have become a hot issue in NAMA negotiations. The United States has been pushing hard on the machinery, electronics, and chemical sectors, with an aim to bring the tariffs down to zero or near zero. It also put pressure on India, China, and Brazil, insisting that emerging economies must participate in arrangements in these sectors. However, what the United States cannot deny is that participation in sectorals is voluntary, a principle confirmed by the Ministers at the 2005 Hong Kong Ministerial Conference. In any sector arrangement, according to the mandate, they should give priority to sectors of export interests to developing countries. In practice, the developed countries have actually excluded sectors of export interests to developing countries, such as textiles and garments, through appealing to issues such as preference erosion. Under these circumstances, I rather doubt that the United States could succeed in persuading India, China, Brazil, and other emerging economies to accept sectoral arrangements only in sectors of export interest to the developed countries.

On services

As the modality of negotiation on services is "request and offer," bilateral negotiations are the basic form for the opening of service markets in this round. According to the initial offers and the improved offers as well as the indications by members at the signaling conference in July 2008, the developing countries have made great efforts in their new offers. For example, out of the 160 sub-categories in the services area, India has offered new commitments on more than 50. Brazil and South Africa offered more than 30. As a result of this round, South Africa and China's commitments would reach the same level as many developed countries in terms of coverage on the number of sub-categories. Actually, according to the service trade agreement, developing members have the flexibility to make their service commitments according to the level of their economic development. Unfortunately, the great efforts by the developing countries were not fully appreciated by some developed countries such as the United States.

If we look at what developed countries have offered in this round, it is much less impressive. For instance, the offers by the developed countries in Mode 4,[3] which developing countries have great export interests in, are very limited. There are not enough new offers on most favored nation exemptions, maritime transport, medical services, education, and the like from the developed members.

In summary, the Chairs' drafts of the agreements as they currently stand have already proven to be of great value for improving market access for all members through this round, including the developed members. It is very unfortunate that the United States does not recognize the value of the result on the table. One should not expect other members to meet all its demands through one single round. One should also understand that you cannot get all you want if you cannot meet the demands of others. A win-win solution comes from concessions from both sides.

It would be a shame if we let the Doha round fail, because its failure would cause great damage to the multilateral trading system. On the other hand, the invisible added value to trade if we can successfully conclude the round would contribute a tremendous enhancement of mutual trust and confidence among members and their business communities. The environment of promoting trade would bring real benefit and help members to expand exports and create jobs.

Efforts for some result from the Doha round

At the G-20 Summit in Seoul and the Asia-Pacific Economic Cooperation (APEC) leaders' meeting in Japan in 2010, leaders gave clear instructions to achieve a balanced and ambitious outcome to the Doha round, according to the mandate and based on the progress already made. These instructions could serve as very important guidance for the negotiators in Geneva to accelerate and intensify the negotiations.

The conclusion of the US-Korean Free Trade Agreement (FTA) is taken by negotiators in Geneva as a positive sign for the Doha round. In the US Congress, there is an effort to push for the agenda to deal with the FTAs with Korea, Colombia, and Panama. It seems that the Korean deal has wide support from the US business community and some of the Republican leaders of the House. If Congress passes this agreement, it would be good news for the Doha round. At least it would show that the two parties could work together instead of constantly looking toward the next election and thereby blocking virtually everything.

However, there is another element we have to consider. What will be the priority of the US administration in its trade agenda? Would President Obama put greater emphasis on the Doha round or on the Trans-Pacific Partnership (TPP)? According to repeated statements made by Ambassador Ron Kirk, President Obama seems to have put the TPP in a more prominent position and called for its conclusion by the next APEC trade ministers' meeting. There is no doubt that the coming TPP arrangement would help the United States to increase its exports and create more jobs at home. But compared with the Doha round, the TPP would be much less significant in serving that purpose. Besides, the shift of focus and the transfer of human resources from the

Doha round to the TPP talks may not help the conclusion of the Doha round negotiations.

Moreover, the current situation in the Middle East and North Africa, the US government debt issue, high unemployment, and the fight against terrorism would prevent President Obama from focusing on trade issues, particularly when faced with the 2012 elections and strong resistance from anti-trade groups within his own party.

On the other hand, the agenda in the Geneva process provides some encouragement for those who would like to see at least some result from the round. The talk about a possible early harvest or a down payment to be decided by the Ministers before the end of this year is an encouraging sign. The Director-General Pascal Lamy has worked hard to collect support from members for some result.

Early harvest or nothing?

I am deeply worried about some proposals from academic circles and non-governmental organizations (NGOs) to totally drop the Doha round. What would members do in the WTO if the round were abandoned? Business as usual? Would members only focus on trade policy reviews, on regular meetings in the bodies under the General Council and on dispute settlement cases? Would they continue to live with the fact that the dispute settlement panelists and Appellate Body members fill the gaps of writing new rules for the world trading system?

These possible scenarios do not sound very attractive. It is probably common sense that there have to be negotiations for new rules among members if the Organization wants to keep itself relevant. Then how could they do it? Could there be a completely new round sometime later? Or could there be new rules or amendments of the old ones adopted at each and every council or committee separately?

To start a new round post-Doha could be even more difficult than the Doha round itself. People have tasted the failure of Seattle. In any new round, one could not ignore the built-in agenda of agricultural subsidies. One could not avoid discussing the tariff cutting formula on agricultural and non-agricultural products. One would have to cover service trade and rules. It may still be difficult to cover so-called twenty-first century issues like export restrictions, labor standards or the environment. In any case, the hard bargaining over the past 10 years would not disappear were a new round to start.

Another choice could be to have no more rounds after Doha. Not even to talk about a single undertaking. Just let the Councils and Committees have their normal functions and set new rules or amend old ones on their own. I personally believe it might be feasible, but it is not in line with the common practice of this Organization and its fore-runner the GATT over the past 60 years and members may not like it because it could not have any trade-offs of their interests in other areas.

So if people really could not drop the round, and at the same time could not afford to just wait till after the next US general election, the only option left could be a kind of early harvest to be adopted at the next Ministerial Conference. I am fully aware that some members are strongly against the idea of an early harvest. Even if they could eventually agree on duty-free quota-free (DFQF) market access for least developed countries (LDCs) on cotton and on trade facilitation, they could not agree to implement them now because they would need these issues to form part of a wider set of trade-offs with other areas of interest.

I would like to make an appeal to those members. It is high time that people gave more consideration to the future of the multilateral trading system rather than to their own national economic interests. As the APEC leaders at their recent Summit reiterated:

> We uphold the primacy of the multilateral trading system and reaffirm that this strong, rules-based system is an essential source of sustainable economic growth, development, and stability. We take considerable satisfaction in the success of the WTO, its existing framework of rules, and its consultative mechanisms in contributing to the beginnings of global economic recovery. The WTO has amply proven its worth as a bulwark against protectionism during a highly challenging period.[4]

I do hope that people take this statement seriously and give thought to the possible ways to save the credibility of the WTO, to deliver the promise of a development round, and to make sure that this Organization is still relevant, particularly at a time when the world has experienced a global financial and economic crisis, upheaval in the Middle East and North Africa and with other great uncertainties facing us.

Certainly there could be more detailed discussions on what issues should be included in the possible package. If members are willing to move along that line, there is still time to finalize the content. In any case, DFQF treatment for LDCs, related amendments to rules of origin, the service waiver for LDCs, and the issue of cotton have to be included in the package. These were decisions taken at the Hong Kong Ministerial Meeting and its immediate implementation is conducive to addressing the great concerns of the poorest countries, which is very much in line with the principle of the Development round. Trade facilitation could bring benefits to all members. It could help trade expansion enormously and bring more benefit to trade even than the further reduction of tariffs. It could also help President Obama to achieve the goal of doubling US exports in the next five years and increasing jobs substantially at home. An early package for the Doha round is probably a suitable one for the Ministers to consider. Without an early harvest of some kind, the Ministers would be wasting their time.

How could we seize the narrow window of opportunity and get the job done?

In my opinion, in order to conclude the round, the developed countries should do as follows:

1.   Stick to the Doha mandate and bear in mind that this is a development round and not a pure market access round. Engage seriously with other members based on the Chairs' texts and not try to re-open the package.
2.   Be prepared to pay for whatever extra efforts are required on improving market access for developing countries. Unilaterally raising ambitions on selected areas will not work and trying to move the goal posts or change the rules of the game in the middle will not work either. Rather, a more realistic and pragmatic approach in terms of ambition would help at the end of the game.
3.   Engage actively the domestic business communities and enhance their understanding of the value of what is on the table and remind them about the damage to their long-term interests if this round fails. The role of the business community in attracting Congressional support for the final deal is crucial.
4.   Past experience shows that without the strong leadership from the United States, nothing will happen. This has been proved by Ambassador Bob Zoellick during negotiations on the July package in 2004 and by Ambassador Rob Portman at the Hong Kong Ministerial Meeting in 2005. Strong leadership does not mean to push hard only; it also means to listen carefully to other members' concerns and sensitivities and try to find a solution through consultation.

On the other hand the developing countries, including the emerging economies, should also be prepared to show flexibilities according to the mandate and the principle of less than full reciprocity. They should actively engage with the negotiators of developed countries and work with them to explore the possibilities of reaching a compromise through give and take at the final stage of the negotiations. The conclusion of the round would be in the interests of all members, particularly the LDCs and the SVEs.

What should we do if we fail to have an early harvest?

Judging from the current political situation, it is highly unlikely that the conclusion of the round will happen anytime soon. The reason is simple. Not only is the United States facing a general election in 2012, quite a number of other countries are also facing elections. Any major concession before these elections could have a negative effect on the campaign of the current government.

Thus, we may not be able to expect anything in 2012, because in an election year one could not expect the leaders to spend time and their political capital on trade issues. The best hope is perhaps in 2013, if the new President of the United States, either President Obama or Mitt Romney of the Republican party, really believes trade could help him improve the economic situation and create more jobs for the country, and therefore puts trade on the priority list of his agenda.

In any event, the choices for members of the WTO in 2013 would be limited. Having traveled to Geneva recently and talked broadly with many Ambassadors, NGO representatives and academic scholars, as well as the WTO Secretariat staff, I found the following options for members to consider:

1. Resume talks based on what was achieved in July 2008. Some members may not like the idea since they believe what is on the table is not enough, and they will claim that things have changed completely and all the issues on the table have become irrelevant. Other members would argue that it is still necessary to address unfinished business. How could members ignore the reality that developed countries continue to provide huge sums of money to subsidize their agricultural production and constrain the opportunities for developing countries, particularly LDCs, to produce and export their agricultural products? No matter whether or not we are going to have a round of negotiations, agricultural subsidies by the developed countries would remain the central issue that members have to tackle.
2. Start a completely new round, a round that would include trade-related investment, competition policy, government procurement, environment, and anything else that may claim to be trade related. I could predict very safely that there will be a terribly heated debate among members in the WTO on the content of the new

round; and it might take years before they could manage to reach consensus on the mandate of the next round of negotiations.

3. Totally drop the idea of having another round at all. Just let all the Councils and Committees do their jobs for legislation, negotiating on new rules and regulations and amending outdated ones. Actually this may not be a bad idea. It would give the General Council and the Ministerial Conference more opportunities to work on substance. They could adopt decisions based on the outcome of the negotiations in the Councils and Committees. There are already quite a number of examples even during the Doha round negotiations. The decisions taken by the Trade-Related Intellectual Property Rights (TRIPs) Council and later adopted by the General Council on TRIPs and Public Health is a typical case. The adoption of the decision on aid for trade and the decision on enhancing transparency of Regional Trade Agreements (RTAs) also indicate what the Committees and Task Force could achieve. It may be that members could consider giving the task of negotiating rules to the Councils and Committees and leaving the issues of market access in agriculture, NAMA, and services that need trade-offs framed in a smaller package.

4. Encourage members to negotiate FTAs and RTAs and at a certain stage try to multilateralize the regionalism. Richard Baldwin has come forward with this concept, which I believe is a brilliant one.[5] At the same time we are keenly aware that it will be a very complicated process and nobody could guarantee that it would succeed. If we look at the current FTAs and RTAs that have been notified to the WTO, they are highly diversified in terms of the level of market access commitments, the scope, and the issues covered. To combine all this in a multilateral framework, we need first of all to have unified rules of origin. This is a tall order since members have not yet reached consensus on non-preferential rules of origin and it is an even more difficult task to agree on preferential rules of origin. On market access commitments, there are many different types of exceptions in the current FTAs and RTAs due to sensitivities of their members. It would be a mission impossible to bring all the commitments together and eliminate all the exceptions by ignoring members' sensitivities. On the scope and the issues to be covered by the multilateral framework, the debate would take a long time on whether trade-related investment, competition policy, government procurement, labor and environmental standards should be included in the multilateral agreement in the same way that many current FTAs and RTAs include them. That debate would last even longer than the Doha round itself.

5. In order to avoid the difficulties faced by the principle of consensus and the single undertaking, members may prefer to go back to plurilateral agreements by applying the concept of critical mass. This idea has been dropped after the Uruguay round, though the United States and European Union are trying to reintroduce it in the NAMA sectoral negotiations. The advantage of this practice is that it is easier to reach agreement among the participants than achieve a consensus among all WTO members. The disadvantage is that there will be a two-tier system in the WTO, unless the plurilateral agreements would not deny the right of free riding by the non-participants. The threshold for the late comers could be high as is the case with the Government Procurement Agreement and Information Technology Agreement.

China's role in the WTO negotiations

China will become a more active member of the WTO over the next decade. After 10 years in the WTO, China has learned a great deal and has more professional people with sufficient experience to support its performance in the WTO. In the future activities in all the WTO bodies and in future negotiations, there will probably be more proposals coming from China or joint proposals from China and its partners.

China will continue to play a positive role in the DDA and any future negotiations. As a major trading nation, China will continue to be a strong supporter of the multilateral trading system. It will make its contribution to a degree compatible with its own level of economic development in order to conclude the Doha round. It will join other members in future negotiations on issues that are of common concern to all members under the current situation. China is not a strong advocate for FTAs and RTAs. China would rather focus on multilateral arrangements to ensure the proper functioning of the WTO. Yet since the Doha round is not going to be concluded anytime soon, and since other members are busy negotiating their own FTAs and RTAs, China has no other choice but to explore its own bilateral and regional arrangements. I believe that this trend could be checked through an earlier conclusion of the Doha round and a possible start of a new round afterwards.

As a developing country, China will continue to work very closely with Brazil, India, South Africa, Argentina and other emerging economies in the effort to make the WTO a more development-friendly and more balanced international organization. We will continue to work closely with the LDCs and small and vulnerable economies, as well as the African, Caribbean, and Pacific (ACP) group, Africa group and other developing country groupings, and lend support to their long-standing positions and demands. I believe that while China will continue to participate actively in whatever small groups there might be, either G-5 or G-7 or G-11, the final decisions have to be the result of inclusive participation of all the WTO Members. The broad Membership has to be kept informed and their voice heard and considered in whatever forms negotiations take. This may lead to some delays in the final decision-making, but it will guarantee that the WTO serves as an international organization that represents the interests of all its members.

China will take on more responsibilities as a major player in the WTO. Yet the responsibilities should be commensurate with its current level of economic development. It will not be realistic to expect China as well as India and Brazil to be treated the same as a developed country. This is not just because its per capita GDP is only $4,000, about one-tenth of the developed country average, but also because of the huge gaps in education, science and technology, economic and industrial infrastructure, environmental situation, social and medical safety nets, and so on that exist. The huge proportion of the rural population and the 150 million poor people living under $2 a day prevent China from assuming the same responsibilities and obligations as developed countries. This is a fundamental principle that China will stick to and there is no room for bargaining or trade-offs.

As a major developing country, China's membership in the WTO helps raise the voice and influence of developing countries. The days are gone when a couple of major developed countries would set the tone and the rest of the members had no other choices but to accept the result of agreements such as the Blair House Agreement. China's participation in the agricultural groups of G-20 and G-33, and its strong support for the legitimate positions of the LDCs, ACP, African and other groupings of developing countries makes the WTO a more balanced organization. It makes sure that whatever decisions the WTO is going to take should be development friendly. It should aim at narrowing the gaps between rich and poor and creating an environment in which poorer countries can develop faster, which would eventually lead to a safer, more stable, and more prosperous world. A decision that seeks to protect the interests of developed countries and address their concerns only, while ignoring the voice of the developing countries, particularly LDCs, would make the poor poorer and the rich richer. A further polarization between the rich and the poor could be a nightmare for the world.

Notes

1 WTO, "Revised Draft Modalities for Agriculture," TN/AG/W/4/Rev.4, 6 December 2008.

2 WTO, "Negotiating Group on Market Access – Fourth Revision of Draft Modalities for Non-Agricultural Market Access – Revision," TN/MA/W/103/Rev.3, 6 December 2008.

3 Mode 4 refers to rules allowing the temporary movement of people into a country in order to provide a particular service.

4 APEC, "Statement on the WTO Doha Development Agenda Negotiations and Resisting Protectionism – Ministers Responsible for Trade Meeting 2011," APEC document 2011/MRT/JMS/1, 19 May 2011.

5 Richard E. Baldwin, "Multilateralising Regionalism: Spaghetti Bowls as Building Blocks on the Path to Global Free Trade," *The World Economy* 29, no. 11 (2006): 1451–1518.

Part IV
Focus on Africa

9 Some consequences of trade liberalization in sub-Saharan Africa

Jomo Kwame Sundaram[1]

A basic premise of the influential Berg Report[2] was that Africa's supposed comparative advantage lay in agriculture. If only the state would stop "squeezing" agriculture through marketing boards and price distortions, the supply-side response to agricultural producers would drive export-led growth. But, contrary to popular assumptions, Africa is at a comparative disadvantage with agricultural exports, relative not only to the developed world, with its protected "green pastures," heavy subsidies, and industrial farming, but also to much of Asia and Latin America as well. Subsequent changes in Africa's exports indicate no significant increase in activities in which African countries ostensibly had comparative advantage. Indeed, after two decades of reforms, Africa's share of global non-oil exports fell to less than half what it was in the early 1980s[3] with the trend continuing over the last decade.

As this chapter shows, Africa has experienced significant deindustrialization since the 1980s with the share of manufacturing in national output declining over the last three decades. In parallel, the continent has been transformed from a net food exporter into a net food importer over the last three decades. Instead, the recent improvements in growth have been largely associated with increased mineral and agricultural exports. Much of the recent increase in food production is for export to countries that have bought or leased land for production for their own food needs or for conversion to biofuels.

High growth in large Asian economies, especially China, has probably contributed most to the recent increase in primary commodity prices, especially for minerals, inducing strong supply responses from many sub-Saharan African countries helped by foreign direct investments from these same big Asian developing countries. However, despite this upsurge, the African share of world exports still remains well below its earlier level. Moreover, the damaging consequences for sustainable development and food security have become apparent, and renewed attention is now being given to the issue as food prices rose sharply from late 2007, and again more recently.

Official development rhetoric continues to imply that small farmers in Africa would benefit greatly if agriculture were liberalized under a comprehensive Doha trade agreement. However, this is unlikely. After all, many food importing African countries would be worse off in future decades without subsidized food imports while very few economies are likely to be in a position to significantly increase their output and exports in the short term. African agricultural production and export capacities have also been undermined by the last three decades of low investment, economic contraction, and neglect.

Severe cuts in public spending under structural adjustment have caused a significant deterioration of infrastructure (roads, water supply, and so on) and have undermined the potential supply response.[4] Even World Bank estimates of the overall welfare effects from multilateral agricultural trade liberalization do not suggest significant gains for sub-Saharan Africa, but stress, on the contrary, the likelihood of losses.[5] Gains from agricultural trade liberalization would largely accrue to existing major agricultural exporters, mainly from the Cairns Group,[6] again of little benefit to most of sub-Saharan Africa.

Agricultural trade liberalization has probably contributed to the decline of African food production, undermining food security. With food production in most rich countries, especially in Europe, heavily subsidized, many African countries have turned to importing food from abroad, with local food producers unable to compete and survive in the face of lower food prices and higher costs of producing food without the benefit of subsidies. Meanwhile, with improved external market access for non-food agricultural commodities, food production has declined, with non-food agricultural commodities growing in significance. Not surprisingly then, sub-Saharan Africa is said to have been transformed from a net food exporter in the 1980s to a net food importer over the last decade (see Figures 9.1 and 9.2).

Meanwhile, greater trade liberalization in manufactures with a Non-Agricultural Market Access (NAMA) agreement would further undermine the potential for African industrialization. Not surprisingly then, much of the mainly import substituting manufacturing capacity developed in the early years after independence, mainly from the 1960s, has collapsed while very little new manufacturing capacity has developed in the continent. Consequently, manufacturing as a share of national output has declined significantly over the last three decades although industrial output has not fallen as much, mainly because of increased mining activities (see Table 9.1 and Figure 9.3).

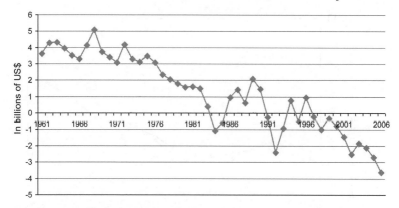

Figure 9.1 Sub-Saharan Africa food trade balance, 1961–2006
Source: FAO statistics from http://faostat.fao.org.
Note: 40 sub-Saharan African countries.

African market access to developed country markets is significantly secured through preferential market access agreements, rather than through past trade liberalization per se. As most sub-Saharan African countries are also classified as least developed countries (LDCs), trade preferences for African countries have been used to play off African developing countries against Asian LDCs, undermining the negotiating positions and strengths of both groups of LDCs. In any case, further trade liberalization threatens to erode the advantages associated with trade preferences.

Additionally, trade liberalization results in an immediate loss of tariff revenue, which can be very significant in developing countries, especially the poorest ones, where tariffs have accounted for up to half of total tax revenue. Reducing these revenues severely reduces their fiscal capacities, and can severely aggravate debt problems by forcing new and increased borrowing in financial markets. Referring to rich countries' claims that developing countries ought to repeal manufacturing tariffs before they can reduce agricultural subsidies, Dani Rodrik asked "[w]hy they need to be bribed by poor countries to do what is good for them is an enduring mystery."[7] Similarly, one might ask why poor countries should agree to multilateral trade liberalization that they need to be compensated for.

"Aid for trade" (A4T) was initially proposed as a means to promote and finance trade facilitation. However, the debate over trade liberalization has recognized that it generally involves both "winners" and "losers," even if the overall outcome is welfare enhancing. Several important policy implications follow from this recognition. First, developing

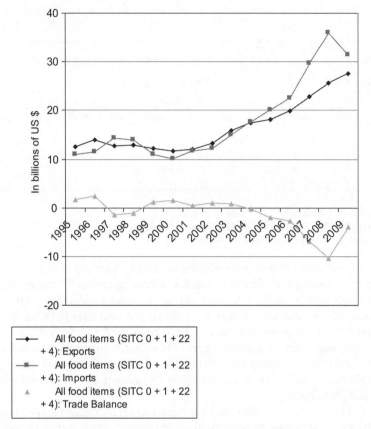

Figure 9.2 Sub-Saharan Africa food trade balance, 1995–2009
Source: UNCTAD statistics from http://unctad.org/en/pages/Statistics.aspx.

countries should be compensated for their loss of productive and export capacities. Less productive enterprises, including small farmers facing subsidized agricultural imports from rich countries, can be expected to be worse off or to go out of business following trade liberalization. In many industrialized countries, losers have been protected to varying degrees—for example, manufacturing workers by welfare, unemployment support, retraining programs, and the like. Second, most developing country governments cannot make up for such lost tariff revenues and, hence, need to be compensated by the richer countries. Third, developing countries—especially LDCs and African, Caribbean and Pacific small island developing states—need to be compensated to accept the erosion of existing preferences resulting from further multilateral trade liberalization.

Table 9.1 GDP by economic activity, sub-Saharan Africa excluding South Africa, 1970–2008 (percentages)

	1970–1979	1980–1989	1990–1999	2000–2008
Agriculture, hunting, forestry, fishing	69	43	30	28
Industry	15	25	29	33
Mining, manufacturing, utilities	12	22	25	29
Manufacturing	7	12	11	8
Construction	2	3	4	4
Services	17	32	41	38
Wholesale, retail trade, restaurants and hotels	6	12	15	14
Transport, storage and communications	3	5	6	6
Other activities	8	15	20	18

Source: UNCTAD statistics from http://unctad.org/en/pages/statistics.aspx

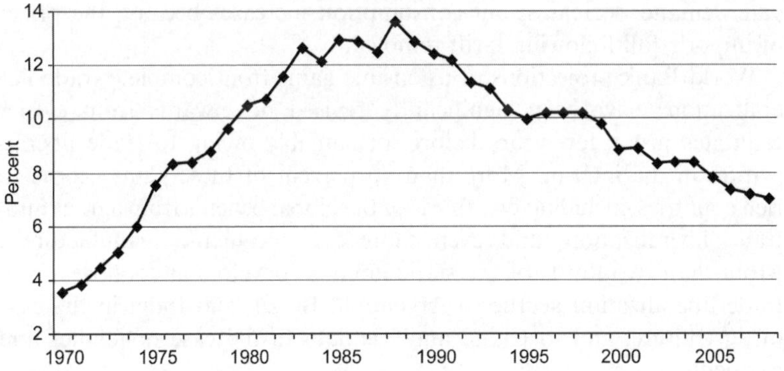

Figure 9.3 Manufacturing share of GDP in sub-Saharan Africa excluding South Africa, 1970–2008
Source: UNCTAD statistics from http://unctad.org/en/pages/Statistics.aspx and author's calculations.

Fourth, and most importantly from a development point of view, there are considerable and uncertain costs involved in developing alternative internationally competitive productive and export capacities and capabilities. Fifth, developing countries have been very emphatic that A4T must be truly additional to promised official development assistance, which has never been delivered in full as promised despite numerous pledges since the 1960s; otherwise, A4T risks becoming an excuse for imposing new conditionalities promoting trade liberalization.

The World Bank has long supported the World Trade Organization (WTO) in promoting trade liberalization, often citing projections made using a computable general equilibrium (CGE) analysis, the so-called LINKAGE model. A CGE model is essentially a system of equations, describing the "behavior" of firms, households, governments, and so on. The LINKAGE model has more than 40,000 equations. The data requirements for parameters and base year variables are tremendous, and trade elasticities, in particular, are often mere "guesstimates" which nonetheless have crucial implications.

An overall positive estimate of gains from trade liberalization relies crucially on a large positive export supply response—which is a heroic assumption when internationally competitive productive and export capacities do not already exist, as in most developing countries, especially the poorest ones. Additional real income—from increased exports and higher consumption—is presumed to outweigh the impact of increased taxes on developing country households needed to compensate for the loss in tariff revenue. If taxes on household consumption are raised, private demand decreases; but consumption increases because the prices of imports fall following tariff removal.

World Bank projections of ostensible gains from complete trade liberalization[8] have been significantly revised downwards from earlier estimates just a few years before, presumably owing to trade liberalization in the interim. More than 70 percent of these gains accrue to rich countries, including two-thirds of the global benefits from agricultural trade liberalization, and even more for non-textile manufacturers. More than two-thirds of the static gains to developing countries from trade liberalization accrue to Argentina, Brazil, and India in the case of agriculture, and to China and Vietnam in the case of textiles and garments.

As full trade liberalization is not under negotiation in the Doha round, Anderson and Martin also considered several possible Doha round scenarios of trade liberalization.[9] Their most realistic scenario projects welfare gains by 2015 of $96 billion, a third of their estimated gains from full trade liberalization, most of which, some $80 billion or 83 percent, flows to rich countries.

Most African governments cannot fully substitute lost tariff revenues with new and higher taxes. The main concessions African developing countries are expected to get from a Doha deal are reduced agricultural subsidies and tariffs in Organization for Economic Cooperation and Development (OECD) countries, but the neglect of both infrastructure and agricultural development over two decades of Bretton Woods institutions' (that is, the World Bank and IMF) structural adjustment programs has left these countries with little capacity to respond to such export opportunities.

What, then, can Africa gain from a Doha deal? How likely are African countries to realize even the paltry $16 billion projected by the World Bank's LINKAGE model for developing countries? Developing economies' aggregate nominal gross domestic product (GDP), according to the United Nations Conference on Trade and Development (UNCTAD) *Handbook of Statistics 2008*,[10] was just above $14 trillion in 2007—making $16 billion, or one-tenth of one percent, look fairly negligible, rather than the big boost to development the Doha round is touted to be.

Another World Bank study analyzed the effects on sub-Saharan African countries of "complete" trade liberalization under a Doha agreement. Its estimates suggest that sub-Saharan Africa could gain substantially because "farm employment, the real value of agricultural output and exports, the real returns to farm land and unskilled labour, and real net farm incomes would all rise substantially in capital scarce SSA [sub-Saharan African] countries with a move to free merchandise trade."[11] According to the simulation results, sub-Saharan Africa excluding South Africa could gain as much as $3.5 billion.[12] The GDP of sub-Saharan Africa excluding South Africa in 2007 was roughly $550 billion,[13] implying total welfare gains of a little more than half of one percent of 2007 GDP. This is much more than the tenth of one percent in expected gains for all developing countries relative to 2007 GDP discussed earlier—but is still not a lot. Some of the poorest and least developed countries in sub-Saharan Africa are also expected to be net losers under "realistic" Doha scenarios.[14]

To be sure, such gains from trade liberalization are one-time increases attributable to theoretical static comparative advantage gains. Such calculations ignore the realities behind the decline of African food agriculture in recent decades, for example. World Bank structural adjustment programs helped undermine the meager competitiveness of African smallholder agriculture. A comprehensive Doha agreement that lowers agricultural subsidies in the North would raise many imported food prices for developing countries, at least in the short to medium term, further reducing many "long-term" welfare improvements these models predict. Hence, it is important to consider the implications of reduced subsidies for food-importing countries as well as for non-food farmers in all countries. These models never predicted the recent food price spikes either.

A more recent "large-scale" investigation, based on the MIRAGE model, produced similar results: rich countries will capture 74 percent of total gains, while middle income and least developed countries will get 24 percent and 2 percent respectively.[15] These welfare gains represent increases—in real income by 2015 relative to the base year level—of three-tenths, two-fifths and four-fifths of 1 percent respectively. Sub-Saharan Africa, excluding Zambia and members of the Southern African Customs Union,[16] should experience an increase in welfare of three-fifths of one percent by 2015 relative to initial GDP. It is not surprising that these numbers are so close to those produced by LINKAGE, because the MIRAGE model is structurally comparable and utilizes the same data set.

Bouët also summarized estimates for full trade liberalization from a variety of other CGE models.[17] First, all the research papers reviewed by him expect trade liberalization to increase world GDP. Bouët cautions, however, that "[t]his conclusion does not mean that all countries or all economic agents are better off. Liberalizing trade creates a 'larger cake', but some can get smaller pieces than others; if efficient redistribution mechanisms are put in place, all agents could experience increased welfare."[18] This too supports the case for the need to compensate losers. Several studies reviewed by Bouët suggest that sub-Saharan Africa will be one of the losers in terms of welfare.[19] Bouët, Mevel, and Orden found that rich countries would gain $19 billion, China and South Asia $1 billion each, while other developing countries would lose $3 billion.[20]

The likely contribution of such different scenarios for poverty reduction varies greatly, and is further limited by the declining contribution of economic growth to poverty reduction because of rising inequality. In view of the historically critical role of trade policy reforms favoring growth and employment for economic development—as opposed to trade liberalization—the consequences of trade liberalization for sustainable development are dubious.[21]

Other estimates—not discussed by Bouët—suggest even more modest gains, with their impacts on poverty and inequality very sensitive to assumptions, definitions, and data quality.[22] Using a simplified, but structurally similar model, Taylor and von Arnim show how heavily trade liberalization simulation results depend on assumptions.[23] Allowing a bit more realism—unemployment, for example—makes clear that Africa will *not* gain, on balance, from trade liberalization. Their exercise suggests that sub-Saharan Africa is likely to experience welfare losses, even assuming the absence of macroeconomic shocks. The region is likely to experience a worsening trade balance, debt problems are likely to increase, and any short-term gains in employment and GDP could evaporate quickly under the pressure of such strained balances.

Even though his model's details differ, Kraev's "alternative" analysis of the effects of trade liberalization on GDP has a methodology and aims compatible with those of Taylor and von Arnim.[24] By endogenizing output, employment, and the current account in a CGE framework, he estimates future risks and past losses arising from trade liberalization. With the current account and employment endogenized, trade liberalization is found to induce macroeconomic volatility—with mostly negative effects for developing regions. Kraev considers two different scenarios. In the first, it is assumed that the trade balance remains unchanged, but that the level of demand is variable (implying the possibility of underemployment of resources). With trade liberalization, imports increase and domestic demand has to decrease to satisfy the external balance constraint. Results in this scenario suggest losses in the order of 10 percent of GDP for sub-Saharan Africa.[25] The second scenario holds GDP constant, and varies the trade balance. As the level of demand remains unchanged, the trade balance worsens considerably, resulting in growing external deficits.[26]

Sandra Polaski introduces unemployment and separates agricultural labor markets from urban unskilled labor markets in an otherwise "standard" CGE model.[27] She concludes that: (i) global gains from further trade liberalization will be very modest; (ii) in sharp contrast to the World Bank's full employment models, developing countries' gains come overwhelmingly from market access for manufactured exports; and (iii) the largest gains will accrue to countries such as China, while the poorest countries (mainly in sub-Saharan Africa) will be net losers. Thus, global gains from any realistic negotiated agreement are close to negligible. "Full liberalization" would bring growth of about half a percent. A "central Doha scenario" could be expected to increase base year global GDP by 0.19 percent,[28] and a "central Doha scenario with 'special products' for developing countries" by 0.18 percent.[29] In contrast to the previously discussed studies, she found that developing countries' aggregate GDP would *decrease* by $6.3 billion, while developed countries' GDP would increase by $5.5 billion with an agreement dominated by agriculture. On the other hand, developing countries' GDP would *increase* by $23 billion, while developed countries' GDP would increase by $30.2 billion with an agreement focusing on manufactures.

Crucially, these gross developing country aggregates obscure the likely impact of trade liberalization on Africa. Sub-Saharan Africa (excluding South Africa) would lose $122 billion, with an agreement focusing on manufacturing trade liberalization, despite the gains for developing countries as a whole.[30] Sub-Saharan Africa (excluding South Africa) would lose $106 billion with an agreement focusing on agricultural trade liberalization.[31] Polaski's findings appear to reflect more accurately the widespread problems of lack of infrastructure, export capacities, and diminished competitiveness in *both* industry and agriculture in sub-Saharan Africa.

Recent advances in international trade theory do not support the case for trade liberalization in sub-Saharan Africa either.[32] "New trade theories" and evolutionary studies of technological development suggest that countries risk being "locked" into permanent slow growth by pursuing static comparative advantage. It is now generally acknowledged that economic growth—particularly the accumulation of capacities and capabilities—precedes export growth. In that sense, trade can foster a virtuous circle, but cannot trigger it. Meanwhile, UNCTAD has long pointed to the importance of growth for trade expansion, and, more specifically, to the weakness of the investment-export nexus that accounts for the failure of many countries to expand and diversify their exports. Also, rapid resource reallocation is not generally feasible without high rates of growth and investment.

Africa's export collapse in the 1980s and 1990s involved "a staggering annual income loss of US$68 billion—or 21 percent of regional GDP."[33] However, "Africa's failures have been developmental, not export failure per se."[34] Dani Rodrik has also argued that Africa's "marginalization" is not the result of trade performance per se, although this may be seen as low by international standards.[35] Another view suggests that Africa trades as much as is to be expected, given its geography and per capita income level. Indeed, "Africa overtrades compared with other developing regions in the sense that its trade is higher than would be expected from the various determinants of bilateral trade."[36]

Thandika Mkandawire notes that the advent of the WTO trade regime was expected to entail losses for Africa from the outset, especially with the loss of preferential treatment (from erstwhile colonial rulers and the European Union under the Lomé Convention).[37] Trade liberalization under WTO auspices has significantly reduced the policy options available to developmental states, especially for trade, industrial or investment policy,[38] though some argue that the WTO regime still leaves room for industrial policy initiatives.[39]

Hence, in summary, there is considerable controversy concerning the structure, assumptions, and resulting estimates from particular models. Overall, though, there is broad agreement that gains for sub-Saharan African countries from any realistically achievable Doha agreement are, with near certainty, negligibly small, if not negative. Besides, it is important to remember that neither CGE models nor theoretical debates about trade liberalization are directly relevant to the WTO negotiations.

Conclusion

Developments since the 1980s have fundamentally changed the environment and conditions for development. Most importantly, economic liberalization—at both national and international levels—has seriously constrained the scope for government policy interventions, including selective industrial promotion efforts. This is especially apparent in international economic relations, but is also true of the domestic policy environment, where policy conditionalities as well as treaty obligations have radically transformed the scope for national economic development policy initiatives.

There has been a widespread and rapid opening up of trade, investment, finance, and other flows. Very often, such liberalization has been externally imposed by the Bretton Woods institutions as conditions to secure access to emergency credit during the debt crises of the 1980s and, more recently, in the wake of currency and financial crises. This has been especially true of much of Africa, which experienced a "lost quarter century" of economic growth from the late 1970s. The 1990s were slightly better with sporadic, but not sustained, growth spurts.

Much of the conventional wisdom regarding African development and poverty is not only misguided, but often harmful. Available evidence suggests that the gains from trade liberalization will be modest for the world economy, and even more so for developing countries, while gains for Africa are even less assured. There is considerable evidence that the main winners from agricultural trade liberalization will be the existing big agricultural exporters from North America, Australasia, Southeast Asia, and the Southern Cone of Latin America. Nonetheless, many well-meaning advocates have joined in the chorus calling for agricultural and industrial trade liberalization as if it will boost development in Africa.

The problems are not limited to sub-Saharan Africa, of course, and apply to the LDCs as well. Recent UNCTAD research on the LDCs, especially in sub-Saharan Africa, for the fourth United Nations LDCs summit in Istanbul in May 2011 point to the following trends over the last decade. As the LDCs' growth, trade, and foreign direct investment stories largely involve Africa, these LDCs' trends for the group as a whole tend to support the preceding analysis. Instead of diversification of exports, LDCs have seen further concentration, which has further increased their vulnerability to exogenous economic shocks as happened with the collapse of commodity prices and trade financing during the 2008–2009 recession.

LDCs' dependence on food imports increased from $7.6 billion in 2000 to $24.8 billion in 2008, even though more than two-thirds of LDC populations earn their living from agriculture. Cereal yields in LDC food agriculture have increased only marginally in the last 20 years and at a much lower rate than the world average. The manufacturing sector accounted for 10 percent of GDP at the peak of the boom in

2007–2008, and thus remained at the same level as at the start of the recent boom. Although LDCs' participation in globally distributed production or service value chains was already quite limited, 27 LDCs experienced further deindustrialization between 2000 and 2008. Also, owing to large profit repatriation from LDCs to investors' home countries, net financial flows associated with foreign direct investment have been negative since 2005. Meanwhile, the share of fuel and minerals increased from 43 to 67 percent of LDCs' total merchandise exports as the share of manufactures declined further during the last decade.

Notes

1 This draws on work done with Rudiger von Arnim and Oliver Schwank to whom I am grateful but do not implicate.
2 World Bank, *Accelerated Development in Sub-Saharan Africa: An Agenda for Action* (Washington, DC: World Bank, 1981).
3 Francis Ng and Alexander J. Yeats, "On the Recent Trade Performance of Sub-Saharan African Countries: Cause for Hope or More of the Same?" Africa Region Working Paper Series No. 7 (Washington, DC: World Bank, 2000), cited by Thandika Mkandawire, "Maladjusted African Economies and Globalization," IDEAs conference, Muttukadu, Tamil Nadu, India, 2002.
4 United Nations Economic Commission for Africa, *Economic Report on Africa, 2004: Unlocking Africa's Trade Potential* (Addis Ababa: UNECA, 2004). Numerous studies have confirmed the importance of good infrastructure for production capacity enhancement and trade facilitation. See Ousmane Badiane and Gerald E. Shively, "Spatial Integration, Transport Costs, and the Response of Local Prices to Policy Changes in Ghana," *Journal of Development Economics* 56, no. 2 (1998): 411–431; and Awuda Abdulai, "Spatial Price Transmission and Asymmetry in the Ghanaian Maize Market," *Journal of Development Economics* 63, no. 2 (2000): 327–349.
5 Kym Anderson and Will Martin, eds, *Agricultural Trade Reform and the Doha Development Agenda* (Washington, DC: World Bank, 2005).
6 The Cairns Group is a group of 19 agriculture exporting countries, composed of Argentina, Australia, Bolivia, Brazil, Canada, Chile, Colombia, Costa Rica, Guatemala, Indonesia, Malaysia, New Zealand, Pakistan, Paraguay, Peru, the Philippines, South Africa, Thailand, and Uruguay.
7 Dani Rodrik, "Don't Cry for Doha," *Daily Star* (Egypt), 5 August 2008.
8 Anderson and Martin, *Agricultural Trade Reform.*
9 Anderson and Martin, *Agricultural Trade Reform.*
10 UNCTAD, *Handbook of Statistics 2008* (Geneva: UNCTAD, 2008).
11 Kym Anderson, Will Martin, and Dominique van der Mensbrugghe, "Would Multilateral Trade Reform Benefit Sub-Saharan Africans?" Policy Research Working Paper No. WPS 3616 (Washington, DC: World Bank, 2005), 26.
12 Anderson and van der Mensbrugghe, "Would Multilateral Trade," 38, Table 2.
13 UNCTAD, *Handbook.*
14 Anderson and van der Mensbrugghe, "Would Multilateral Trade," 48, Table 12.

15 Antoine Bouët, "The Expected Benefits of Trade Liberalization for World Income and Development: Opening the 'Black Box' of Global Trade Modeling," International Food Policy Research Institute *Food Policy Review* 8 (Washington, DC: IFPRI, 2008).

16 The Southern African Customs Union consists of Botswana, Lesotho, Namibia, South Africa, and Swaziland.

17 Bouët, "The expected benefits."

18 Bouët, "The expected benefits," 56.

19 Bouët, "The expected benefits," Table 4.2.

20 Antoine Bouët, Simon Mevel, and David Orden, "More or Less Ambition? Modeling the Development Impact of US-EU Agricultural Proposals in the Doha Round," IFPRI Information Brief (Washington, DC: IFPRI, 2005).

21 Ha-Joon Chang, *Bad Samaritans: Rich Nations, Poor Policies and the Threat to the Developing World* (London: Random House, 2007); Erik S. Reinert, *How Rich Countries got Rich – and Why Poor Countries Stay Poor* (London: Constable, 2007).

22 For example, Frank Ackerman, "The Shrinking Gains from Trade: A Critical Assessment of Doha Round Projections," Working Paper No. 05–01, Global Development and Environment Institute, 2005.

23 Lance Taylor and Rudiger von Armin, *Modelling the Impact of Trade Liberalisation: A Critique of Computable General Equilibrium Models* (Oxford: Oxfam International, 2006).

24 Egor Kraev, *Estimating GDP Effects of Trade Liberalization on Developing Countries* (London: Christian Aid, 2005).

25 Kraev, *Estimating GDP Effects*, 14, Table 3.

26 Kraev, *Estimating GDP Effects*, 15–16, Tables 4 and 5.

27 Sandra Polaski, *Winners and Losers: Impact of the Doha Round on Developing Countries* (Washington, DC: Carnegie Endowment for International Peace, 2006).

28 The "central Doha scenario" assumes that developed and developing countries decrease tariffs on agricultural (manufactured) products by 36 percent (50 percent) and 24 percent (33 percent) respectively. Export subsidies are eliminated completely, and domestic support is reduced by a third in all regions.

29 Polaski, *Winners and Losers*, 22, Table 3.1.

30 Polaski, *Winners and Losers*, 26, Figure 3.4.

31 Polaski, *Winners and Losers*, 28, Figure 3.8.

32 Andrew B. Bernard, J. Bradford Jensen, Stephen J. Redding, and Peter K. Schott, "Firms in International Trade," *Journal of Economic Perspectives* 21, no. 3 (2007): 105–130.

33 World Bank, *Can Africa Claim the 21st Century?* (Washington, DC: World Bank, 2000), quoted in Mkandawire, "Maladjusted African Economies."

34 Gerald K. Helleiner, "Introduction," in *Non-traditional Export Promotion in Africa: Experience and Issues*, ed. Gerald K. Helleiner (London: Palgrave, 2002), 4.

35 Dani Rodrik, *The New Global Economy and Developing Countries: Making Openness Work* (Washington, DC: Overseas Development Council, 1999).

36 David T. Coe and Alexander D. Hoffmaister, "North-South Trade: Is Africa Unusual?" *Journal of African Economies* 8, no. 2 (1999): 228–256; Faezah Foroutan and Lant Pritchet, "Intra-Sub-Saharan African Trade: Is It Too Little?" *Journal of African Economies* 2, no. 1 (1993): 74–105.

37 Thandika Mkandawire, "Maladjusted African Economies and Globalization," *Africa Development* 30, nos. 1 & 2 (2005): 1–33.
38 Irma Adelman and Erinc Yeldan, "Is This the End of Economic Development?" *Structural Change and Economic Dynamics* 11, no. 1–2 (2000): 95–109; Vadiraj Raghawendracharya Panchamukhi, *WTO and Industrial Policies* (Geneva: UNCTAD, 1996); Dani Rodrik, "Can Integration into the World Economy Substitute for a Development Strategy?" World Bank ABCDE-Europe Conference, Paris, 26–28 June 2000.
39 For example, Alice Amsden, "Industrialization Under New WTO Law," UNCTAD X High Level Round Table on "Development Directions for the Twenty-First Century," Bangkok, 12 February 1999.

10 Africa and the Doha round

Richard E. Mshomba

At its best, the World Trade Organization (WTO) helps all member countries make the most out of their similarities and differences for the benefit of all. The WTO serves to promote trade through negotiations and agreements to reduce trade barriers. Trade is an important tool for development. Membership in the WTO includes the poorest and richest countries in the world. Some of those rich countries were colonizers of the poor countries, the poverty of which can be attributed, in part, to colonialism. Some of the WTO members have mature democratic systems, and some are under a one-party system, a monarchy, or a dictatorship. These differences not only produce diverse economic interests—they also explain diverse capacities to negotiate. In this chapter I briefly consider the history of African countries in the General Agreement on Tariffs and Trade (GATT) and its successor, the WTO. I then examine the capacity of African countries to negotiate. Although that capacity is limited, African countries are making remarkable strides. Finally, additional challenges and opportunities for the WTO and African countries in the Doha round of negotiations will be addressed. Negotiations in the WTO will always be complex and at times contentious, as demonstrated by the stalemate in this round of negotiations. Nonetheless, the stalemate provides opportunities for retrospection and charting new paths for negotiations.

African countries in the GATT and the WTO

Since the end of World War II (WWII), nations have made efforts to address political and economic issues in the world through international institutions. The United Nations was founded in 1945 to promote peace and international cooperation. The International Bank for Reconstruction and Development (IBRD) (and latterly, albeit slightly differently, the World Bank) and the International Monetary Fund (IMF) were also established in 1945 to provide long-term and short-term loans, respectively.

Multilateral trade negotiations have also been part of formal global politics and diplomacy since the end of WWII. The GATT was established in 1947 with the mission to liberalize trade. It was formed from parts of the International Trade Organization (ITO), a proposed specialized agency of the United Nations. The ITO never came into existence, however, because the US Congress refused to ratify its founding Charter, claiming that it would undermine the national sovereignty of the United States in trade policy. Although the GATT was technically only a provisional treaty throughout its 48 years of existence, over time it actually amounted to increasingly complex agreements, administered and enforced by its operating body. These agreements were designed to reduce barriers to trade. There were eight rounds of negotiations under the GATT. The first seven rounds of negotiations were launched in Geneva (1947); in Annecy, France (1949); in Torquay, England (1950–1951); and again in Geneva (1955–1956, 1961–1962 [the Dillon round], 1964–1967 [the Kennedy round], and 1973–1979 [the Tokyo round]). The eighth round, launched in Punta del Este, Uruguay (1983–1993 [the Uruguay round]), was the one from which the WTO was born. Each round of negotiations sought and accomplished, to varying degrees, a reduction of trade barriers among members.

African countries have always been involved in these trade negotiations, albeit, for the first two decades, as appendages to their colonial powers. Many writers have argued that the GATT had failed to address the development needs of developing countries because of:

a)   the passive and defensive role of developing countries in the GATT;
b)   the lack of participation of developing countries in exchanging concessions; and
c)   the focus of developing countries on special and differential treatment (SDT) for developing countries as their main objective.[1]

Faizel Ismail challenges those assertions by pointing out that from the onset, developing countries argued against the proposed most favored nation (MFN) principle that would treat developed and developing countries the same.[2] Developing countries also challenged, successfully, a voting system that would have taken into account the economic size of a country in determining its voting power. Instead, decisions under the GATT were made by consensus, implying that each member had a veto power.

Regarding the lack of participation by developing countries in exchanging concessions,[3] Ismail explains that in many cases the bargaining conditions precluded developing countries from participating.[4] In other words, it is not that they did not want to participate, but rather that they were excluded. In addition, developed countries did not make any serious attempt to reduce trade barriers that were relevant for products from developing countries. Finally, regarding SDT, he narrates its evolution as developing countries continued to emphasize their development needs. Nonetheless, developing countries were also pushing for increased market access for their products.

African countries were part of the GATT from its inception by extension.[5] While only 23 countries signed the original treaty establishing the GATT in 1947, participation in the GATT was extended to colonies of GATT members. To the extent that colonialism was, by design, fundamentally an exploitative political and economic system, the extension of GATT rights and obligations to the colonies was also seen as a means for exploitation. When independence came, a colony to which GATT benefits and obligations were applied could join the GATT immediately as a full contracting party.

The assertion that developing countries participated actively in the GATT does not apply to African countries. With the possible exception of South Africa, African countries' participation in the GATT, particularly in the first seven rounds, was marginal at best. Moreover, African countries were more interested in their economic relations with European countries than in their relations with the GATT in general. European countries were the most important trading partners for African countries, mostly because of colonial ties. To continue this relationship, European countries and independent African countries signed the Yaoundé Convention in 1963, under which most dutiable imports from African countries entered the European Community (EC) duty-free.

The Yaoundé Convention was succeeded by the Lomé Convention in 1975 which, in turn, was replaced by the Cotonou Agreement in 2000 in the WTO era.[6] Even when the EC established its Generalized System of Preferences (GSP) program in 1971 under the GATT, which was to benefit all developing countries, African countries preferred to use the Yaoundé Convention and later the Lomé Convention because they were more extensive in their coverage.[7] In fact, while the establishment of GSP programs was a victory for developing countries in general, to African countries it caused erosion in the margin of preference in their exports to the EC.[8] African, Caribbean, and Pacific (ACP) countries had exclusive preferential market access to the EC. Not surprisingly, for African countries, special and preferential treatment has been a starting point in all their negotiations with developed countries.

Of course, special and preferential treatment can be controversial even among African countries because of their different compositions of exports and imports. More importantly, whether utilized or not by the intended targeted countries, once special and preferential treatment is in place, it becomes a barrier to reducing MFN tariffs. It is no wonder that the consideration of special and preferential treatment is part of all negotiations.

African countries' capacity to negotiate

As of September 2011, the WTO had 153 members, including 42 African countries. In addition, 31 countries were observers, including nine African countries. Only two African countries, Eritrea and Somalia, had neither membership nor observer status.

There is no doubt that the negotiating capacity of African countries has improved considerably compared with the period of the Uruguay round (1986–1993). The Uruguay round was long and arduous, requiring many skilled people in various fields. The round resulted in many complex agreements. The agreements themselves, let alone their likely long-term impact, were not always clear to all participants. This was particularly the case for sub-Saharan African countries, which had relatively very limited technical and diplomatic representation in the negotiations. Whereas developed countries had specialists for each specific area of negotiation, the sub-Saharan African countries that participated in the negotiations were represented by generalists. For example, in the final negotiations of the Uruguay round in 1993, Japan had more than 100 representatives, Tanzania had two, Ghana had one, and Angola had none.

Competent and hardworking as those few sub-Saharan African representatives may have been, they were too few in number and their resources too limited to fathom all the intricacies of economics, law, science, strategy, and politics involved. It should be noted that the United Nations Conference on Trade and Development (UNCTAD) did provide valuable technical assistance to developing countries. In addition, developing countries, on their part, used a group system to share information and formulate strategies together, where they could identify common interests. Even though these initiatives, especially the UNCTAD technical assistance, helped to bridge the information disparity between developed and developing countries, there was still significant uncertainty. Accordingly, sub-Saharan African countries wanted to retain their policy options wherever possible. They signed the agreements because they knew it would be difficult to join the WTO later; they subsequently requested and attended workshops by the WTO to help them understand the agreements better. Those workshops and other training programs have become long-term features of the WTO, as exemplified by annual WTO regional trade policy courses for mid-level government officials from developing countries. In sub-Saharan Africa, there are two such programs, one for English-speaking countries and one for French-speaking.

Thus, one challenge facing the Doha round of negotiations is that African countries are in no hurry to sign any new agreements when they are still trying to comprehend fully and implement the ones negotiated under the GATT. Furthermore, the African group in the WTO and other coalitions to which African countries belong, such as the ACP group, the G-77, the G-33, and the least developed countries (LDC) group, have become forces to be reckoned with.[9] In addition, African countries often receive political and technical support from international non-governmental organizations (NGOs) that often seem to be skeptical of freer trade agreements.

Although sometimes NGOs and members of civil society do not fully appreciate the advantages of freer trade, African countries cannot avoid working with them. In the late 1990s, NGOs were quite effective in articulating the negative impact of the Trade-Related Intellectual Property Rights (TRIPs) Agreement for developing countries. They played a pivotal role in the outcome of a lawsuit that was brought by an association of 39 pharmaceutical companies against South Africa. The association had challenged a South African law that was aimed at easing access to HIV/AIDS antiretroviral drugs through the use of parallel importing and compulsory licensing, which are permitted by the TRIPs Agreement. After a three-year legal battle, with NGOs criticizing the plaintiffs for their lawsuit, the Pharmaceutical Manufacturers' Association in April 2001 withdrew its court case against the South African government.

Perhaps no single issue has galvanized the African group more and given them more substantial experience in WTO negotiations than the TRIPs Agreement. They were pressured by developed countries to sign an agreement that was certainly going to be painful. As a result, almost immediately, African countries had to fight for amendments that would allow them access to cheap medicines. After more than 10 years of negotiations, the WTO in 2007 approved an amendment to the TRIPs Agreement to ease the access of developing countries to cheap medicines.[10] This experience has shown African countries the benefits of working together and being persistent. It has also made them even more hesitant about any new agreements. Most importantly, the experience the African group acquired and the coalitions it forged in the process are assets transferable to other endeavors.

While African countries have become more experienced in WTO negotiations, their capacity to negotiate in the WTO is compromised by several factors. These include membership in multiple coalitions, dependence on aid, a lack of coherent domestic policies, unfulfilled promises, and a lack of adequate transparency.

Ideally the leverage in negotiations in a "democratic" organization like the WTO should come only from the merits of a country's position on a given issue and how it is able to articulate that position. However, in reality, leverage in the WTO, as in other multinational negotiations, usually comes mainly from a country's economic strength. Since most African countries have relatively small economies, their leverage usually comes from negotiating as coalition blocs. The negative side of belonging to multiple coalitions is that it spreads thin the scant diplomatic and technical resources that African countries possess. In fact, proposals from those coalition groups are usually the product of a few core countries, determined by technical capacity, the personalities and experience of diplomats, and what is at stake. In those African countries where the agricultural sector is the backbone of the economy, there is a lot at stake in the outcome of the Doha round negotiations. However, for a country like Angola, which is heavily dependent on oil exports and facing virtually no barriers (in the importing countries), the outcomes of most negotiations in the WTO are inconsequential.

The point here is that while African countries have been able to build coalitions among themselves and with other countries, these coalitions are often tenuous because of the diversity of developing countries and their various economic interests. An example would be the different interests that food exporting countries and food importing countries would have in regards to agricultural export subsidies in developed countries. Even US cotton subsidies, which have been criticized probably more than any other agricultural subsidies, are not harmful to all poor countries. Those subsidies depress the world price of cotton. Certainly the economies of LDCs that depend heavily on cotton exports, such as Benin, Burkina Faso, Chad, and Mali, experience economic losses due to such subsidies. However, LDCs such as Bangladesh and Lesotho, which import cotton, benefit from those subsidies. Even in the LDC group, interests vary. These differences will only grow over time as more developing countries diversify their exports and also as they develop special trade agreements with developed countries.

The situation is further complicated by the fact that the WTO does not have criteria that would place developing countries in clear sub-groups according to the size of their economies and export sectors. Most African countries are in an awkward situation because the constraints imposed by various agreements are often not aimed directly at them. The constraints are usually targeted at large developing countries, such as Argentina, Brazil, China, India, and South Africa. Such countries are typically capable of taking advantage of any available loopholes. Of course, South Africa is in the African group, and for various strategic, historical, and institutional reasons, African countries tend to be in coalitions with other large developing countries, even if their interests are not completely in harmony. As is to be expected, the large developing countries want it both ways. They want to be acknowledged as such and therefore to be in the Group of 20 Finance Ministers.[11] However, when it comes to agreements in the WTO, which tend to provide long transitional periods and more policy space for developing countries, they want to be lumped together with small developing countries. Suggestions to explicitly place them into their own category are often rejected with the claim that it is a strategy by developed countries to "divide and rule."

Also compromising the capacity of African countries to negotiate in the WTO is their dependence on aid. It is an understatement to say that most sub-Saharan African countries are dependent on aid. On average, Africa received about 35 percent of the world total net official development assistance (ODA) from 2000 to 2009. In 2009, the top 10 aid recipients in Africa (in dollar amounts), listed in descending order (with the country receiving the most aid listed first), were Ethiopia, Tanzania, Côte d'Ivoire, Democratic Republic of Congo, Sudan, Mozambique, Uganda, Kenya, Nigeria, and Ghana. Together these countries received 47 percent of the total ODA to Africa in 2009.[12] ODA varies significantly from country to country, whether measured in terms of dollar amounts, ODA per capita, or ODA as a ratio of gross national income. Aid is also quite volatile. The distribution of aid is determined mainly by bilateral negotiations, even when pledges for aid may have been made in a multilateral setting.

There is never a shortage of rationale for aid in general and aid for trade in particular in the WTO negotiations. The rationale articulated in the aid for trade initiative includes: (a) to enable African countries to participate in the WTO negotiations more effectively; (b) to finance the cost of implementing WTO agreements, such as establishing new institutions and revamping old ones; (c) to address supply-side constraints; and (d) to alleviate adjustment costs, such as those emanating from decreases in tariff revenues and from the erosion of the margin of preference. However, the dependence on aid and the bilateral negotiations that determine its distribution compromise African countries' capacity to negotiate in the WTO. Diplomats are not so naïve as to approach the WTO negotiations single-mindedly, without considering their countries' aid dependency, when clearly the donor countries have full discretion on the disbursement of aid.

If the diplomats from developing countries happen to be independent minded and seemingly stubborn, developed countries have a way of reminding them about their dependency. Developed countries have more direct and less public ways of pressuring a country to conform to their wishes. For example, US embassies in Africa usually distribute US position papers to their host countries before WTO meetings, both as a courtesy and to forewarn them not to "rock the boat." An African country's head representative in the WTO negotiations tells how he once received a call from a US trade official in Geneva alerting him that his position (the position of the African diplomat) on a particular issue was not compatible with that of his boss in the capital—the minister of trade. Apparently, the US official had called the African minister of trade and charmed him with some promise of continued aid to his country and the two agreed they would straighten out the African official in Geneva so he would be receptive to the US position on the issue. The US official was just being "kind" to let his "colleague" in Geneva know.

Compromising the situation even further is that most African leaders operate with a mindset that aid is the lifeline of their economies. This mindset not only compromises their capacity to negotiate in the WTO and other multilateral settings, but can also limit creativity, resourcefulness, and effective public discourse. The dependence behavior sometimes manifests itself as a total embarrassment.

In 2001, Philadelphia hosted the US-Africa Business Summit. A presentation was organized by the University of Pennsylvania at which some African ministers were invited to speak with some US entrepreneurs and Wharton business students about investment opportunities in Africa. It surprised everyone that the African officials quickly started talking about the need for assistance: "Help us to build roads, help us to build schools," and so on. One courageous and frustrated African graduate student raised his hand and said something like this: "We are not from the State Department. Most people here want to know why they should consider investing or working in Africa. So far you have done a very good job telling them why they shouldn't."

Requests for aid and complaints that aid is insufficient are almost reflex reactions by African countries in the WTO negotiations. The "aid for trade" initiative has only formalized those reactions. However, whatever the rationale for aid might be, this instinctive dependence on aid compromises African countries' capacity to negotiate. Aid should not be linked to negotiations for removing trade barriers and other trade distortions. African countries should evaluate the impact of potential agreements on their own merit. Aid can facilitate trade reforms, but it should not be the reason for reaching an agreement.

Turning now to how domestic policies affect the capacity to negotiate, there is no doubt that coherence in domestic policies allows a country to articulate its position in any negotiations in an authoritative way. This is not always the case for African countries, as manifested in their changing positions on agricultural prices. The following example illustrates part of the inconsistency.

In 2005, at the G-8 meeting in Scotland, African leaders were pleading for aid and for the removal of farm subsidies in developed countries. Those subsidies reduce world prices of agricultural products, hurting farmers in Africa. A great deal of suffering in Africa has been attributed to farm subsidies in developed countries; some have described them as "subsidies that kill."[13]

Only three years later, in 2008, at the G-8 meeting in Japan, African leaders were present again. The pressing problem this time was that food prices were too *high* and, again, developed countries were partially to blame. Those countries were using corn for combustion instead of human consumption. High prices for agricultural products were a threat to political stability in Africa and other parts of the world. Internally, some countries (not only African countries) imposed restrictions that hurt farmers. For example, some countries imposed price controls and placed restrictions on exports, even to members of their regional economic blocs.[14] Some went so far as to deny small farmers the right to sell their own produce, even domestically. As an example, but not an isolated one, the District Commissioner of Morogoro, in Tanzania, in 2008 warned that those who sell food crops would be prosecuted for "inviting hunger."[15] Imagine—someone who has produced food to be prosecuted for inviting hunger! What would be the fate of those who had never touched any farm tool? As good as the intentions of government leaders may have been, threatening farmers in this way is bad for three main reasons: (i) it violates farmers' fundamental right to decide for themselves what to do with the fruit of their labor; (ii) it is likely to hurt, not help, farmers and their families financially; and (iii) it is likely to hurt everyone else, too, because it backfires and leads to farmers producing less food.

Every time food prices go up, the political pendulum shifts from a concern about low incomes for farmers to the plight of the net buyers of food. A strong position against agricultural subsidies cannot be maintained if a country is also fearful of high agricultural prices, even though those prices may benefit its farmers. The point here is not that African leaders should only focus on farmers or urban residents exclusively, but rather to suggest that the dilemma they face regarding agricultural prices is largely due to the lack of a coherent, long-term, agricultural policy. Without a coherent policy, the capacity of African countries to negotiate is compromised, because their position will fluctuate with prices instead of being firmly determined by economic principles and long-term development goals.

In some ways, the behavior of developed countries has diminished the willingness and capacity of African countries to negotiate. Developed countries often make promises they do not keep and pledges they do not honor, thus making African countries skeptical of negotiations. For example, promises by developed countries to remove agricultural subsidies have not been matched by real action.

It must be noted that African countries engage with developed countries in other forums, including the United Nations, the IMF, the World Bank, and the G-20. What happens in those forums has an impact on WTO negotiations. For example, promises of financial aid made by G-20 countries that go unfulfilled, become a reason, valid or not, as to why African countries cannot take developed countries at their word regarding promises to reduce protection. In addition, while the G-20 can play an important leadership role, it is also accused of exclusivity. This is the same accusation some African countries make against the "Green Room" process in the WTO, from which they feel excluded. African countries have called for transparency within the WTO to improve the decision-making process. They have often argued that the lack of transparency hurts the credibility of the WTO, complicating negotiations and compromising their ability to participate.

Additional challenges and opportunities for the WTO and African countries

In the last 10 years, the Doha round has become the lens through which people view the WTO. The failure to conclude the round after 10 years of negotiations, and the clear indications that even when and if it is concluded the agreements will be less far reaching than originally envisioned, has undoubtedly hurt the reputation of the WTO.

Everything expressed now about the Doha round, whether from the African perspective or any other, has the benefit of 10 years of hindsight. African countries feel that their concerns have not received the full attention and response they deserve. Among other expectations, African countries entered into the Doha negotiations with the hope that the agricultural sector would be brought into greater harmony with their development objectives. Likewise, they hoped that special and preferential treatment would be retained; even if it was decreased because of the erosion of the margin of preference, they hoped that loss would be counterbalanced by financial aid and other forms of assistance.

The Doha round can fairly be described as a disappointment or even an embarrassment. It appears that the euphoria associated with the WTO finally being able to launch its first round of negotiations blinded people's vision. Two years earlier in Seattle, the WTO had attempted unsuccessfully to launch a new round of negotiations, in part because of the dissatisfaction of developing countries. In response, WTO members regrouped and armed themselves with a development agenda.

Notwithstanding its ambition to reduce trade barriers with the ultimate goal of increasing development, especially in poor countries, the Doha round had a mercantilist undertone camouflaged in "buzz" phrases such as "special products" and "policy space." Regarding "special products," some countries proposed criteria that could be subject to such broad interpretations that virtually every product could be given the status of "special." Consider this description of "livelihood security" proposed by the G-33 in 2005:

> Livelihood security relates to the adequate and sustainable access to resources or assets (i.e. education, land, capital, social networks, etc.) by households and individuals to realize a means of living. Moreover, alternative employment opportunities are simply not available to illiterate, aged and/or unskilled people, and agriculture presents almost the only option, including in developing countries with high levels of rural illiteracy as well as those which do not have adequate safety-nets. The situation becomes aggravated in the case of perennial crops as opposed to annual crops.
>
> Another crucial characteristic that defines livelihood security in developing countries is that low income or resource poor, disadvantaged or uncompetitive farmers have very low risk thresholds, and it is not possible for them to shift from their traditional product to another easily since this involves both considerable resources as well as high levels of risk. Therefore, it is not so much a question of the importance of a particular product in the total production structure in agriculture, but the characteristic of farmers producing the product that drive agricultural policy in developing countries in this case.[16]

While this description has merit, it would fit all agricultural products in Africa—those produced by subsistence farmers and also those produced by big farmers who employ unskilled labor.

Regarding policy space, there is no doubt that countries, especially developing countries, need policy space to be able to implement domestic policies that would enable them to achieve their development goals. However, freer trade agreements are often presented as if they are not part of what should be in the policy space. They are seen as crowding out other policies, rather than complementing them. That is a mercantilist attitude.

At its core, a mercantilist approach to trade puts a disproportionate emphasis on the benefits of exports than on imports, a view that goes back for centuries.[17] While this view was vigorously challenged by a number of British philosophers, including the renowned David Hume and Adam Smith,[18] the mercantilist sentiment is ubiquitous, though at varying degrees at different times and for different countries.

Of course, African countries are not any better or worse than other countries in their desire to have foreign markets opened to their goods with the least reciprocity possible. However, as most of them are poor, they want to take full advantage of being "underdogs." They approach the WTO negotiations as if they are doing the world a favor by liberalizing trade. Therefore, they feel they should be compensated and rewarded for it. They are often quick to point out the implementation and adjustment costs of trade reforms, but reluctant to acknowledge and estimate the cost of protection.

Developed countries are big on preaching the merits of free trade but resist granting complete duty-free quota-free (DFQF) access for all products originating from LDCs that have membership in the WTO. Instead, they have offered to extend DFQF access to imports from LDCs covered by 97 percent of tariff lines. However, it is known that the remaining 3 percent can cover a very large percentage of important exports from LDCs. Thus, the impact of such an offer would depend very much on the spirit by which developed countries would implement it. Understandably, LDCs have asked for DFQF access for all of their exports to developed countries. However, LDCs would make an even stronger case if they proposed granting complete DFQF access to *all* WTO countries for all products originating from LDCs. That means every LDC would also be open to all other LDCs' products. That would expand the market for LDCs' products and at the same time increase competition among LDCs, which is one of the main benefits of trade.

This is not to suggest that trade is a "magic bullet." Trade is, nonetheless, an important tool for economic growth. Trade steers countries toward an efficient use of resources, an infusion of new technologies, and greater competition. Of course, economic growth is not automatic. Other factors, such as macroeconomic instability, civil war, health pandemics, and corruption can drag an economy down. Even when trade leads to economic growth, it does not necessarily translate into improvement in people's standard of living. Trade must be complemented by other policies, including effective education and health policies, for economic growth to bring about development. But this does not mean that diplomats have to be apologetic about trade.

One would expect WTO language always to emphasize the benefits of freer trade. However, in the diplomatic world where candid observations are often perceived as politically incorrect and thus avoided, and ambiguity is often considered ingenuity, there is no wonder no one cries out "the emperor has no clothes" when, for example, an assertion like *non-distortionary subsidies* is made even for large countries. In reality, except in cases where there are positive externalities, referring to a subsidy (by a large country) as non-distortionary is a misnomer. Subsidies by large producers always affect world prices, directly or indirectly.

Many studies will analyze the Doha round of negotiations and inform us more as to why it has not been successful. However, it is important not to confuse the WTO with its initiatives. The WTO and the Doha round are not synonymous. As an organization, the WTO has many more responsibilities than completing a round of negotiations. Undoubtedly, the reputation of the WTO has been bruised, but its relevance should not be underestimated, especially during global economic slowdowns when the sentiment for protection gets stronger.

Imperfect as it might be, the WTO plays a key role in monitoring and enforcing trade laws, thus providing a more predictable trade environment. The WTO is not simply about negotiating new trade laws. One must therefore critically question the assertion by Paul Collier that poor countries have no reason to be in the WTO. He writes:

> What are the countries of the bottom billion doing in the WTO? ... It does not have resources to disburse to countries, nor an objective that its staff must achieve with such resources. It is not a purposive organization but rather a marketplace. The WTO secretariat is there merely to set up the stalls each day, sweep the floors each evening, and regulate the opening hours. What happens is made by the bargaining ... But the markets of the bottom billion are so tiny that even if their governments were prepared to reduce trade barriers, this would not confer any bargaining power on them. If the U.S. government decides that the political gains from protecting cotton growers outweigh the political cost of making American taxpayers finance a hugely expensive farm bill, the offer of better access to the market in Chad is not going to make much difference.[19]

As discussed earlier, it is no secret or surprise that a country's economic strength is important in determining its leverage in negotiating agreements. But this phenomenon is not unique to the WTO. Collier's comments on the WTO seem to imply that bargaining is an invention of, or an imposition by, the WTO. However, bargaining between poor countries and rich countries would take place with or without the WTO. Notwithstanding the fate of the Doha round, the WTO plays an important role in facilitating negotiations between very diverse countries. In fact, in some ways the impasse of the Doha round reflects the maturity and democratic nature (though this is not to be exaggerated) of the organization. It is highly unlikely that poor countries would be better off relying solely on bilateral bargaining, rather than actively engaging in multilateral bargaining and forming coalitions with other WTO members. The unity of developing countries contributed in no small part to developed countries agreeing to bring the agricultural and textile and apparel sectors into the WTO. At least now poor countries can challenge the United States on its cotton subsidies, as Benin and Chad have done through the dispute settlement system as third parties, as well as through the "cotton initiative" that they launched jointly with Burkina Faso and Mali.[20]

Another dynamic is playing out in the WTO era, and it is both a challenge and an opportunity. More countries now have "big economy" status, much more so than during the GATT era. This evolving dynamic makes the negotiations both more uncertain and, at the same time, more balanced. A persistent challenge associated with large economies is the potential for elections in those countries to delay negotiations, usually until a new government is formed. With more countries now having that "big economy" status, it seems there will always be some election somewhere that can delay trade talks and increase uncertainty.

The increased number of large economies is reflected in the growing role of the G-20. In 2009, the G-20 replaced the G-8 as the premier global economic forum; and the G-20 seems better poised to handle emergencies. It does not, however, seem well positioned to handle long-term negotiations the results of which, one way or the other, may not cause the total collapse of economies. Nonetheless, the growing number of large economies brings more balance in the negotiations. It is no longer the case that only the European Union and countries like Japan and the United States have a strong voice. The positions of countries like Argentina, Brazil, China, India, and South Africa, even individually, now also carry noticeable weight in the negotiations and, therefore, must receive attention.

Perhaps the failure of the Doha round has to do with it being too ambitious. Maybe the WTO was trying to achieve too much, hoping to make up for lost time. It had failed to launch a new round of negotiations in an earlier try. Now the stalemate in the Doha round is an opportunity for the WTO to examine its strategies and ambitions and to set priorities.

Notes

1 Faizel Ismail, *Reforming the World Trade Organization: Developing Countries in the Doha Round* (Jaipur and Geneva: CUTS International and Friedrich Ebert Stiftung, 2009), 12.
2 Ismail, *Reforming*. The MFN principle means a member country must treat all other members equally in respect to trade policy. If a member country lowers the tariff rate on a commodity entering from one member country, for example, it must likewise lower the tariff rate on that commodity from all other member countries.
3 Exchange concessions imply reciprocity, that is, quid pro quo.
4 Ismail, *Reforming*.
5 South Africa and Southern Rhodesia (Zimbabwe) were among the original contracting countries of the GATT. However, at the time, each of these countries was under a White minority rule that was notoriously repressive of the majority Black Africans.
6 The Cotonou Agreement has not fared well. It was not covered by the Enabling Clause adopted in 1979 under the GATT that allowed developed countries to discriminate against other developed countries in favor of developing countries. The Cotonou Agreement has been evolving into Economic Partnership Agreements, that is, reciprocal agreements between the European Community and African, Pacific, and Caribbean countries.
7 The GSP is a program under which developed countries provide preferential reduction or removal of trade barriers on products from developing countries. The program has been implemented under the auspices of the GATT and the WTO. The GSP program is an exception to the MFN provision.
8 The margin of preference is the difference between MFN tariffs and the special and preferential tariffs for goods coming from developing countries. The margin of preference erodes whenever MFN tariffs are lowered for goods covered by preferential programs.
9 All 42 African countries in the WTO are members of the African Group. All sub-Saharan African countries are members of the ACP Group. The G-77 is a coalition of developing countries founded in 1964 to promote their interests in multilateral negotiations at various forums. The membership of the G-77 grew from 77 countries when it was founded to over 130 in 2011. All African countries are members of the G-77. The G-33 is a group of over 40 developing countries in the WTO, including 14 African countries, that have made their voices heard regarding special products and a special safeguard mechanism. Of the 33 least developed WTO member countries, 26 are African. The African Group, the ACP Group, and the LDC Group also coordinate under an umbrella called the G-90.

10 For a detailed account, see Richard Mshomba, *Africa and the World Trade Organization* (New York: Cambridge University Press, 2009), Chapter 3.
11 The Group of 20, or G-20, is a group of advanced and emerging economies. Since its inception in 1999, the G-20 holds annual meetings of finance ministers and central bank governors from those countries. South Africa is the only African country that is a member of the G-20. This is not to be confused with the G-20 within the WTO, which is a coalition of developing countries that formed in the run-up to the Cancún Ministerial Conference.
12 Data available from www.oecd.org.
13 Nicholas Kristof, "Farm Subsidies That Kill," *The New York Times*, 5 July 2002, 19.
14 This in itself hurt the capacity to negotiate as a regional bloc.
15 *Mwananchi*, "Watakaouza chakula Moro kushtakiwa" [those in Morogoro who will sell food crops to be prosecuted], Dar-es-Salaam,Tanzania, June 2008.
16 G-33, "Special Products – Contribution by the G-33," JOB(05)/230, 12 October 2005, 2, www.tradeobservatory.org/library.cfm?refid=77130.
17 Thomas Mun, *England's Treasure by Foreign Trade* (London: John Grismond, 1664, reprinted Oxford: Basil Blackwell, 1928).
18 See David Hume (edited and introduced by Eugene Rotwein), *Writings on Economics* (Madison: University of Wisconsin Press, 1970); and Adam Smith, *An Inquiry into the Nature and Causes of the Wealth of Nations* (Dublin, 1776).
19 Paul Collier, *The Bottom Billion: Why the Poorest Countries Are Failing and What Can Be Done About It* (New York: Oxford University Press, 2007), 170–171.
20 Mshomba, *Africa and the World Trade Organization*, Chapter 2.

11 The Doha Development Agenda

Prospective outcomes and African perspectives

Pradeep S. Mehta, Bipul Chatterjee, and Joseph George

The Doha Development Agenda (DDA or Doha round), launched in December 2001 at the fourth Ministerial Conference of the World Trade Organization (WTO), is intended to address the development interests and concerns of developing and least developed countries (LDCs) and thereby empower them to participate effectively in the multilateral trading system. The Doha round came in the immediate wake of the adoption of the United Nations Millennium Development Goals (MDGs) by world leaders who recognized that it was their responsibility to lay foundations for a more peaceful, prosperous, and just world. They further pledged greater cooperation to address global economic challenges of which trade is a key element of MDG8 (Global partnership for development). Thus, the conclusion of the DDA could be considered as part of delivering the MDGs.[1]

Given the larger role of the DDA negotiations and immense expectations raised around it, the urgency of its conclusion is now greater than ever. However, complex politicking and vast issue coverage have regrettably prolonged the negotiations even though the round has proven to be remarkably robust, surviving numerous setbacks. Though important advances have been made in several areas, a final agreement remains elusive; and the negotiations remain stranded by the lack of consensus on a number of topics in which the divide is largely between developed and advanced developing countries.

The DDA, at the outset, promised due consideration of the special developmental needs of the disadvantaged WTO members and delivery on "development" through the application of the principle of less-than-full reciprocity, whereby developing countries are allowed to offer lesser/fewer commitments and concessions in return for what they get. Also, it mandated the review and strengthening of a number of special and differential treatment (SDT) provisions along with technical assistance and capacity building (TACB) programs for developing countries, particularly LDCs.

However, almost as the negotiations commenced the focus immediately shifted to controversial market access issues in agricultural and industrial goods. In the agriculture negotiations, trade-distorting farm subsidies in developed countries, predominantly in the European Union and the United States, have been at the epicenter of standoffs. While developed countries have been defensive on this issue, they have taken offensive positions in the area of industrial goods, demanding larger tariff cuts generally and steeper cuts on specific industrial sectors/products from advanced developing countries like China, India, and Brazil. Hence, a successful conclusion to the round primarily hinges on the resolution of outstanding issues in the negotiations on agriculture and industrial goods. Disagreements on the development dimension of the DDA are also responsible for the stalemate. Most developing countries, the majority being the African countries, considered development as a major Doha mandate and have refused to set aside development issues from the ambit of the ongoing talks.

As far as the developing countries are concerned, a pro-development approach was meant to address the earlier and perceived skewed nature of the multilateral trade system that enabled the developed countries to garner most of the gains from international trade. For most developing countries it was crucial to secure a bigger "share in the growth of world trade commensurate with the needs of their economic development" as promised in the Doha Ministerial Declaration.[2] Further, the DDA outcome should contribute positively towards fulfilling their aspirations on rural development and food security. The issues that developing countries brought to the agenda in this regard included SDT, TACB, better market access for developing countries' exports to developed countries' markets, and balanced rules that provide policy space to developing countries.

Developing countries are rightly concerned that with a change in focus from development issues to market access the DDA may not be able to deliver on its developmental objectives. This question is particularly sensitive for the WTO's African members, more than half of which are LDCs. It is in this context that this chapter takes stock of certain broad challenges facing the DDA and the proposed ways of addressing these challenges, as well as analyzing the outstanding concerns of African countries along with prospective outcomes of the round that would benefit them.

Broad challenges facing the DDA and a possible way forward

At the core of the current state of affairs in the Doha round lie the stark differences in the interests of the developed world on the one hand and developing countries and LDCs on the other. The single most crucial test facing the participants in the DDA is to resolve these differences and reach a consensus sooner rather than later because the round cannot afford further delays. This is especially so as with the passage of time realities change, making it increasingly difficult for the negotiating process to keep up with the pace of change in the external environment. Further delays would severely affect the relevance of the expected final outcomes of the round. In addition, since the DDA has been working with a fixed agenda set in 2001 and slightly modified in the July 2004 Framework, the more the round is prolonged the more it affects the WTO's capability to address its ever growing obligation to deal with new and emerging issues.

So that the round can be brought to a timely and relevant conclusion it is important that the following issues are addressed:

- First, in order to expedite the negotiations it is crucial that major players, especially the United States, take leadership by relaxing their rigid positions on key issues. It has been observed that internal political differences have been constraining several major member countries from delivering on their responsibilities towards constructive participation in the round. This poses a tricky situation for the multilateral trade system because it has limited control over internal political issues of its members and should not be held hostage to such domestic political interests.
- Second, new developments in the world economy have directly and indirectly affected the course of the negotiations. A case in point is the impact of the recent global economic crisis on the progress of the DDA. Domestic political economy concerns and the pressures for protectionism in the aftermath of the crisis slowed down the DDA talks. There still exists a looming threat of economic downturn in the G3 countries (the United States, European Union, and Japan) along with signs of food and fuel supply shocks at the global level that may again hold back the progress of DDA. These are also exogenous factors over which the WTO has limited control and members should be conscious so as not to allow such obstacles to cause more delays.

In order to overcome these challenges, a concerted effort must be made to put pressure on the major players to resolve the internal political differences that have been constraining their participation in the round. Such an effort can be made only in coordination with other global development institutions and international coalitions/bodies, since the exogenous factors that may affect the negotiations can hardly be predicted with precision and acted upon by the WTO alone. Very strong grounds for strengthening this coordination already exist and this must be achieved by reasserting the strong links of the DDA with the achievement of the MDGs, especially the vision about global partnership for development.

An example to substantiate this point may be drawn from the experiences in the recent past. When the financial crisis erupted in late 2008, the G-20 mobilized the international community's response to the crisis. While the primary focus was on mutual support and coordination of response actions among its member countries, the G-20 also arranged for significantly increased international assistance to developing and transition economies. This was achieved, in particular, through expanded lending by the multilateral development banks and the International Monetary Fund (IMF), which also eased the terms of the resources provided to low income countries, including cancellation of interest payments due through 2011. This helped to a large extent in easing the pressure on countries to resort to protectionism and consequently reinstated confidence in trade liberalization and multilateral trade negotiations.

Based on this experience and with a view to avoid dilution of focus on the ongoing negotiations, the WTO should continue to document and publicize trade distortive protectionist measures adopted worldwide and thereby put pressure on its members to prevent them from adopting defensive trade policies. In this regard, the fact that the G-20 members committed themselves to resisting protectionist policies[3] and requested the main international trade agencies to monitor country activities is further evidence of the fact that WTO negotiation processes may benefit from global coalitions with common goals.

Remaining issues in the DDA and possible outcomes

The main focus of the DDA negotiations, as envisaged in the Doha Declaration and its subsequent modification in July 2004, has been on the removal of trade barriers in agriculture, industrial goods (Non-Agricultural Market Access [NAMA]), and services as well as some other issues such as the framing of an agreement on trade facilitation measures, special negotiations for improving disciplines on antidumping, subsidies and countervailing measures, fisheries subsidies, the relationship between the Agreement on Trade-Related Intellectual Property Rights (TRIPs) and the Convention on Biological Diversity, and geographical indications (the last two under the intellectual property rights negotiations). The mandate of the round requires negotiations in all areas including these to be concluded simultaneously under the "single undertaking" arrangement.[4]

It can be argued that the major negotiating areas that hold the key to the conclusion of the DDA are agriculture, NAMA, and services. Since the December 2005 Hong Kong Ministerial Conference significant advances have been made in agriculture and NAMA negotiations as reflected in the draft negotiating texts circulated by the respective Chairs in December 2008. Though progress in services market access negotiations has been relatively slow after the "signaling conference" held in July 2008 wherein members exchanged indications on their own new and improved commitments as well as the contributions expected from others, positive improvements, particularly in the areas of domestic regulation and the implementation of LDC modalities, were noted by the Chair in his March 2010 report to the Trade Negotiations Committee.[5] The remaining outstanding issues from the perspective of developing countries are as follows.

Agriculture

- Securing deeper cuts in tariffs in each tier for developed countries and shorter periods to implement these cuts than those proposed in the December 2008 text.[6]
- Securing developing countries' right to self-designate an appropriate number of tariff lines as special products with the limit raised to 20 percent of tariff lines, including raising the proposed maximum limit of 5 percent of tariff lines that can be fully exempted from any cuts. Removal of the condition that tariff cuts on special products would have to average 11 percent.
- Securing deeper cuts in overall trade-distorting domestic support (OTDS) by developed countries than those proposed in December 2008 text, with separate disciplines and further reduction commitments in each component of OTDS through an appropriate tiered formula.
- Securing review and revision of "blue box" and "green box" criteria for making the support measures included therein less trade-distorting, and the development of strict disciplines to curb the tendency of evading reduction commitments through "box shifting."
- Securing special commitments for substantial cuts in cotton subsidies and separate disciplines to expedite trade in tropical products.
- Securing the right to retain monopoly status for state trading enterprises in developing countries.

NAMA (industrial goods)

- Developing country participation in sectoral negotiations should be voluntary.

- Securing agreement not to introduce an "anti-concentration clause" that may limit the instruments for safeguards.

Services

- Securing substantial easing of entry (immigration) and qualification requirements for movement of professionals under Mode 4.
- Redressing the distortions in the economic needs test that restricts the free movement of professionals.

Given the "single undertaking" principle on which the DDA negotiations are being conducted, impasse in the negotiations is most likely to be resolved by conceding to each other's interests in agriculture and NAMA negotiations by developing and developed country groups respectively as envisaged in the Hong Kong Ministerial Declaration. Accordingly, modest increments in market access commitments beyond the tariff and subsidy cuts in agriculture and NAMA already written into the current negotiating modalities may be expected. Under such a scenario, tariff cuts on industrial goods based on the accepted modality may have to be supplemented with deeper tariff cuts on sectors/products of priority interest to the proponents of sectors such as chemicals, electronics/ electrical goods, and the like. This scenario would also entail stricter disciplines on agricultural subsidies, with deeper cuts on already agreed OTDS as well as the inclusion of more trade-distorting subsidies under OTDS. A substantial commitment to cut down cotton subsidies with separate disciplines may also be part of this package.

In addition, to make any Doha deal work, countries have to come up with concrete commitments to liberalize trade in services. To date, these negotiations have not yielded offers that would enhance market access and require a substantial acceleration of the request/offer negotiations in services. The movement of natural persons remains heavily regulated, and proposals for the negotiation of the issue in the context of the round have found resistance from developed countries. Deeper commitments on market access in this area could yield substantial gains for developing countries as well as economic welfare benefits for developed countries.

Scope of African concerns in the DDA

Out of the 41 African countries that are members of the WTO, 16 are developing countries and the rest are LDCs. Though there are some differences between the negotiating positions and demands of LDCs and other developing country members, especially as the LDCs are exempted from binding commitments, African countries, whether developing or least-developed have generally presented a common front in the WTO because they face similar economic conditions, perhaps with the exception of a few like South Africa.

African representation in the DDA has been predominantly through various formal as well as issue-based coalitions.[7] The Africa group in the WTO includes all the 41 countries. African countries are further represented in the African, Caribbean, and Pacific (ACP) group, based on their special trade relationship with the European Union, and the G-90 group, which combines the ACP, Africa and LDC groups. In addition, reflecting their special interests and development status, various subsets of the Africa group have been members of other coalitions, including the Cotton Four,[8] the G-20 (which fights for improved agricultural market access),[9] G-33[10] ("friends of special products," which pursues mainly defensive agricultural interests), NAMA-11 (which fights for lower tariff cut commitments for developing countries' non-agricultural products), and the LDC group.

The formation of the Africa group in 1995 notably advanced the participation of member countries from the continent that had been suffering from a lack of institutional development and negotiation capacity. The coalition has wielded strong influence in the course of DDA negotiations. During the initial years following its formation, the Africa group did not have a clear negotiation position on many negotiating areas outside the purview of direct issues pertaining to LDCs.[11] In due course, the group members came forward to take clear positions on each of the DDA negotiation issues, recognizing that they have a significant bearing on the future development of African economies.

The ACP and Africa groups have been in agreement with the proposals of the G-20 and G-33 on agriculture and the NAMA-11 on industrial goods. Going by the proposals tabled by the Africa, ACP and LDC groups, the most important concerns of African countries have been: (i) cotton subsidies; (ii) food security concerns faced by net food importing developing countries (NFIDCs); and (iii) preference erosion. Besides these, their main demands have been securing an early harvest for LDCs as well as expanding the reach and coverage of aid for trade (A4T), Generalized System of Preferences (GSP) schemes and TACB programs. The highlights of the proposals of the African coalitions are as follows:

• The elimination of all forms of subsidies granted to cotton producers by developed countries; providing duty-free quota-free (DFQF) access for imports of cotton from LDCs; and setting up a mechanism to deal with the loss of revenue that cotton producing countries in Africa are facing as a result of declining cotton prices resulting from developed country subsidization.[12]

- Green box subsidies, especially those provided as decoupled income support, insurance against income loss, and investment aid should be subjected to eligibility criteria such as low levels of income, status as a producer or landowner, landholding and production level, in a fixed and unchanging base period. Also, there should be thresholds placed on the criteria.
- DFQF market access for all products originating from all LDCs and an early harvest arrangement approved for DFQF.[13]
- Fully addressing the issue of erosion of preferences through appropriate and meaningful trade solutions.
- The exemption from tariff reductions on industrial goods under NAMA negotiations for countries included in paragraph six of the July 2004 Framework; and the additional flexibilities for developing countries enshrined in paragraph eight of the July 2004 NAMA framework should be treated independently of the tariff formula, that is, lower developing country formula cuts cannot be offset by reducing the availability of paragraph eight flexibilities.[14]
- The strengthening disciplines on export prohibitions and restrictions provided under Article 12.1 of the Agreement on Agriculture.
- Clarifications and modifications in the existing provisions of Article XXIV of the General Agreement on Tariffs and Trade (GATT) 1994 to incorporate SDT for developing countries; the introduction of the notion of non-reciprocity in regional trade agreements between developed and developing countries; and to preserve the Enabling Clause to continue to provide the legal basis for South-South regional trade agreements. (The Enabling Clause, or as it is officially known the "Decision on Differential and More Favourable Treatment, Reciprocity and Fuller Participation of Developing Countries," was adopted in 1979 and provides the legal basis for preferential trade agreements in favor of developing countries.)
- Clarity on implementation of the proposed LDC modalities as part of the final services package, covering principles for the provision of technical assistance and mechanisms and procedures for LDCs to have maximum flexibility in the services negotiations.

A comparison between outstanding issues in the DDA and African concerns gives an optimistic picture, as the ongoing negotiations maintain the scope of addressing the core issues concerning African LDCs. Though a gradual shift from development aspects to market access issues has occurred over the course of the negotiations, it is evident that a final package cannot materialize without substantial commitments on agricultural subsidy reductions and adequate SDT provisions. While the issue of agricultural subsidies is high on the agenda of agriculture negotiations, LDC modalities in services already have general acceptance, pending implementation specifics.[15]

One of the key observations emerging from the demands of the African countries is that their expectations of the round are not solely based on flexibilities through SDT, aid, and technical assistance, as is commonly perceived.[16] For instance, recognizing the importance of services in their economic and social development, LDC group members insisted that the LDC modalities not only should address the need for additional time and resources to make their sectoral commitments for opening up services markets, but also guarantee that Members shall give special priority to providing effective market access in sectors and modes of supply of export interest to LDCs. In this case and also in NAMA negotiations, the representation of the African countries shows a sense of urgency arising from the realization that delays in liberalizing trade may mean delays in their overall economic development and poverty alleviation.

With regard to flexibilities and safeguards for developing countries and LDCs, promising results can be expected from the DDA. As stated in the Doha Declaration[17] and reaffirmed in the July Package of 2004,[18] the provisions for SDT, which are an integral part of the WTO agreements, shall be reviewed with a view to strengthening them and making them more precise, effective, and operational. Prior to the 2005 Hong Kong Ministerial, the General Council had instructed the Committee for Trade and Development to review the outstanding agreement-specific proposals on SDT and report back with clear recommendations for decisions.[19] This review includes provisions aimed at increasing the trade opportunities of developing countries and LDCs, transitional time periods for implementing agreements and commitments, flexibilities in commitments made, and the use of policy instruments as well as provisions requiring all WTO members to safeguard the trade interests of developing countries and LDCs.

Another significant source of benefit for the African countries lies in the reappraisal of provisions related to TACB as well as the Agreement on Trade Facilitation that is being negotiated under the round. The Draft Agreement on Trade Facilitation has been one of the major achievements of the round. The Agreement would oversee policy reforms in customs procedures and related areas that cut transaction costs for exporting and importing both goods and services. The broad disciplines of the Agreement have already been framed and contain improvements over

Article V of the GATT (Freedom of Transit) as well as Article VIII (Fees and Formalities connected with Importation and Exportation) and Article X (Publication and Administration of Trade Regulations).[20] Taking into account the high cost of implementing trade facilitation reforms, the prospective agreement allows horizontal exemptions, or, in other words, a mechanism of voluntary choices for developing countries and LDCs in selecting the provisions that are to be legally binding for them. This allows poorer member states to strike a balance between self-enforcing reforms in the areas covering Article V, VIII and X in which voluntary reforms are already underway and opting out of binding commitments that are difficult to comply with in the immediate future.

This presents the African countries with an opportunity to take up trade reforms through formal commitments wherever implementation costs are minimal and supplement the reforms through adequate infrastructure building by taking advantage of technical and financial assistance provided for in the Agreement. Many provisions in the proposed Agreement give ideal guidelines for disciplining and improving trade facilitation conditions with respect to the publication of information and consultation, mechanisms for advance rulings and prompt and transparent appeal procedures, the elimination of impartiality, border agency cooperation, periodic review and the reduction of formalities and documentation requirements, the usage of international standards and the harmonization of trade facilitation procedures, and the elimination of pre-shipment inspection among other things. Binding commitments will also help to reinforce and accelerate already initiated reforms in these areas at the national and regional level. Arguably, most of these reforms are highly relevant for land-locked countries dependent on transit facilities as in the case of many African LDCs.

Additionally, A4T allocations, though outside the purview of the DDA, offer opportunities for making investments in infrastructure, and improve trade policy and regulation as well as productive capacity. Therefore, using A4T as a complementary factor rather than a substitute, the management of aid flows should be integrated into national trade policy-making process. From the perspective of African recipients, the success of this strategy depends on linking A4T initiatives with the negotiating areas in the DDA in such a way that aid projects facilitate effective utilization of the outcomes of the round.

Conclusion

It is more or less clear that the future of the Doha round lies in reciprocal exchanges in agriculture vis-à-vis NAMA between the developed country block and the large and advanced developing countries, coupled with improvements in reciprocal offers in services by all negotiating parties. The ACP and Africa groups have pledged unequivocal support to the position expressed by the NAMA-11 group of developing countries favoring the principle of "double proportionality" (that is, a balance between NAMA and agriculture negotiations).[21] This would mean enhanced market access for developing countries in agriculture, which coupled with Mode 4 of the General Agreement on Trade in Services is considered to be key areas of economic gains for African countries.

However, following the points discussed in the previous sections, the overall benefits for African countries will depend on how the details of the final deal turn out with respect to three broad aspects: (i) the extent and coverage of the removal of agriculture subsidies, particularly in cotton given its positive implications for enhanced market access and negative implications for NFIDCs in terms of food inflation; (ii) the extent and coverage of SDT provisions that would benefit all African countries, along with A4T, GSP and TACB programs, particularly allocations to which African LDCs would be eligible; and (iii) the overall package for LDCs and small and vulnerable economies and remedial measures for the erosion of preference margins enjoyed by African countries in general.

A dilemma facing the predominantly agricultural-based African economies is the possible impact of subsidy cuts on access to internal price stability and parity conditions. While expected increases in world market prices may enhance the price competitiveness of certain agricultural exports, the need to continue subsidized protection for domestic producers to maintain that price competitiveness still would remain. As most African countries are net importers of food, the comfort of subsidized imports may get eroded, leading to a rise in their import bills. However, the phased elimination of cotton subsidies by the United States and the European Union with a short implementation period should be high on the agenda for the benefit of African members. The elimination of annual cotton subsidies to the tune of US$3 billion will enable West African producers to gain 5–12 percent of the value of their cotton exports.

In addition, in the general context of talks on agricultural subsidies, the concerns of the NFIDCs should be recognized and addressed through measures including the granting of a special status to such countries as was done in the Uruguay round. As noted earlier, one of the most important issues for African countries is food security, but no firm agreement has yet been reached on how to address this in the agriculture negotiations. All except 12 African countries may benefit from such a food security plan, either as LDCs or as NFIDCs.

Another crucial area for Africa is to seek ways and means to address preference erosion for their products in developed country markets following most favored nation tariff cuts. The focus in this area is currently on deepening GSP schemes for LDCs over the most favoured nation reduction rates to check preference erosion as well as on capacity building programs and relaxations in rules of origin clauses to enhance the utilization of preference schemes. Most African countries have severe problems in expanding their exports to markets that already exist. Therefore, additional emphasis must be placed on enhancing market access through improved rules of origin, support to deal with non-tariff barriers, and A4T.[22] This is especially so because the retained preference margins through GSP schemes would have to be forgone in the medium term and African nations should use aid and technical assistance to enhance their competitiveness with urgency using the time window available to them before preferences cease to exist.

Other key demands that need to be pursued to ensure minimum assured benefits for Africa are: (i) additional flexibilities for trade in industrial goods envisaged under paragraph eight (NAMA) of the July 2004 Package over and above the flexibilities that would be granted through lower tariff cuts and a longer implementation period; (ii) early harvest and full utilization of the TACB programs envisaged under the proposed Agreement on Trade Facilitation (this would also partly address the implementation issues that would arise once the round is concluded); (iii) fast tracking of the implementation of the Task Force on Aid for Trade recommendations through the provision of additional, non-conditional, predictable, sustainable, and effective aid; (iv) the implementation of full DFQF market access to products originating from all LDCs including arrangements for the early harvest of this commitment so that the LDCs can start benefiting at the earliest; (v) the review of Article 27.3b (patentability of plant and animal varieties) of the TRIPs Agreement that should result in providing rightful protection of genetic resources and traditional knowledge and effective implementation of the TRIPs and Public Health Agreement that ensures affordable access to generic drugs in countries with limited or no pharmaceutical manufacturing capacities; and (vi) exclusion of fishing-access agreements from the definition of subsidies, specifically the government-to-government transfer of fishing-access fees.

In the area of services negotiations, the expectations are centered on the implementation of LDC modalities and substantial improvement in offers from developed countries and advanced developing countries on market access to services exports from LDCs through Mode 4, specifically the easing of barriers for entry of unskilled labor. These outcomes along with the general market access opportunities that are expected and accompanied by the already agreed safeguards and flexibilities would help to deliver the developmental expectations of African countries.

Besides these areas, common concerns from the region have been raised in the past, which need further pursuance, including the removal of various existing non-tariff barriers (such as restrictive import policy, environmental standards, eco-labelling, laboratory test for dyes, unrealistic certification measures, export subsidies, technical barriers on service trade, anti-dumping and countervailing measures) in the major import markets. Though to varying degrees supply-side constraints are common to all African countries, the solutions for these should be sought as a regional block. Fresh demands must be raised for adequate financial resources and technology transfers to address low capacity to meet product quality standards and infrastructural bottlenecks. It is of the utmost importance for African governments to form a regular regional consultative mechanism to pursue these common developmental goals.

Nevertheless, it cannot be ignored that unilateral policy reforms by member states are essential to achieve actual results. The usage of aid projects for trade related capacity building, intra-regional customs cooperation for smooth transit facilities and so on are obligatory voluntary measures in this regards. Given that huge expenditure outlay is to be expected in order to expedite the process, supplementary support must be sought from relevant multilateral agencies for trade-related infrastructure (such as transport, energy, logistics), and financial and capital market development, as well as other areas in order to reduce transaction costs. Promoting improvements in infrastructure and the business environment would open up opportunities for the private sector, both in terms of trade and of investment and thereby enable African countries to take advantage of the DDA outcomes. Therefore the "delivery on development" of the DDA from the point of view of Africa's development should be evaluated in the context of both favorable outcomes of the round as well as unilateral support measures initiated by African member states.

Notes

1 The expected outcomes of the DDA have been treated in the literature as having significant bearing on the achievement of MDG targets. Moreover, Goal 8 of the MDGs recognizes a wider role for trade issues, including Aid for Trade initiatives, that goes outside the ambit of the DDA. See United Nations MDG Gap Task Force, *The Global Partnership for Development: Time to Deliver* (New York: UN, 2010), 27–42. Also see the sister volume to this book, Rorden Wilkinson and David Hulme, eds, *The Millennium Development Goals and Beyond: Global Development after 2015* (London: Routledge, 2012).

2 WTO, "Doha Ministerial Declaration," WT/MIN(01)/DEC/1, 20 November 2001, paragraph 2.
3 Each G-20 Summit Declaration from September 2009 to mid-February 2010 included a call and promise to resist protectionist pressures. As a result, recourse to new trade restrictions by G-20 members was less pronounced later, after the initial shock of the financial crisis, and the overall extent of these restrictions has been limited.
4 See WTO, "Doha Work Programme, Preparations for the Sixth Session of the Ministerial Conference, Draft Ministerial Text," JOB(05)/298/Rev.1, 1 December 2005, for details of the Doha Work Programme.
5 WTO, "Council for Trade in Services – Special Session – Negotiations on Trade in Services – Report by the Chairman," TN/S/35, 22 March 2010.
6 WTO, "Revised Draft Modalities for Agriculture," TN/AG/W/4/Rev.4, 6 December 2008.
7 Africa's concerns in the Doha round are contained in the Addis Ababa Declarations of 20 March 2009, 3 April 2008, and 15–16 January 2007; the Nairobi Ministerial Declaration of 12–14 April 2006; the Arusha Declaration of 12–14 April 2006; the Arusha Development Benchmarks of 21–24 November 2005; the Cairo Road Map on the Doha Work Programme of 5–9 June 2005; and the Kigali Consensus of 27–28 May 2004.
8 Benin, Burkina Faso, Chad, and Mali.
9 Not to be confused with the G-20 of Finance Ministers.
10 G-33 includes the African member states of Congo, Côte d'Ivoire, Kenya, Madagascar, Mauritius, Mozambique, Nigeria, Senegal, Tanzania, Uganda, Zambia, and Zimbabwe.
11 For example, the Africa group was regularly reminded that, while it was legitimate for it to focus on the DFQF issue, it should steer clear of the subsidies issue since most of its members would not in any case be obliged to make any commitments on subsidies. See for details, Arsene M. Balihuta, "African Group and DDA: Maintaining Solidarity of a Large Coalition," in *Reflections from the Frontline: Developing Country Negotiators in the WTO,* eds, Pradeep S. Mehta, Atul Kaushik, and Rashid S. Kaukab (Geneva and New Delhi: Academic Foundation and CUTS International, 2012), 313–328.
12 See WTO, "WTO African Regional Workshop on Cotton, Cotonou, Republic of Benin, Note by the Secretariat," WT/L/587, 23–24 March 2004; and WTO, "Proposed Elements of Modalities in Connection with the Sectoral Initiative in Favour of Cotton, Communication from the African Group," TN/AG/SCC/GEN/2, 22 April 2005 for details of proposals on cotton subsidies; and for analytical exposition, see Daniel A. Sumner, "Reducing Cotton Subsidies: The DDA Cotton Initiative," in *Agricultural Trade Reform and the Doha Development Agenda,* ed. Will Martin and Kym Anderson (Washington, DC: World Bank, 2005), 271–292.
13 See Jane Kennan and Christopher Stevens, "Implications of the Hong Kong Ministerial Declaration on Duty-free and Quota-free Access for Least Developed Countries," in *After Hong Kong: Some Key Trade Issues for Developing Countries,* ed. Ivan Mbirimi (New Delhi: The Academic Foundation and Commonwealth Secretariat, 2007), 35–110.
14 See Hakim Ben Hammouda, Stephen Karingi, Romain Pérez and Mustapha Sadni-Jallab, "Can the Doha Round Benefit Africa's Industrial Sector?" African Trade Policy Centre, UN Economic Commission for Africa, Work

in Progress Paper No. 45 (Addis Ababa: UNECA, 2006); and UNECA, "Report of the Workshop for the African Group Countries on: WTO NAMA Negotiations on Non-Tariff Barriers," (2010), www.uneca.org/atpc/events/NTBs2010/ReportWorkshopNegotiationsNonTariffBarriers-apr2010.pdf, for a detailed exposition of African members' interests in NAMA negotiations.

15 In September 2003, the Committee on Trade in Services adopted the "Modalities for the Special Treatment for Least-Developed Country Members in the Negotiations on Trade in Services," TN/S/13, 5 September 2003.

16 African countries' participation has often been characterized as being excessively reliant on flexibilities and aid. Alternative views and evidences can be found in UNECA, "The Doha Round and African Development: Turning Words into Deeds," UNECA Position Paper Series (Addis Ababa: UNECA, 2003); Peter Mandelson, "Doha Development Agenda: The Round for Africa," Statement to the Third African Union Conference of Ministers of Trade, Cairo, 8 June 2005; and Mareike Meyn, "The WTO Doha Round Impasse: Implications for Africa," Overseas Development Institute Briefing Paper No. 41 (London: ODI, 2008).

17 WTO, "Doha Ministerial Declaration," paragraph 44.

18 WTO, "Doha Work Programme: Decision Adopted by the General Council on 1 August 2004," WT/L/579, 1 August 2004, section 1D.

19 See WTO, "Committee on Trade and Development – Special Session – Report to the General Council," TN/CTD/7, 10 February 2004.

20 See WTO, "Negotiating Group on Trade Facilitation – Draft Consolidated Negotiating Text," TN/TF/W/165, 14 December 2009.

21 See WTO, "Negotiating Group on Market Access – Market Access for Non-Agricultural Products – Communication from the NAMA-11 Group of Developing Countries," TN/MA/W/86, 8 June 2010.

22 See Bernard Hoekman and Susan Prowse, "Economic Policy Responses to Preference Erosion: From Trade as Aid to Aid for Trade," World Bank Policy Research Working Paper 3721 (Washington, DC: World Bank, 2005); and Sheila Page, "A Preference Erosion Compensation Fund: A New Proposal to Protect Countries from the Negative Effects of Trade Liberalisation," Overseas Development Institute Opinion Paper 35 (London: ODI, 2005) for detailed expositions.

12 The Doha Development Agenda and the WTO can deliver on Africa's development priorities

Peter Draper, Memory Dube, and Morisho Nene

The purpose of this chapter is to critically assess whether the concerns of the poorest, particularly in Africa, have been taken sufficiently into account in the formulation of the Doha Development Agenda (DDA) and, flowing from this, the prospects and possibilities for achieving an outcome to the round that is tailored more appropriately to the challenges confronting Africa. Geographically the focus is confined to sub-Saharan Africa since North African countries are closely linked to the European economic sphere and are culturally distinct. Accordingly we begin by setting out in broad terms the contours of sub-Saharan African development challenges. Throughout we relate those challenges to the outlines of the multilateral trading system. We then turn to the DDA itself. We highlight the main features of the DDA package from our sub-Saharan standpoint, and address gaps in it as highlighted in the preceding discussion of development challenges in relation to the multilateral trading system. This sets the scene for a brief discussion of the potential for plurilateral agreements to transcend the impasse in the World Trade Organization (WTO); we discuss investment as one potential investment plurilateral in order to illuminate the issues at stake. We conclude with some thoughts about what needs to be done in and beyond the DDA in order to better address African development challenges through the multilateral trading system.

Africa's development challenges in relation to the multilateral trading system

Most, if not all, countries in the sub-continent suffer from chronic supply-side deficiencies, essentially meaning their capacities to produce and supply goods and services into domestic, regional, and international markets are severely limited. In trade parlance this means that network services infrastructure (communications; energy; finance; transport) are seriously deficient in almost the entire sub-continent, with the partial exception of South Africa and its immediate neighbors in the Southern African Customs Union (SACU).

Partly related to this, many African countries perform poorly in the plethora of global competitiveness surveys, which is a function of poor regulatory capacities and problematic procedures governing the conduct of business. Consequently the region's competitiveness is severely hampered, which in turn inhibits *diversification* away from commodity exports, on which the sub-continent overwhelmingly relies, into value-added manufacturing and agricultural processing. Whereas regional markets do provide some potential for exporting value-added goods,[1] in practice such exports are dominated by a handful of regional leaders: South Africa, Kenya, and Nigeria in particular.[2]

These aggregate patterns suggest two core issues of interest to Africa concerning the outcomes of the DDA: attracting network services foreign direct investment (FDI), and ensuring continued access for primary product exports into predominantly northern markets.

Regarding network services, the key issue is to ensure that foreign investors, and nascent domestic investors, have secure access to those markets on mutually acceptable terms. This suggests that a liberalization agenda is in order, but one balanced between host nation regulatory rights and investor obligations. These issues are covered under bilateral investment treaties (BITs), but the problem with these arrangements is that investors can play divide and rule, whereas host governments feel impelled to offer more generous concessions than their competitors. Since the sub-continent faces a renewed "scramble" for resources there may therefore be merit in exploring—beyond the DDA—the possibility of negotiating *multilateral rules governing investment*, particularly investor obligations. We return to this point later.

As for market access for African exports, the major concern is with agricultural goods. However, paradoxically the European system of preferential market access granted to former colonies, from which African states have historically benefitted, has set the sub-continent up in a "Faustian bargain" with the European Union (EU)—the major agricultural export destination. Since African states generally enjoy better market access than the major agricultural exporters in the Cairns group and elsewhere, they have little incentive to see their margins eroded through an ambitious agriculture pact. Not surprisingly therefore, the Africa group has advocated less ambition in EU tariff reduction commitments in the agriculture talks. However, this also means the incentives to reform domestic agricultural production are diminished, which in turn contributes to locking African producers into primary agricultural exports.

Reinforcing this trend is the global tendency to practice tariff escalation. This inhibits processed agricultural exports from Africa, and diversification into manufactures to the extent this is feasible. Furthermore, elaborate standards regimes for agricultural and industrial products in developed countries constitute major non-tariff barriers—a problem that all developing countries face.

Two other issues compromise developing country exports in general, and African exports in particular: emerging climate change regimes, and policy reactions in developed countries to the global economic crisis and what this reveals about gaps in the WTO's regulatory architecture. Concerning climate change negotiations trade and competitiveness concerns have moved to center stage, particularly over "carbon-leakage." Essentially, developed countries worry that as they implement carbon-reduction measures with teeth, thereby penalizing their companies, so those companies will relocate production to developing countries that have not taken on substantial mitigation obligations. Furthermore, those developing countries generally have less punitive environmental laws, and so it may be possible to transfer older, more polluting technologies to them. The net result could be job losses in developed countries while carbon emissions are either not reduced or increase, and the planet "cooks" anyway.

These concerns lead logically to potential trade policy remedies. Three are under discussion in various forums. First, so-called "border carbon adjustments" would impose taxes on imports in "trade exposed industries" from countries that have not adopted substantial mitigation targets. Second, "production process methods" have a broader applicability than the carbon mitigation discussion but are nonetheless relevant. Third, in the DDA negotiations member states continue to haggle over liberalization of environmental goods and services. This connects to a broader debate in the climate change negotiations over the terms under which developing countries can access advanced clean energy technologies and how such access will be financed.

For sub-Saharan Africa the sector of greatest concern is agriculture, where most of the rural poor make their living. "Climate protectionism" is already manifesting in new or stringent product standards and labeling for valuable exports such as fruits and vegetables. Mitigation of carbon emissions in the transportation sector is an additional source of concern for the region. To the extent it is implemented it would presumably affect all countries, but the effects could be sharpest in the developing world. Aviation measures, for example, could penalize the tourism trade, which is a significant revenue source for many countries in Southern Africa. Furthermore, road transportation is crucial to cross border trade in the region so any measures in this sector would have to be closely watched.

Regarding the global economic crisis, "murky protectionism" remains an abiding concern.[3] Eric Ogunleye documents the contours of impact of African trading partners' protection measures on African trade and finds substantial incidence of harm (80 percent of total measures versus 20 percent that were liberalizing).[4] Not surprisingly these mostly affected the more diversified economies, particularly South Africa (80 measures) followed by Egypt, Tunisia, Morocco, and Kenya (56, 40, 33, 31 measures respectively). This reinforces the general truism in trade protection, that those goods with the least value-added generally attract the least protection. Ogunleye notes that a substantial portion of these measures are concentrated in the agricultural sector in which the WTO's rules specifically allow for developed countries to increase payments to their farmers in times of declining global prices, including export support payments.[5] This points to the urgency of concluding the Doha round in order to further discipline the use of agricultural subsidies.

Yet the gaps in the WTO's regulatory regimes go much further than this, as evidenced by the wide array of crisis responses.[6] Specific problem areas from the standpoint of African countries include:

- *Subsidies disciplines on finance*, in light of huge bailouts to the financial sector. While these were necessary in order to prevent the wholesale collapse of the Western financial system, their continued implementation raises questions about whether the recipients might use them to build market share in relatively rapidly growing emerging markets while restricting lending at home, thereby constituting unfair competition. A few African economies are developing their financial sectors quite rapidly now[7] and hence have an interest in this issue.
- *Policies affecting movement of workers.* Ogunleye notes that a number of European countries in particular tightened their immigration procedures, which in turn has an impact on African skilled temporary migrants with attendant consequences for sending remittances back home.[8] Many poor families in Africa rely on these remittances.
- *Investment conditionalities*, such as the French government prevailing on the oil company Total not to shut down its refinery at Dunkirk, which in turn meant rationalization in another national jurisdiction, potentially Nigeria. This reinforces the need for multilateral rules on investment, as discussed earlier.

Consequently, even if the Doha round were to be completed, there is a large agenda arising from, and transcending, the economic crisis that could and should keep the WTO busy for years to come. At the very least this suggests a more focused agenda for the WTO in the future, together with reform of its decision-making dynamics.[9] More concretely, once the Doha round conundrum has been resolved, we advocate the membership turn to plurilateral agreements in order to modernize the WTO's rules architecture. Later in the chapter we take one theoretical example of a plurilateral agreement—investment—and explore its dynamics from an African perspective in order to shed light on the concrete implications of this approach.

Does the Doha round's architecture address African challenges?

This is a complex question to answer, given the DDA's breadth; the following brief survey is necessarily selective.

We begin with a core principle underpinning the DDA: special and differential treatment (SDT) in terms of trade liberalization obligations. While no-one would argue with this principle, it is driven by a pre-occupation with market access. As noted earlier, African countries stand to gain little in terms of the market access components of the negotiations since they supply very little into global markets; indeed they stand to lose substantially through preference erosion should serious commitments ensue. On the other hand, trade liberalization is necessary for development but not sufficient.

So can the WTO facilitate development and not just adjustment to WTO rules as SDT currently does?[10] Arguably the best avenue for this is aid for trade (A4T). Maximizing the benefits of A4T assistance requires the identification of national priorities that should be embedded in a national development plan or strategy.[11] This is particularly important because trade policy is part of a development policy package and not an end in itself. Most of the major questions about the A4T agenda were resolved by the report of the task force on A4T. The focus is now on mobilizing additional funding for economic official development assistance (ODA) using traditional channels of disbursement, both multilateral and bilateral, with the WTO using its convening power to raise support for the segment of ODA that addresses economic infrastructure and capacity building. This speaks directly to African development priorities. However, A4T is not part of the DDA package, but is rather a complement to the DDA. This means that any agreements on A4T will not be subject to binding dispute settlement. Yet the history of donor delivery on ODA commitments is checkered; therefore it is not obvious that African countries should rely on external subsidies to "deliver development" from above. Instead, they have to redouble their own efforts and work out how best to leverage the DDA towards this end.

In this light we turn to the regulatory agenda. African countries were closely involved in rejecting three of the four Singapore issues (investment, transparency in government procurement, and competition policy) at the Cancún Ministerial in 2003. This was primarily a rejection of standards designed in and for developed countries from being applied to developing countries, and is also a reflection of the skewed nature of these trade negotiations where African countries lack the requisite analytical and negotiating capital,[12] and in many cases the capacity to implement negotiated outcomes. Similar caution is warranted in negotiating intellectual property rights.

These concerns are understandable and in accordance with SDT; but beyond the DDA they are possibly misplaced for some negotiating issues. Earlier we made the case for reconsidering multilateral rules on investment from an African standpoint; to this we could add the importance of clarifying rules on government procurement since this was one of the main instruments of protection developed countries resorted to during the economic crisis. But these are post-DDA issues.

Trade facilitation remains one of the biggest hurdles to trade in Africa. It covers such aspects as energy, transport, logistics, finance, technology, skills transfers, and bureaucratic efficiency.[13] However, the pre-requisites for a development oriented trade facilitation agreement include other resources outside of the WTO's scope and control, such as coordination of different ODA projects and cooperation with international agencies and institutions concerned with development. Such capacity to coordinate and cooperate with other institutions does not reside within the WTO. Nonetheless, this is one aspect of the DDA on which there does seem to be widespread consensus that the draft agreement is appropriately framed. And these negotiations have adopted the novel approach of linking implementation of commitments to actual delivery of financial and technical support, or A4T.

The services agenda is also of major importance. On the "defensive" front African countries should offer greater liberalization of access to network services markets through FDI. In return, they should aim to secure commitments in Mode 4 negotiations concerning temporary movement of skilled Africans to developed country markets. Since remittances are now such a large contributor to financial inflows into African economies this potential win-win situation, while politically complex to deliver owing to developed country concerns over immigration, should be pursued as a top priority. Ultimately the key long-term negotiating card Africans hold is the dire need for developed countries to reform their pension systems and allow temporary migration to plug skills gaps in their rapidly aging populations.

On the market access front the core issues of agricultural and Non-Agricultural Market Access (NAMA) remain of interest to African countries. Negotiations on agriculture have been aimed at improving market access for developing countries in developed country markets; the reduction and elimination of all forms of export subsidies; and the disciplining, reduction, and elimination of domestic support for farmers.[14] Liberalization of trade in agriculture and the elimination of trade distorting measures are critical to many sub-Saharan African countries' development. The lack of homogeneity among African countries and complexity of the situation with regard to the agricultural negotiations also present a development challenge. This is best captured in the cotton issue, which has become the litmus test for African countries regarding whether the DDA can deliver on development for Africa. Furthermore, the liberalization of agricultural trade will affect net food importing countries that have benefited from the deflated prices of farm commodities, while disciplining food aid (a form of export subsidy) may also threaten those countries that depend on it, at least in the short term. Notwithstanding these threats the overall aim should be to incentivize African farmers to produce more, while minimizing short-term damage to fragile home nations arising from the vulnerabilities outlined here. In this sense the DDA seems to be appropriately balanced.

The NAMA negotiations are another area of critical development potential for developing countries. Liberalization of trade in industrial goods in major markets (developed and developing) will theoretically allow African countries to move away from their reliance on commodity exports and allow them to export value added goods. Their own liberalization will also encourage imports of many products critical to consumption and production. However, in keeping with SDT least developed countries (LDCs)—33 of which are to be found in sub-Saharan Africa—will not be expected to reduce their tariff rates, although they will be expected to bind them. They may also receive duty-free quota-free (DFQF) market access to 97 percent of developed country markets at the conclusion of the round. In a replay of the agricultural "Faustian bargain" this DFQF access has been constructed to exclude products of broader (that is, non-African) LDC export interest, a good example being that of clothing exports from Bangladesh that are excluded.[15] Hence on the DFQF front as in the agriculture talks the DDA is protecting margins on products of export interest to African countries and as such is appropriately specified.

However, the problem is not that African countries need new markets but that they face constraints in trying to expand their exports to markets that already exist and need improved rules of origin and support to deal with non-tariff barriers such as sanitary and phytosanitary standards and technical barriers to trade that continue to restrict African exports. Unfortunately the DDA is not a good forum for addressing these non-tariff barrier concerns since these regulatory frameworks remain inherently unilateral in their application; sensitive to domestic consumer lobbies in developed country markets; out of the control of governments in the case of the plethora of private standards; and controlled by developed country multinational corporations through international standards setting bodies. Consequently it will be very difficult for African negotiators to penetrate this web of institutionally embedded interests.

A case for plurilaterals: investment

As argued earlier, the future of the WTO lies substantially in transcending current decision-making dynamics. One aspect of this is plurilateral agreements.[16] But the issues that may be subject to plurilateral accords are complex and contentious. To illustrate this we consider one of those—investment—from the standpoint of African interests in the subject.

The rapid growth of foreign investment into developing countries has increased the need for transparent regulation covering investor rights and obligations. Developed countries are concerned with the restrictions that some FDI recipient countries impose in order to protect and develop domestic industries, and rules to prevent capital flight. The fact that they were unable to agree on the mooted multilateral agreement on investment, negotiated under the auspices of the Organization for Economic Cooperation and Development during the 1990s, demonstrates how difficult it is to secure agreement on this subject. Developing countries have firmly resisted the establishment of a multilateral framework for the regulation of investment which is seen as intruding into "policy space." This was a key issue in the Cancún WTO Ministerial in 2003, where African countries, together with other developing countries, played a pivotal role in preventing this "Singapore issue" from being included in the Doha round.

Consequently, investment is regulated through a patchwork of BITs; provisions in regional trade agreements; and multilateral instruments within the framework of the WTO: Trade-Related Investment Measures (TRIMs); the General Agreement on Trade in Services (GATS); the Agreement on Subsidies and Countervailing Measures (SCM); Trade-Related aspects of Intellectual Property Rights (TRIPs); and the Government Procurement Agreement.

Having generally shown an aversion to the establishment of a multilateral framework on investment, African countries allow these investments to be governed by BITs. BITs have come to be regarded as guarantees of protection for investors, particularly investors in a developing country, because they often attain greater standards of legal protection than those afforded by the domestic law of that country. While these BITs do not generally affect the host country's regulation of the admission of foreign investment, they provide extensive rights for the investors and obligations for the host government. This has resulted in concerns that BITs tend to be uneven and accord more rights and legal recourse to investors than they do to host countries, loading them with a host of obligations instead. The SCM Agreement, Agreement on TRIPs, and the Government Procurement Agreement have an indirect bearing on investment and are not discussed here.[17]

TRIMs and GATS, both products of the Uruguay round, are more central to the issue. TRIMs deals with trade-related investment measures imposed on foreign investors, while GATS deals with investments in the services sector. Neither is an investment agreement per se; rather they cover trade-related aspects of investment.

In bringing investment into the General Agreement on Tariffs and Trade (GATT)/WTO agenda, developed countries aimed to proscribe a range of restrictions imposed on investors by developing countries. Developing countries were opposed to the initiative on the grounds that the GATT had no business regulating investment, barring its effects on trade. The compromise was TRIMs. The TRIMs Agreement calls on countries to notify their existing TRIMs and eliminate them within the specified time period. Essentially, it prohibits the use of trade-related measures that would violate the national treatment principle in GATT Article III, and Article XI covering the general elimination of quantitative restrictions. The agreement provides an illustrative and non-exhaustive list of the kind of measures that would be inconsistent with GATT Articles III and XI. The TRIMs agreement does not impose any regulation on investment but rather clarifies and prohibits the use of measures that were already disallowed within the GATT framework. Notably, export performance requirements, although trade distortive, are not regulated by TRIMs because they do not violate Articles III and XI. Where the export performance requirements involve the use of export subsidies, then these are partly regulated by the SCM agreement, which prohibits the use of export subsidies in relation to all non-agricultural products. The general exceptions available under GATT 1994 also apply to the TRIMs agreement. Good examples would include the Article XX general exception, as well as the temporary exceptions (subject to consultations and review after two years) that the GATT avails to developing countries under Article XVIII of GATT for economic development and safeguard measures for balance of payments purposes. Usually, any general exception applicable to a commitment under GATT would also be applicable to the TRIMs agreement.

Countries agreed to review TRIMs five years after its entry into force. The review was initiated in 1999 but the developed-developing country divide has impeded any agreement on the subject.[18] Developing countries want the flexibility to use TRIMs for development purposes while developed countries would like to see the maintenance of the status quo. Concerning the review, the African group proposed that the provision allowing for temporary exceptions to the prohibition of TRIMs should apply for a period of six years for African countries and that extension of transition periods should be granted to LDCs. In the 2005 Hong Kong Ministerial Declaration, LDCs were granted permission to maintain existing TRIMs for a new transition period of seven years and also to introduce new TRIMs; but the latter could only be maintained for five years, subject to renewal.

The financial and regulatory advantages enjoyed by foreign investors are often counteracted by the TRIMs applied by African countries. However, these TRIMs have also been shown to be ineffective in their desired objective. The same arguments against the protection of domestic markets prevail. Where TRIMs are utilized, most commonly local content requirements, domestic industry is not exposed to competition and therefore is less able to increase its competitiveness. The investor might also not be able to produce high quality and cost-effective products as a result of the domestic inputs he or she is obliged to use. This contributes to reduced international competitiveness. The end result may be that the host country achieves import substitution but not industrial development. The consumer also suffers through high prices brought on by the lack of import competition and the inefficiencies caused by import substitution.[19]

The GATS agreement deals more directly with investment through its Mode 3, or commercial presence. This refers to the supply of a service by one member's service supplier, in the territory of another member state. The largest extent of services trade liberalization commitments in the WTO so far are said to have been undertaken in Mode 3.[20] Members make both market access and national treatment commitments. These can be further divided into general obligations and specific commitments.

General obligations include the most favored nation principle, whereby parties to GATS are prohibited from distinguishing between WTO members when it comes to the treatment of services and service providers in their domestic markets. Specific commitments are determined by the market access commitments made in scheduled sectors. The schedules determine the application of market access and national treatment obligations. Unless a member commits to offering national treatment it is at liberty to discriminate between domestic and foreign "like" services and service providers. In scheduling their commitments members may impose such restrictions as:

- limitations on the total number of service suppliers;
- limitations on the total value of service transactions or assets;
- limitations on the number of service operations or total quantity of service output;
- limitations on the number of natural persons employed;
- measures that restrict or require specific types of legal entity or joint venture; and
- limitations on the participation of foreign capital.

Unless specifically scheduled, these restrictions must generally not be maintained.

Generally GATS affords African countries the flexibility to select the sectors in which they want investment, to impose whatever conditions they see fit, and also to retain foreign ownership restrictions in scheduled sectors. Hence GATS Mode 3 is more flexible than the BITs African countries seem to favor. Furthermore, the TRIMs and GATS agreements have the advantage of imposing transparency obligations through notification of policies and commitments. Also, disputes are governed by the WTO Dispute Settlement Understanding rather than investor to state arbitration. Additionally, TRIMs and GATS intrude less into the domestic policies of host countries than BITs, which usually contain "standstill" or "preservation of rights" clauses regardless of changed circumstances. In other words BITs do not contain flexibilities as is the case in the WTO. However, the multilateral frameworks do not have provisions for investor protection and rights.

Overall, a multilateral agreement on investment would not be ill-advised for developing countries. Indeed, some scholars think that the WTO is the best forum for African countries to pursue negotiations on investment issues.[21] Three factors are given to explain this point of view. First, the WTO will take into account special concerns of developing countries. Second, the WTO will give the possibility to bring all developing countries into the agreement and therefore reduce the risk of being out-maneuvered by developed countries; and third, it will ensure coherence between the investment agreement and other WTO agreements.

Given the skewed economic relations between developed countries and developing countries, particularly African, a multilateral agreement on investment would have to include caveats. African countries are wary of any agreement that would take away their sovereign rights over investment regulation and place it in the hands of a legal instrument that would, given the skewed negotiating dynamics, reflect developed country interests—as BITs tend to do. The main interest is investor obligations, or regulation of investor practices. The provisions of paragraph 22 of the Doha Declaration are worth noting here: " ... any framework should reflect in a balanced manner the interests of home and host countries, and take due account of the development policies and objectives of host governments as well as their right to regulate in the public interest."[22] This provision should find favor with developing countries because it creates room for development policies and also takes the public interest into consideration. The emphasis here, at least for developing countries, should be on curtailing investor practices in host countries that are detrimental to development.

In this regard an issue of great interest to Africans nowadays is the investment in arable lands by a variety of investors, mostly from the traditional Western investor countries, the Gulf states and Asian countries, often from China and India. In recent years investors from major developing countries have begun to acquire thousands of hectares of agricultural land in Africa. The major problem with this investment is that the agricultural production realized by those investors will be mostly, if not completely, exported to their home countries. This kind of investment could increase the risk of famine and food shortages on the African continent.

In this light, the international law framework tends to provide hard rights for foreign investors in the form of BITs, and this often leads to subordination of domestic law.[23] New obligations under a plurilateral investment code should bind foreign investors to domestic regulations in the first instance. But they could make provision for crisis contingences such as export restrictions on food in the event of a crisis. Such provisions should be reasonable and enforceable, and should not discriminate against foreigners—that is, they should apply to domestic investors too.

A possible basis for building a framework for an agreement on investment from an African perspective is the Extractive Industries Transparency Initiative (EITI). It seeks transparency, strengthened accountability, and good governance, which in turn create greater economic and political stability. The key with EITI lies in its principles, one of which states that "we affirm that management of natural resource wealth for the benefit of a country's citizens is in the domain of sovereign governments to be exercised in the interests of their national development." This initiative would provide a good template for the prevention of resource stripping in the investment framework.

The key to this framework would be the balancing of investor and host country rights and obligations. Paragraph 22 of the Doha Declaration could form the cornerstone of such a framework.[24] It should not be about unfettered liberalization of investment but should give African countries enough room for development considerations. Provision should be made for national treatment and most favoured nation treatment, and for those countries concerned with policy space the "bottom up" approach of GATS could be employed, with countries choosing the level of liberalization for different sectors.

Conclusion

Overall, in our assessment the DDA is appropriately structured to take account of African sensitivities and needs, albeit there are some question marks over the potential of the A4T agenda to adequately address supply-side constraints and step up to the increasingly rigorous non-tariff barriers encountered in accessing developed country markets. However, since the WTO is not a development agency its failure to do this is not necessarily an indictment, in our view. Of more importance to us is that African countries do more to help themselves, particularly by grasping the nettle of network services liberalization in their own interests and using this to pressure developed countries to liberalize their procedures governing temporary migration of skilled African workers to their markets.

In the medium term, beyond the DDA, African negotiators should also look seriously at an offensive agenda in a possible investment plurilateral negotiation. This requires buying into the notion of more limited negotiating rounds possibly confined to single issues and entailing subsets of the membership.[25] While this approach holds some dangers, not least the systemic implications of a weakening of the multilateral trading system as it stands today, once we resort to negotiating plurilaterals among subsets of the membership, in our view the benefits are likely to substantially outweigh the costs because scarce negotiating resources could be focused much more than is currently the case. And with proper application of the SDT principle, as is being pioneered in the trade facilitation talks, African countries could turn out to be major winners, rather than losers, in this scenario.

Notes

1 UNCTAD, *Economic Development in Africa Report: Strengthening Regional Economic Integration for Africa's Development* (Geneva: UNCTAD, 2009).

2 Peter Draper, "Rethinking the (European) Foundations of African Economic Integration: A Political Economy Essay," OECD Development Centre Working Paper No. 293 (Paris: OECD, 2010).

3 Richard Baldwin and Simon J. Evenett, eds, *The Collapse of Global Trade, Murky Protectionism, and the Crisis. Recommendations for the G 20* (London: Centre for Economic Policy Research, 2009); Simon J. Evenett, ed., "Tensions Contained … For Now: The 8th GTA Report," (London: Centre for Economic Policy Research, 2010), http://globaltradealert.org/sites/default/files/GTA8_0.pdf.

4 Eric K. Ogunleye, "Effects of Post-Crisis Foreign Trade Policy Measures on Economic and Trade Performance in Africa," *Global Trade Alert*, 5 May 2010.

5 Ogunleye, "Effects of Post-Crisis," 40.

6 Simon J. Evenett and Bernard Hoekman, "Policy Responses to the Crisis: Implications for the WTO and International Cooperation," www.voxeu.org, 6 July 2009.

7 Rand Merchant Bank "Africa Markets Update," 15 November 2010.

8 Ogunleye, "Effects of Post-Crisis," 44–45.

9 World Economic Forum, *Everybody's Business: Strengthening International Cooperation in an Interdependent World – Report of the Global Redesign Initiative* (Geneva: World Economic Forum, 2010); Peter Draper, "Whither the Multilateral Trading System? Implications for (South) Africa," South African Institute of International Affairs Occasional Paper No. 64 (2010).

10 Frank J. Garcia, "Beyond Special and Differential Treatment," *Boston College International and Comparative Law Review* 27, no. 2 (2004): 291–318.

11 Joseph E. Stiglitz, "Two Principles for the Next Round, or, How to Bring Developing Countries in from the Cold," in *Developing Countries and the WTO: A Proactive Agenda*, ed. Bernard Hoekman and Will Martin (Oxford and Malden, MA: Blackwell, 2001), 7–24; and Alexander Keck and Patrick Low, "Special and Differential Treatment in the WTO: Why, When and How?" Staff Working Paper ERSD-2004-03 (Geneva: WTO, 2004).

12 Michael Friis Jensen and Peter Gibbon, "Africa and the WTO Doha Round: An Overview" *Development Policy Review* 25, no. 1 (2007): 5–24.

13 Phil Alves, Peter Draper, and Nkululeko Khumalo, "Africa's Challenges in International Trade and Regional Integration: What Role for Europe?" South African Institute of International Affairs Occasional Paper No. 32 (2009).

14 James Scott and Rorden Wilkinson, "The Poverty of the Doha Round and the Least Developed Countries," *Third World Quarterly* 32, no. 4 (2011): 611–627.

15 Mareike Meyn, "The WTO Doha Round Impasse: Implications for Africa," Overseas Development Institute Briefing Paper No. 41 (London: ODI, 2008); and Scott and Wilkinson, "The Poverty of the Doha Round."

16 Draper, "Whither the Multilateral Trading System."

17 The SCM agreement is only relevant to the extent that it includes some commonly used investment incentives in its definition of incentives but it

does not address the subject with specific reference to measures imposed upon foreign investors. TRIPs provides for the intellectual property rights protection of foreign investors as well as exceptions to such protection. The Government Procurement Agreement deals with transparency and non-discrimination issues in public procurement requirements for the procurement of foreign products and products produced by locally domiciled foreign investors. See OECD Directorate for Financial and Enterprise Affairs, "Relationships between International Investment Agreements," Working Paper on International Investment No. 2004/1 (2004).

18 Edwini Kessie, "Trade Related Investments Measures (TRIMS)," (2009), www.unitar.org/ny/sites/unitar.org.ny/files/9Dec_TRIMs.pdf.

19 Japan Ministry of Trade, Economy and Industry, "Trade Related Investment Measures," (Tokyo: Ministry of Trade and Industry, 2008), www.meti.go.jp/english/report/downloadfiles/gCT0328e.pdf.

20 Offah Obale, "The GATS and Foreign Investment," Powerpoint presentation at the Second Annual Forum of Developing Country Investment Negotiators, Marrakesh, Morocco, 3–4 November 2008, www.iisd.org/pdf/2008/dci_forum_gats.ppt.

21 A.V. Ganesan, "Strategic Options Available to Developing Countries with Regard to a Multilateral Agreement on Investment," UNCTAD Discussion Paper No. 134 (Geneva: UNCTAD, 1998); Douglas H. Brooks, Emma Xiaoqin Fan, and Lea R. Sumulong, "Foreign Direct Investment in Developing Asia: Trends, Effects, and Likely Issues for the Forthcoming WTO Negotiations," ERD Working Paper Series No. 38 (Manila: Asian Development Bank, 2002).

22 WTO, "Doha Ministerial Declaration," WT/MIN(01)/DEC/1, 20 November 2001.

23 Carin Smaller and Howard Mann, *A Thirst for Distant Lands: Foreign Investments in Agricultural Land and Water* (Winnipeg: International Institute for Sustainable Development, 2009).

24 WTO, "Doha Ministerial Declaration."

25 Draper, "Whither the Multilateral Trading System?"

Appendix

GLOBAL POVERTY SUMMIT JOHANNESBURG

19 January 2011
GPS/DDA/TF/S/1

THE JOHANNESBURG STATEMENT ON THE DOHA DEVELOPMENT AGENDA

Almost a decade since the Doha Development Agenda (DDA) was launched the negotiations have yet to yield an outcome that contributes meaningfully to the alleviation of poverty and the promotion of economic development. The further continuation of this situation arrests the necessary process of reforming international trade rules to improve the transparency and democratic accountability of decision-making and promote sustainable growth within the poorest countries.

There are a number of issues that pose significant threats to the livelihoods within the poorest countries which need to be treated with the greatest seriousness. Among these, ensuring food security, promoting sustainable forms of development, and putting in place safeguards that enable vulnerabilities to external shocks to be mitigated, are among the most pressing. Moreover, the length of time that the negotiations have taken threatens to render aspects of the agenda obsolete.

A successful conclusion requires a willingness, commitment and seriousness from all World Trade Organization (WTO) Members as well as determined yet flexible leadership from developed, developing and least-developed members alike. It also requires active engagement with national and global business and civil society communities to encourage support for the negotiations.

To meet its development objectives and to make a substantial contribution to poverty reduction and the enhancement of human well-being, a concerted effort is required to bring the DDA to an early and satisfactory conclusion. However, conclusion of the round for the sake of urgency alone is not acceptable, and the objective of improving the role played by the multilateral trade system in the achievement of development must be maintained. To this end, WTO Members should remain faithful to the DDA's original mandate, redouble their efforts to place development at the heart of the negotiations, and bear in mind that the business of enhancing the contribution of trade to the development of the poorest and most vulnerable will not halt with the conclusion of a development-centred outcome.

The pursuit of agreement in the following areas will go a considerable way towards ensuring that an equitable and opportune outcome of the negotiations is realised, and these objectives ought to be secured as a matter of urgency. As such, we encourage WTO Members to:

I. An "Early Harvest" for LDCs

1. Agree and implement prior to the conclusion of the DDA **duty-free and quota-free access** into the markets of all developed WTO members, and those developing members in a position to do so, for all products originating from least-developed countries.
2. Press for the establishment of an **annual reporting mechanism** on the implementation of duty-free and quota-free market access. This should be seen as going beyond the annual reporting mechanism currently in operation in the Committee on Trade and Development through its pursuit of the implementation of legally binding commitments. The WTO Secretariat should oversee this mechanism and should be provided with the necessary resources to fulfil this role comprehensively.
3. Simplify and liberalise **rules of origin** to reduce the bureaucratic burden on least-developed countries and to allow their firms to import inputs from the most efficient suppliers, thereby enhancing their competitiveness while also enabling them to make better use of duty-free and quota-free access.
4. Fast-track the elimination of **export subsidies and trade-distorting domestic support** in the developed countries on agricultural products that are of export interest to least-developed countries, particularly in the areas of sugar, groundnuts, dairy products and fish. In particular, the immediate elimination of export subsidies and domestic support that have been a major cause of the decimation of cotton farmers and a threat to livelihoods in the "cotton four" countries, Benin, Burkina Faso, Chad and Mali needs to be addressed as a matter of urgency.

5. Secure substantial improvements in the offers from developed members, and developing countries in a position to do so, on market access to services exports from least-developed countries through **Mode 4** of the General Agreement on Trade in Services (GATS). This should include providing better access for the temporary movement of workers and for outsourcing in various areas including health, education and call centres from these economies.

6. Reform and expedite the **accession** process so that acceding countries are not required to undertake commitments beyond those that are currently agreed to by existing WTO members at the same level of development. Commitments by acceding developing and least-developed countries and small and vulnerable economies (SVEs) should also be consistent with their development needs and capacities.

II. Capacity Building and Aid for Trade

7. Provide relief for least-developed countries and SVEs for any **erosion of preferences** resulting from the conclusion of the DDA through the provision of effective financial and technical co-operation by the developed countries. Any adjustments made for the loss of preferences should be designed to encourage sustainable diversification and to cushion any negative effects of the reform process accompanied by a realistic transition timeframe.

8. Pursue the early implementation and full utilisation of the technical assistance and capacity building programmes envisaged under the proposed **Trade Facilitation** Agreement.

9. Secure additional, substantial and predictable **Aid for Trade**, to enable developing countries to avail themselves of the opportunities that trade opening provides as well as to increase investment in training that enhances the capacity of developing countries to participate in negotiations. This aid should be unconditional and not linked to negotiations for removing trade barriers and other trade distortions. The WTO should be mandated to monitor commitments on Aid for Trade and to build this into the Aid for Trade Global Review Process starting with the July 2011 meeting.

III. Non-agricultural Market Access (NAMA), Policy Space and Balanced Rules

10. Agree that all developing country commitments should be commensurate with their level of development; that is, commitments should

be made on the basis of **less than full reciprocity**. Special and differential treatment should remain a guiding principle in the negotiations.

11. Recognise the rights of developing countries to employ **industrial policies** to promote new industries including the use of procurement preferences and financial market interventions.

12. Establish a mechanism providing SVEs with the **flexibility** not to implement a specific discipline, if such non-implementation is properly justified for development interests. This should be understood as operationalising the principle of special and differential treatment, and targeted capacity building should be utilised to assist the country to meet the implementation of the remaining obligations. The Monitoring Mechanism currently being negotiated in the WTO Committee on Trade and Development Special Session could be used for such a purpose.

13. Pursue a much more ambitious programme to address **non-tariff barriers** (including technical barriers to trade, sanitary and phytosanitary measures and standards) faced by developing and least-developed countries in developed country markets.

14. Ensure that the outcome of the NAMA negotiations creates significant new market access to products of interest to developing countries and addresses the issue of **tariff escalation** in developed countries, enabling the beneficiation and processing of their raw materials.

IV. Intellectual Property Rights

15. Thoroughly reform the **Agreement on Trade-Related Aspects of Intellectual Property Rights** (TRIPs) to: (i) make the TRIPs and Public Health amendment more effective, enabling developing countries to use these flexibilities to provide more affordable medicines for public health; and (ii) include a mandatory disclosure of origin requirement for patents to prevent biopiracy of developing country genetic resources and traditional knowledge, in accordance with the Convention on Biological Diversity.

V. Agriculture and Food Security

16. Ensure that the outcome of the Doha Round creates fundamental reforms in developed country agriculture by making real and effective cuts in domestic support programmes. **Export subsidies** in developed countries should be eliminated at the

end of 2013 as agreed at the 2005 Hong Kong Ministerial Conference.

17. With due regard to the export interests of developing countries, adequate flexibilities should be provided for the Special Products of developing countries and an appropriate **Special Safeguard Mechanism** created to address the rural development, food security and livelihood concerns of developing countries.

The Johannesburg Global Poverty Summit
Johannesburg 17–19 January 2011

Index

A4T (aid for trade) 7, 11, 100, 137,
177, 193, 195, 196, 197, 198, 199,
201, 206–7, 214; dependence on
aid 176, 177–78; Johannesburg
Statement 123–24, 219; MDG8
199; Task Force on Aid for Trade
150, 198, 206; trade facilitation
159; Trade Facilitation Agreement
124, 219; trade liberalization
159–61
ACP (Africa, Caribbean, and Pacific
group) 127, 138, 151, 152, 173,
175, 185, 193, 197
Africa: ANC 106; bilateral
agreement/BITs 9, 12, 210, 212;
challenges 7, 96–97, 101, 202; a
changing world 95–97; coalitions
151, 176–77, 185, 193, 197;
colonialism 171, 173; concession
162; deindustrialization 10, 157,
158; dependence on aid 176,
177–79; development 97, 126–30,
199; EU 75, 203; GATS 212;
GATT 171, 172–74, 194; growth
157, 161, 167; income poverty 6,
73–75; infrastructure 95, 100, 137,
158, 162, 168, 199, 202–3; lack of
coherent domestic policies 176,
179–80; LDCs 3, 188, 192–93;
marginalization 3, 120, 121, 166,
173; market access 159, 195, 197,
198–99, 203, 206, 208;
multilateralism 97, 210, 213; PTAs
95, 96, 97, 101; regional
integration 95; TRIMs 211;
unemployment

22, 115, 160, 164, 165; US-Africa
Business Summit 178; WTO 97,
174–80, 185, 192–93, 205–6
(challenges and opportunities
180–85); *see also* DDA and
Africa; developing country;
LDCs; sub-Saharan Africa; SVEs
Africa Group 79, 86, 151, 176, 177,
185, 200, 203; beginnings 193, 200
Agah, Yonov Frederick 8, 121–40
agreements, conventions, treaties 2,
40; Agreement on Agriculture,
Doha 64–67, 68, 98, 194;
Agreement on Agriculture,
Uruguay round 25, 27–28, 57–58,
63–64; ATC 25; Cotonou
Agreement 173, 185; critical mass
agreement 39, 40, 43, 45, 46, 53,
151; Economic Partnership
Agreements 96, 185; EITI 213–14;
FTA 145, 150, 151; Government
Procurement Agreement 2, 151,
209, 210, 216; Lomé Convention
166, 173; "partial harvest"
approach 51–52; PTAs 94, 95, 96,
97, 99, 101; RTAs 130, 136, 150,
151, 209; Sanitary and
Phytosanitary Measures 99, 130;
SCM 209, 210, 215–16; single
undertaking 2, 32, 51–52, 82, 135,
146, 151, 190, 192; Technical
Barriers to Trade Agreement 129,
130; Trade Facilitation Agreement
52, 124, 190, 195–96, 198, 219;
TRIMs 130, 209, 210–12;
Yaoundé Convention 173; *see also*

194, 195, 198, 201; SSM 98;
sub-Saharan Africa 208; trade
liberalization 159, 160, 167–68;
TRIMs 211; TRIPs 13; *see also*
DDA, "early harvest"; SVEs
Lee, Donna 6–7, 72–90
"less than full reciprocity" principle
9, 23, 25, 31, 113, 133, 135, 148,
187, 220
liberalization 19, 52; developed
country 95; employment 21; gains
from 18, 20, 23, 33–34; market
liberalization 9, 10, 11, 37, 42, 52;
NAMA 20, 22, 208; regional
liberalization 95; role of
liberalization within development
22, 32; services 46–47, 49, 50, 65,
68, 192; tariff liberalization 10, 21,
23, 96; United States 44; *see also*
market access; trade liberalization
Like Minded Group 25

marginalization 93, 117; Africa 3,
120, 121, 166, 173
market access 3, 5; Africa 159, 195,
197, 198–99, 203, 206, 208;
agriculture 3, 98–99, 107, 127,
128, 143, 188, 204, 208; DDA 11,
27, 37–40, 117, 122, 123, 144–45,
188; DDA deadlock 37, 39–40,
134; Johannesburg Statement 219;
market liberalization 9, 10, 11, 37,
42, 52; *see also* DFQF;
liberalization; NAMA; tariff;
trade liberalization
MDGs (Millennium Development
Goals) 187, 199; food security 58;
MDG8 187, 190, 199
Mehta, Pradeep S. 11, 187–201
mercantilism 11, 53, 115, 117, 182;
WTO 103, 116, 181
MFN (most favored nation)
principle 53, 94, 138, 172, 174,
185, 198, 211
Mshomba, Richard E. 10, 11, 171–86
multilateralism 39, 50, 93, 117, 147,
172, 183, 209; Africa 97, 210, 213;
asymmetrical multilateral trade
32, 103; bilateral/multilateral
agreement comparison 212; cotton

negotiations 78, 80, 81; crisis of 7,
93; DDA deadlock, moving
forward 9, 39–40, 48, 115, 133,
138; developing country 212–13;
investment 203, 205, 207, 209–13;
South Africa 103, 104, 105, 106,
113; WTO 50–51; *see also* GATS;
TRIMs; TRIPs

NAMA (Non-Agricultural Market
Access) 9, 11, 37; Africa 99, 127,
128, 158, 193, 208–9; BRICs 30,
141–42; China 143; DDA 27,
30–31, 32, 44–45, 116, 128–29,
134, 141–42, 143–44, 188, 191
(deadlock 132, 134, 188;
recommendations to 191–92,
196–97); developing country 9,
30–31, 32, 143, 188; diversification
30; EU 30, 44, 112–13;
Johannesburg Statement 123, 124,
219–20; liberalization 20, 22, 208;
NAMA-11 8, 105, 112–13, 114,
193, 197; sectorals 144;
standard-setting 99, 209; Swiss
formula 108, 116, 143; uncertainty
reduction 44; United States 30, 44,
141–42; *see also* tariff
natural resources 214; prices rise 7,
97, 101; raw material production
19, 30, 220; *see also* environmental
issues
Nene, Morisho 11–12, 202–16
NGO (non-governmental
organization): Africa 175; DDA,
criticism 108–9, 110, 146;
Environmental Working Group
75–76; Open Secret 79; TRIPs
175; *see also* civil society

ODA (official development
assistance) 177, 206, 207
OECD (Organization for Economic
Cooperation and Development) 1,
40, 57, 126, 209
OTDS (overall trade-distorting
domestic support) 98, 111, 188,
192; elimination/reduction 27, 77,
123, 125, 127, 128, 142, 191, 208,
218; *see also* subsidy

Routledge Global Institutions Series

1 **The United Nations and Human Rights (2005)**
   A guide for a new era
   by Julie A. Mertus (American University)

Books currently under contract include:

The Regional Development Banks
Lending with a regional flavor
by Jonathan R. Strand (University of Nevada)

Millennium Development Goals (MDGs)
For a people-centered development agenda?
by Sakiko Fukuda-Parr (The New School)

Peacebuilding
From concept to commission
by Robert Jenkins (The CUNY Graduate Center)

UNICEF
by Richard Jolly (University of Sussex)

The Bank for International Settlements
The politics of global financial supervision in the age of high finance
by Kevin Ozgercin (SUNY College at Old Westbury)

International Migration
by Khalid Koser (Geneva Centre for Security Policy)

Human Development
by Richard Ponzio

Religious Institutions and Global Politics
by Katherine Marshall (Georgetown University)

The Group of Twenty (G20)
by Andrew F. Cooper (Centre for International Governance Innovation, Ontario) and Ramesh Thakur (Balsillie School of International Affairs, Ontario)

The International Monetary Fund (2nd edition)
Politics of conditional lending
by James Raymond Vreeland (Georgetown University)

The UN Global Compact
by Catia Gregoratti (Lund University)

Institutions for Women's Rights
by *Charlotte Patton (York College, CUNY) and Carolyn Stephenson (University of Hawaii)*

International Aid
by *Paul Mosley (University of Sheffield)*

Global Consumer Policy
by *Karsten Ronit (University of Copenhagen)*

The Changing Political Map of Global Governance
by *Anthony Payne (University of Sheffield) and Stephen Robert Buzdugan (Manchester Metropolitan University)*

Coping with Nuclear Weapons
by *W. Pal Sidhu*

Global Sustainability
by *Tapio Kanninen*

Private Foundations and Development Partnerships
by *Michael Moran (Swinburne University of Technology)*

Integrating Africa
Decolonization's legacies, sovereignty, and the African Union
by *Martin Welz (University of Konstanz)*

Feminist Strategies in International Governance
edited by *Gülay Caglar (Humboldt University of Berlin), Elisabeth Prügl (Graduate Institute of International and Development Studies, Geneva), Susanne Zwingel (SUNY Potsdam)*

The International Politics of Human Rights
edited by *Monica Serrano (Collegis de Mexico) and Thomas G. Weiss (The CUNY Graduate Cetner)*

For further information regarding the series, please contact:
Craig Fowlie, Publisher, Politics & International Studies
Taylor & Francis
2 Park Square, Milton Park, Abingdon
Oxford OX14 4RN, UK
+44 (0)207 842 2057 Tel
+44 (0)207 842 2302 Fax
Craig.Fowlie@tandf.co.uk
www.routledge.com